Living Systems, Evolving Consciousness, and the Emerging Person

Psychoanalytic Inquiry Book Series

Volume 26

 *Psychoanalytic*
Inquiry Book Series

Living Systems, Evolving Consciousness, and the Emerging Person

A Selection of Papers from the Life Work of Louis Sander

Edited by Gherardo Amadei and Ilaria Bianchi

Routledge
Taylor & Francis Group
NEW YORK AND LONDON

Routledge
Taylor & Francis Group
711 Third Avenue
New York, NY 10017

Routledge
Taylor & Francis Group
27 Church Road
Hove, East Sussex BN3 2FA

First issued in paperback 2014

Routledge is an imprint of the Taylor and Francis Group, an informa business

© 2008 by Taylor & Francis Group, LLC

International Standard Book Number-13: 978-0-88163-464-8 (Hardcover)
International Standard Book Number-13: 978-1-138-00593-8 (pbk)

Library of Congress Cataloging-in-Publication Data

Sander, Louis W.
  Living systems, evolving consciousness, and the emerging person : a selection of papers from the life work of Louis Sander / Louis Sander.
    p. ; cm. -- (Psychoanalytic inquiry book series ; v. 26)
  Includes bibliographical references and index.
  ISBN 978-0-88163-464-8 (hardback : alk. paper)
  1. Infant psychiatry. 2. Infant psychology. 3. Mother and infant. 4. Developmental psychobiology. I. Title. II. Series.

  [DNLM: 1. Social Adjustment--Collected Works. 2. Adaptation, Psychological--Collected Works. 3. Child--Collected Works. 4. Child Development--Collected Works. 5. Consciousness--Collected Works. 6. Infant--Collected Works. 7. Mother-Child Relations--Collected Works. W1 PS427F v.26 2008 / WS 105.5.A8 S214L 2008]
  RJ502.5.S36 2008   616.89'17--dc22

                                                        2007019703

Visit the Taylor & Francis Web site at
http://www.taylorandfrancis.com

and The Analytic Press Web site at
http://www.analyticpress.com

Editors' Notes

This book project started, toward the end of the nineties, from my request (G. A.) of Louis Sander to have access to his non-published material. A correspondence between us developed from my initial contact, and I still remember the emotions conjured up when I received his first, kind letter of response, handwritten in tiny handwriting but completely intelligible. The correspondence continued, little by little, regarding plans to collect, for the first time, those items that Sander himself deemed could best explain "a life's work." I am grateful to Sander for having entrusted me with the task of editing his book, which, after arranging 13 chapters, I then shared with I. B., who was becoming interested in infant research and moving from the theory to the observation of infant development. The work is therefore born from meetings, not only of minds, but also of people—namely, between us, Sander, and the BPCSG (Boston Process of Change Study Group), that today seeks to develop Sander's continually inspiring theories.

The complexity of Sander's writings, the necessity to eliminate repetitions inevitably present in work that spanned decades, the need to lighten the studies' methodological explanations (but in a way that still allowed the reader access to the acute interpretations of the results suggested by the author), and lastly, the importance of arriving at a complete book (rather than a collection of papers)—all required time and attention. Knowing this could not have been done to perfection, we hope to have created a suitable work that does justice to the necessity of sharing, in its final united form, the work of a great scientist who, in our opinion, has a poet's soul in him, as demonstrated by various passages in his writing, as in the case of the final chapter that mingles existential and spiritual issues. It was our unforgettable honor to have worked on it. We believe we have done so with care, and certainly with love and respect.

Contents

PART 3

Foreword

Some people can see the forest but not the trees. Some people can see the trees but not the forest. Some people can see both and some rare people not only can see the forest *and* the trees but also appreciate the complexity of the entire ecological system. Louis W. Sander is such a rare person. As Dr. Sander states in chapter 8, the real problem for infant research is the **translation** of principles governing the developmental processes to their incorporation within the exchanges and interactions that will be the shaping forces in new infant–caregiver systems. The extent of "forest" covered by Sander is vast indeed: the formulation of basic principles of processes that govern all living systems, ranging from the cellular level to the level of human consciousness. And the focus on "trees" is penetrating indeed: richly documented research findings comparing specific mother–child pairs over both brief and long segments of time. By examining findings from the specific pairs and comparing them to other pairs, Sander's studies reveal both continuities and discontinuities of the development. Sander tracks and demonstrates the integration of two processes: the increasingly complex levels of getting together between caretaker and neonate, infant, and child (the relational aspect), and the increased complexity of the neonate's, infant's, and child's coherence of organization and growing awareness of self and other (the intrapsychic aspect).

I present this highly condensed summary of critical aspects of the conceptual range that Sander covered to whet the reader's appetite for a remarkable tour of infant studies revealed by one of the most renowned masters of the field. I need to mention several other orienting comments. Sander writes about systems: living systems, mother–child systems, and family systems. In 2007 that hardly seems worthy of comment, but Sander was conceptualizing development in terms of systems when the analytic field was locked into a language of psychic structures that tended toward a linear conception of energic vector forces operating in an exclusively intrapsychic domain. Sander's contribution is seminal to our contemporary approach to nonlinear systems evolving in an intersubjective, interactive field of fitting together and achieving moments of meeting through mutual recognition. I encourage the reader to appreciate Sander's view of evolution in its broadest context, and as it moves to open the *potential* available to every mother–infant pair as they negotiate specific tasks of fitting together or adaptation over a span of time. Finally, I regard Sander as a semantic magician. In seamless appreciative writing, he offers a positive rendering to a host of theoreticians such as Hartmann, Erikson, Bowlby, Winnicott, Trevarthen, Spitz, and Edelman, all of whose writings use different language and present concepts often disparate to each other and, I believe, to Sander's theses. Sander generously selects the aspect of their discoveries that he values while avoiding the polemics common to many analytic discourses.

In the mid-1970s, I attempted to review and integrate the theories of ego psychology, Mahler, and Kohut on the development of the sense of the self (1975) and the development of the sense of the object (1979). This effort propelled me into the burgeoning field of infant research, and the confusing crosscurrents of its pioneers. In a wonderful moment of inspiration, I flew out to Boulder, Colorado and spent an afternoon with Lou Sander. He graciously offered his time to me despite my neophyte status in a field in which he was an acknowledged expert. The foundations of the approach I used to apply infant studies to existing theory in *Psychoanalysis and Infant Research* (Analytic Press, 1983) grew out of that afternoon spent with Lou.

I believe I can speak for everyone who knows Lou that he is a gentle man and a gentleman with a brilliant mind. To me, Lou's greatest contribution is his ability to appreciate complexity, recognize paradox, and never lose sight that the goal of the quest is the recognition of the unique qualities of each human evolving in his or her unique ecological setting.

This presentation of Dr. Sander's papers would not have been possible without the support of the Koehler Foundation (Stiftung) and Lotte Koehler of Munich. Dr. Koehler, a practicing psychoanalyst, is to many who know her well, the generous benefactor who prefers to offer her support quietly and with little personal acknowledgment. Nonetheless, in my mind, I dare to refer to Lotte as the patron saint of infant studies, whose foundation has helped to bring into both the English and German literature works by Basch, Stern, Mahler, Beebe, and many others as well as me. I will add that since she is an analyst of great critical discernment, for an author to receive her support is a high honor.

Finally, I will place Dr. Sander in the trajectory of a half-century of studies of infancy and their application to psychoanalytic treatment of children and adults. Dr. Sander's work draws directly on the 1954 Boston University longitudinal study of mother–child interactions over the first 18 months of life, and is largely but not entirely a Boston story. From the 1950s on, Boston has been a center of research touching on pediatrics: T. Berry Brazelton, on child's analysis; Samuel Kaplan, Steve Ablon, Judy Yanof, Jim Herzog, Alexandra Harrison, on infant research; Sander, Gerald Stechler, Edward Tronick, Karlen Lyons-Ruth; and Evelyne Schwaber, Arnold Modell, and Jeremy Nahum on adult analysis. By 1980, at a self psychology meeting in Boston organized by Samuel Kaplan and Evelyne Schwaber, papers on infant research and developmental theory were presented by Stechler, Stern, and Sander to over a thousand attendees. By 1980, Sander's findings and conceptualizations spread far beyond Boston as an inspiration to many. Furthermore, he was in Colorado where excellent infant studies were being carried out first by René Spitz, and then by a group around Robert Emde. And a connection of all these pioneers extended to the richly productive group in New York of Daniel Stern, Beatrice Beebe, and Patricia Nachman, and later Beebe and Frank Lachmann. This mini-survey is completely subjectively biased in that all those I have mentioned are my heroes and mentors. How does it all come together and what is Sander's role in it? Louis W. Sander is an integrator and innovator whose motto could well be the title of chapter 12: "Thinking Differently." I suggest that the principal influence he has had on the field of research in psychoanalysis is to encourage everyone to "think differently." Many years ago Evelyne Schwaber described to me how Sander had led her to think differently in her influential work on empathic listening. And on the practical level of psychotherapeutic treatment, we have the Boston Change Process Study Group bringing Sander's many contributions together to make the intersubjective world of analyst–analysis and an experience of recognition and innovative artistry.

Joseph D. Lichtenberg, M.D.
Bethesda, Maryland

REFERENCES

Lichtenberg, J. (1975). The development of the sense of self. *J. Amer. Psychoanal. Assn.*, 23: 413–484.
____ (1979). Factors in the development of the sense of the object. *J. Amer. Psychoanal. Assn.*, 27: 375–386.
____ (1983). *Psychoanalysis and Infant Research*. Hillsdale, NJ: The Analytic Press.

Preface

This collection of previously published papers and unpublished works can be viewed as a story of the gradual emergence of an overarching idea through the course of a life's work. The idea is one that describes an essential principle of process for living systems—that there is a continuing impetus, both energizing and motivational, that moves the system toward enhanced coherence in its engagement with its surroundings as it achieves increasing inclusiveness of complexity. The papers have been selected from a career of developmental research within the framework of psychoanalytic thinking. One might say they represent an outcome of a search for basic principles governing life as an ongoing creative process. As principles they should be found to be operative at each and every level of complexity in living systems—from that of the single-cell organism to the organization of human consciousness. Hopefully, the implications of this idea will emerge in the reader's thinking, as he or she goes through the papers.

The sequence of papers is an example of the emerging complexity in my thinking over many decades. It was a thinking that began with my struggle to integrate in some real way a simple rural childhood that had generated a deep devotion to and fascination with the wonders of nature that I had grown up within—with the deeper actualities of the structure and function of the anatomy, biochemistry, and physiology of the human body, brain, and mind that I encountered as I pursued a degree in medicine, and then tried to apply to the healing process at the clinical level. As time went on, I became aware that an ever-present background to this ongoing task was the emergence of my own integrative core—my "self." The underlying impetus to pursue this open-ended, bumpy trajectory was these dim but endless questions: "But, who am I? Who do I want to be? What difference does it make?"

As Freud began his thinking within the realm of biology underlying behavior at the human level, so have I in this collection, but with an important difference. We begin here not with the individual organism, but with systems thinking and the view of the living system as one that brings together both the organism and its environment of evolutionary adaptation as a coherent entity—one that provides continuity of the life of both the individual and of the system over time. Thus it is not just the organization of the individual but of the system that is being portrayed, both being within an essential process of creativity that proceeds in spite of change or discontinuity over its evolutionary trajectory.

My thinking on this matter began with the work of the biologist Ludwig von Bertalanffy (1952) in the 1930s and 1940s, which he summarized in his book *The Problem of Life*. He proposed two essential principles: a principle of organization and a principle of primary activity—two essential, mysterious features of all living matter that we have as yet to fully explain: namely, (a) how the enormous spectrum of complexity of components in every living thing from the unicellular creature to the human being organizes itself into—and then is held within—the unity, or coherent wholeness, of the individual entity—the organism—over time; and (b) how the impetus energizing this organizational process must come from within the organism; it is not something imposed from without. This makes the continuity of life, in each organism that lives and each living system that endures over time, a matter of self-organization, self-regulation, and self-correction. Continuity of life in both the individual and the system depends, then, on the proper functioning of some principle of wholeness, or coherence, or unity. At the human level we have coined the word *state* to describe the degree of coherence or wholeness, which might be called health, of the individual within its system. The perception of one's own state and that of the "other" is an ever-present background for regulation of human interaction. It also describes the condition of energy flow in the individual-surround living system, an expanding flow as the complexity and inclusiveness of the system expand. Such a state of wholeness becomes motivational, as an essential impetus by which "coherence" is continuously being sought, or being reachieved, in an ongoing creative organizing process, as the individual moves toward an increasingly inclusive complexity of engagement with its surroundings.

Among the principles of process that govern living systems are others, such as "the device of specificity," proposed by biologist Paul Weiss (1949), or that of "rhythmicity." When we move from principles of process governing the action of the individual within the living system to principles governing the exchanges—the adjustments or negotiations necessary to reach the essential connectedness between individual and system that provide the continuity of life—we encounter the requirement of a major principle, long known in the world of biology. It is the principle of *adaptation*, which refers to the mutual modifications among the diversity of interacting components that are necessary to achieve the essential specificity of connection, or the "fitting together" that is required to generate this vital coherence or unity of the whole. This requires the resolution of a basic paradox: On the one hand there is the uniqueness or singularity of each new individual in the ongoing creation of diversity. On the other hand, diversity must still permit changes at the level of both the individual and the system that are required to reach the harmonious coherence—the "fitting together" or connectedness—that allows the life of both individual and system to continue. At the human level we can ask, how can we be both "distinct from" and "together with" at the same time? Here, *at the level of the human system*, we propose that "resolution" involves movement toward a next, higher level of inclusiveness in the conscious organization of each component. It is an expanded inclusiveness involving what we have termed a *recognition process*—a shift in the organization of consciousness that *allows* each to be different—together—while *maintaining* the essential coherence in our organization as a system.

In this collection of papers, then, we are suggesting that one can view the evolutionary process—from the level of the creation of life on this planet to the organization of consciousness—in terms of a set of basic principles essential for continuity of life in living systems. These govern the process of the emergence of an incredible diversity of forms, the construction of increasingly inclusive ecologies, to the emergence of the human species. At the present moment, instead of a process within the perspective of evolutionary time, we are at a point at which we think of the organization of human consciousness as a functional actuality of our existence *now*. We think of it as an *outcome* of the evolutionary process and not in terms of human consciousness as being within the "direction" of a process of change over longer spans of time in the history of time and evolution—an overarching creative process moving us toward a global ecology that we are within but, on the level of the individual, as yet do not conceive. The evolution of human consciousness will reach a new level of both complexity and unity, and a new domain of creativity once we comprehend the inclusiveness and overarching direction of the creative process we are within and the principles that govern it.

Preface to German Edition

Louis Sander, now more than 80 years of age, is an infant researcher who is also trained in psychoanalysis. He is the "grand old man" of modern infant research. Major representatives of developmental theory including Daniel Stern, J. M. Hoffmann, T. Berry Brazelton, the attachment researcher Allan Sroufe, Gerald Stechler, Karlen Lyons-Ruth, Beatrice Beebe, and Frank Lachmann regard him as a major teacher, influencing their own work. Authors such as Jessica Benjamin, Arnold Modell, Stephen Mitchell, and Edward Tronick have discussed and borne tribute to his work.

This preface is, in a manner of speaking, a declaration of love for the scholar Louis W. Sander, on the part of a psychoanalyst whose practice was strongly influenced and enhanced by the knowledge of his research outcomes and his interpretations based on the most modern theories. L. Sander became, so to say, one of her "patron saints."

Freud had emphasized the great significance of early childhood development for the adult personality. In the course of their "transference" onto the analyst, acquired modes of acting, thinking and feeling enabled a reconstruction of their probable origin and the manner in which they had been worked through.

Sander's work opened the opposite route—namely, an attempt at *predicting* the *probable* future of a later adult on the basis of observational data from childhood. I experienced this in my first "intellectual meeting" with Sander. This occurred indirectly, through a clinical case presentation by Evelyne Schwaber in 1978 in Chicago at the first International Conference on the Psychology of the Self, published in 1980. At the end of the lecture, she reported that she had given Louis Sander some data on the early history of her patient and asked his opinion about the personality and defense structures a person with such a background was likely to develop. The data she offered him was sketchy: he came "from a middle-class professional family, and his parents told him that he cried for the first year and a half and did not talk until age two. Sander replied: Drawing upon the information that this was from a middle-class professional family, I would believe that the basic biological needs of hunger and warmth and so on were not at issue, that the crying would be principally for social interaction, then, not physical care. If we are to speculate what the 'archaic' elements of the transference might be, I would say first of all that this infant was exposed to states of overwhelming disruption, unrelieved by any outside input.

There would be a basic fear, then, of annihilation, or disruption, or explosion, or fragmentation that would follow from the states of overwhelming physical disorganization that go with such crying. One might say there would be a fear of being overwhelmed by one's own state, and that there would be a sense of helplessness if such states threatened. There might be a great deal of recourse to self-stimulation—in contrast to the impotence he had experienced in producing contingent effects elsewhere in his world. He may have a need to be in control of his life situation himself, lest there be an overwhelming state which might ensue. Thus, there would be a great need to control situations potentially triggering his own feelings and his own world; the lack of response of his world to his crying would be connected with a sense that relationships are not to be counted on to come to him, and that they would be available only if he could elicit them. This would be connected with a certain 'distance' that would go with his lack of basic trust in the possibility of anyone 'meeting' him from a point outside himself. Fundamentally, he would really have had to get on by himself, distant from social relationships.

"The parallels between what was discovered in the analytic situation and what was predicted by the infant researcher are striking" (Schwaber, 1980: 240–241). Formulating such a prognosis requires knowledge of the need in early childhood to be comforted to prevent a derailment of regulation, as well as empathy with the inner condition of the crying infant. Sander's developmental diagnoses and their interpretations reveal deep human insight, empathy, and sympathy. Here, reference is due especially to his work "Development as a Creative Process" (chapter 13, pp. 231–246), written upon the death of his colleague of many years, Ellen Stechler. The clinical example above gives an inkling of the enormous importance of Sander's work for therapeutic practice. Of course, such a preview on the possible personality development of a child with such a past can only be a guess. The follow-up studies of Sander's originally observed children showed that no reliable data could be obtained. But, infant research as done by Sander opens to the clinician possibilities to form hypotheses of how the patient became the person he is now, hypotheses which have to be proved or disapproved in the clinical work.

At the time, I thought, "if it's that simple, then you have to learn it." I read Sander's publications, including the essay reprinted in this volume (chapter 1, pp. 3–24) "Issues in Early Mother–Child Interaction" (1962). But it wasn't so simple. I had to familiarize myself with many new theories. In explaining his diagnoses, Sander went beyond libido theory and drew on information theory and cybernetics, as well as the theory of nonlinear dynamic systems. His premise is that every living organism regulates itself and simultaneously engages in an intensive exchange with its life-supporting environment. Particularly in the mother–child system, mutual regulation and self-regulation are closely intermingled. Neither the self-regulating individual nor the influences of its environment can be regarded independently. As Sander writes, all behavior has to been seen in its specific context. A mother with her individual personality and her child with its particular predispositions form a system in which certain issues are regulated and mutual adaptations emerge. Through the process of maturation of the child, the regulatory balance of the mother–child system is disturbed. As a result, a new adaptation is required of the mother and of the child on a more complex and differentiated level.

What have I learned?

My first psychoanalytic teacher was René Spitz. On his deathbed, he summoned his closest pupil, Robert Emde, to hand down his psychoanalytic legacy. It was: "Survival, Adaptation, Evolution." Precisely these aspects are given their due in the life work of Louis Sander, most prominently in his last seminal paper (chapter 12, pp. 25–51) entitled "Thinking Differently: Principles of Process in Living Systems and the Specificity of Being Known" (2002). In earlier years, he had already postulated that mother and child form *one* developing *system* in which, as a result of the genetically induced adaptation of the infant, the latter accomplishes certain maturational steps. These lead to alterations in the infant's behavior, which in turn call for a new adaptation within the mother–child system. For the first 36 months of life, Sander distinguished seven successive "issues" with their initial constellations, and he described their negotiation outcomes as well as possible disturbances. This is elucidated in the paper reprinted here, which was based on the observation of 30 mother–child pairs at regular intervals over a period of 36 months. In 1988, in the publication "The Event-Structure of Regulation in the Neonate–Caregiver System as a Biological Background for Early Organization of Psychic Structure" (chapter 7, pp. 149–161), Sander described—again, in minutely detailed interpretation of his observations of very early mother–child interaction—how the sense of identity and sense of self-as-agent develop. Today, his theses have been corroborated many times over by intersubjectivists, attachment theory, and neuroscience.

In his last paper, the culmination of his life's work (chapter 12, pp. 211–230), he extends his thesis on the reciprocal influence between the part and the whole, individual and environment, on adaptation, self-regulation and mutual regulation to encompass the entire spectrum of development: from the molecular biological level through the organelles in monocellular beings and organs in multicellular beings, and on to the level of consciousness and to the therapeutic situation. In doing so, he explains fundamental concepts brought forth by such scholars as Von Bertalanffy, Prigogine, Edelman, W. Singer, and others.

To express this very simply: Sander regards organism and environment, mother and child, as *one* system engaged in development in an ever-changing flow of time, place, and movement. He advances from thinking in terms of structures to thinking in terms of processes. A major role is attributed to the resolution of oppositional pairs, such as continuity versus discontinuity, self-agency and specificity versus synchronicity or binding in Singer's sense (i.e., simultaneous neural firing)—but above all to the resulting self-organization and its development, particularly in the context of the early mother-child relationship. When two organisms are connected by the same *rhythm*, recurrent patterns will emerge, having features of both self-similarity and of singularity. This *rhythmicity* enables "being distinct from each other" and "being together with each other" at the same time.

An example would be a newborn establishing a 24-hour cycle of sleep-awake rhythms in adaptation to being fed by the mother. Both share a common directionality. The child becomes a system within a larger system held together by its synchrony. This leads to varying rhythms of mutual engaging or being-together-with and disengaging or being-distinct-from, as also occurs in looking and looking away. With increasing age and particularly with the acquisition of language, the child gradually disengages from the dyad between the 18th and 36th month. (It is to be noted that disengagement does not mean disconnection).

Language acquisition enables the child to communicate its *inner* experience and intentions. The empathic mother confirms the child's inner perceptions. This makes communication between mother and child possible on a new level, namely, that of symbolic representation and language. An exchange on inner awareness takes place. In Sander's view, it is the infant's experience of an "other" being aware of what the infant is aware of within himself that lends this experience the feeling of being real. Sander calls this process "*recognition*." It is a matter of experiencing "*shared awareness*." The awareness shared by mother and child is an important step in the development of a higher order consciousness as described by Edelman as a *dyadic expansion of consciousness*, a development promoted by exchange and cooperation between mother and child.

For the senso-motor and senso-secretional processes of previous phases were not yet conscious, although they do remain in the memory as "implicit relational knowledge." As early as the Mahler Symposium on May 8, 1982 in Philadelphia, Sander had asserted that the first self was a "state-self." The perception, shared with the mother, of inner feelings makes self-perception and the perception of a self-organizing core within oneself possible for the first time. This lays the basis for a feeling of continuity. The organism, which in a more primitive phase requires regularity in its environment in order to maintain its stability, thus achieves a greater independence from external shifts and changes. In his last paper, "Thinking Differently," Sander postulates a developmental line of the "experience of recognition," characterized as the specific experience of a moment in which one knows that one's own experience is validated and truly recognized by another. Sander's statements correspond to a certain extent to the recent hypotheses of Fonagy and colleagues to the effect that the child becomes aware of its inner state due to marked mirroring by the mother.

Sander thus introduces into the framework of psychoanalysis concepts that were of great significance for me toward understanding the relationship between analyst and patient. He not only surmounts the model of libido and defense by advancing from one-person psychology to that of the dyad but also describes the latter as a *system*—*one* system which negotiates, on certain levels of development, tasks emerging from the imbalance caused by the epigenetic maturation of the child. From Sander, I learned to take into account the strategy of the child and the caretaker within this process—e.g., in the regulation of the "state-self"—as it is re-lived in the transference, and learned the importance of "negotiation" in the analytic process. This aspect, in conjunction with clinical descriptions, opened my perspective to the re-discovery of "Gestalten" in adult patients: forms originating in their early interaction and adaptation or mal-adaptation to the mother-child system.

One thought from Sander's work that particularly enhanced my clinical practice was the import of "recognition" and "shared awareness." In my experience, shared awareness plays a very important role in analytic treatment. If the analyst is immediately able to give the patient this feeling, it greatly promotes the positive transference. Usually, however, only a strenuous process of "negotiation" between patient and analyst leads to shared awareness. It is already a sign of good progress when the analyst can communicate to the patient that what he or she is saying may not immediately be understood properly, and can ask the patient to persist in explaining *his or her version* until both have reached a mutual understanding of the significance and meaning attached to what the patient is feeling or wishes to express. It should be kept in mind that, in Sander's view, only that which has been shared with another can become psychic reality.

Sander is among the pioneers of modern infant research. He is now a member of the much-discussed "Boston Process of Change Study Group" initiated by Daniel Stern, a circle of infancy researchers and psychoanalysts who—based on the findings of modern infant research—are attempting to discover how change occurs in the intersubjective field during treatment, what process precedes it, and why a qualitative leap takes place at a particular juncture, the so-called "now-moment." Thus, Sander remains at the foremost front of research.

Unfortunately, much of Sander's work is scattered in various journals, books, and handbooks, some of which are hardly accessible. It took a great effort to convince him that it would be desirable to publish his most important research outcomes and their interpretation in a single volume. It was Gherardo Amadei who was finally able to overcome Sander's hesitation, and the book first appeared in Italy. Amadei, in close cooperation with Sander, served as the editor. Credit for the English edition by The Analytic Press is due to Joe Lichtenberg. A translation being published by Klett-Cotta will make the work of L.W. Sander more well-known in the German-speaking community.

The reader is given a description of the advancement of the developmental process and of the principles according to which this might be achieved, derived from the integration of the state-of-the-art in molecular, bio-, neuro-, and psycho-research. It is to be hoped that readers of this book will not only expand their scientific knowledge and incorporate new insights into their professional practice, but also appreciate that accurate scholarship is founded on more than just clean and correct scientific methods and statistics. Sander's findings in developmental psychology and his *explanations* of them are also based on deep human *understanding*, empathy, and sympathy.

Lotte Köhler

REFERENCE:

Schwaber, E. (1980), Self Psychology and the Concept of Psychopathology: A Case Presentation. In: *Advances in Self Psychology*, Goldberg, A. (ed.). New York: International Universities Press, 215–251.

Part 1

Part 1 begins with observations of the adaptive process over the first 3 years of life within the diversity of human infant–caretaker systems. These cases illustrated for us the increasingly complex levels of fitting together between infant and caretaker that must be achieved over that time. It was an experience that required us to think from the level of biology to the way feeling, emotion, and meaning become organized in the development of human consciousness.

The descriptions of mother–child interactions over the first 18 months of life are drawn from the 1954 Boston University Pavenstedt longitudinal study in early child development, entitled "The Effect of Maternal Maturity and Immaturity on Child Development." As a way of comparing the three samples of mother–child pairs over the first 3 years of life that were selected for this study, we organized the comparison data in relation to the way each mother–infant pair negotiated a sequence of seven tasks of "fitting together," or adaptation over this span of time. The organization of these observational data led to the formulation of a number of basic principles of process governing all living systems, ranging from the cellular level to the level of human consciousness.

1

Issues in Early Mother– Child Interaction

One of the principal aims of our longitudinal study of early personality development, begun at the Boston University School of Medicine–Massachusetts Memorial Hospital's Medical Center in 1954, was the investigation of the mother–child relationship. The study was of a naturalistic exploratory type, planned to provide frequent opportunities to observe mother and child together in a variety of situations over the first 6 years of life. Only primiparous mothers were selected to keep the factor of mothering experience comparable in the groups. Detailed descriptions were made at each contact of the behavior of the mother, of the child, and of the interaction between them. Thus, for each mother–child pair a longitudinal descriptive account was obtained of the progression of outstanding characteristics their interaction demonstrated in these well-defined situations over the years of the study. Comparable observations have been gathered on 22 of the mother–child pairs from birth through the 36th month of life. We have begun to analyze this extensive interactional material, and are presenting in this paper one of the avenues of approach to this task that we are following at present. This approach consists of dividing the interactional data gathered for each pair into a sequence of time segments and making evaluations of interactions prominent in each segment. We are using these evaluations to study the proposal that in this early period there are a series of issues that are being negotiated in the interaction between mother and child. The paper will present the theoretical considerations and the observational materials that have suggested such a possibility.

In investigating the early mother–child relationship, we wished especially to study the way a particular maternal personality exerted its influence on the child and on the course of his development. In the original research design, primiparous mothers were chosen whose personalities showed the widest contrasts we could find along a range of emotional maturity and immaturity, in order that we might observe clear-cut contrasts in their behavior with their infants. We felt that this would make interactional behavior more readily assessed in relation to the developmental course taken. Such obvious interactional contrasts were encountered in the sample of mother–child pairs. We were faced with the task of weighing their importance in relation to the course of development that followed and of comparing similar interactions across the sample of mother–child pairs.

Ernst Kris (1950) discussed the difficult problem of investigating the mother's personality "in order to establish a link between her behavior and the symptomatology of the child." He stated: "The situation in a specific crucial period can no longer be described only in terms of psychosexual development; equal consideration has to be given to that of the aggressive impulses, to the development of the ego, and to that of object relations" (p. 36). He suggested as an example that the particular balance existing in a parental relationship in respect to "the alternatives between indulgence and deprivation (discipline)" might have a phase-specific appropriateness, requiring more of one at one point and more of the other at another to improve the infant's chances for successful conflict solution.

In *A Genetic Field Theory of Ego Formation* (1959), Spitz presented in detail his concept of the part played by the adequacy or inadequacy of object relations in the epigenesis of early ego development. In this publication, he asked the question: "Will disturbances in infantile object relations result in deficient ego formation according to the critical period at which they occur?" (p. 84). After describing the relationship between "synchronicity" and integration, he proposed that a "developmental imbalance" results when asynchrony exists between a maturational period of early ego development and particular features of object relations appropriate to it. The question that at once arises is this: Which features of object relations are appropriate to which periods of early ego development?

This question was extensively dealt with by Erikson (1950a, 1950b) in his presentation of stages of development and the interactions that are associated with each. He discussed the influence on later developmental outcome of cultural variations in these interactions, as well as variations stemming from individual personality characteristics of caretaking figures. In the first two stages of his schema, covering the first 3 years of life (which is the span we are studying in our interactional analysis), he described in considerable detail the interactional elements we have selected for evaluation in our mother–child pairs. Furthermore, he described these features as alternatives with a considerable range of possible variation between the extremes. He implied that, in the individual's object relations, some point of equilibrium will be struck in this range between alternatives that will be characteristic for that individual. For example, in regard to the alternative of supply versus frustration experienced in the establishing of the particular ratio of trust versus mistrust that will be characteristic for a given child, Erikson (1950b) wrote: "Now, while it is quite clear what *must* happen to keep a baby alive (the minimum supply necessary) and what *must not* happen, lest he be physically damaged or chronically upset (the maximum early frustration tolerable), there is a certain leeway in regard to what *may* happen; and different cultures make extensive use of their prerogatives to decide what they consider workable and insist upon calling necessary" (p. 57). Each individual mother also possesses the same prerogative. She exercises it in accord with the consistencies that characterize her particular personality makeup. This factor touches on certain considerations that underlie our approach to the evaluation of interactions in the various periods of early ego development, and that are discussed now briefly before we turn to the specific interactional elements of early object relations we have selected for study.

If the behavioral consistencies that characterize a mother's particular personality makeup could be viewed from the position of the infant's experiences with them, they could be conceived as coming to be represented by certain expectancies or anticipations that the infant would develop in respect to these features of his relationship with the mother. It might take a certain period of time before a trend was established and the *expectancy* became an accurate estimate. The simple repetitive situations that are a part of the daily life of mother and child in this early time of life should lend themselves admirably to a solid set of reliable anticipations about many dimensions of the mother's behavior. A longer span of time for the same degree of certainty to be established would be required in the face of maternal inconsistency or marked expressions of ambivalence in her activities. The estimate should finally approach the point on the range between alternative possibilities for each element of early mother–child interaction that would be characteristic for the pair.

We have tried to capture these relationships in our evaluation of interactions by representing the reaching of such a point as the negotiation of an *issue of interaction*. The *New Century Dictionary* gives several definitions for the word *issue*. It can mean "a point in question," or it can mean "an outcome." A third definition puts these two together as "a point, the decision of which determines the matter." The issue would be negotiated when the child's expectancy for the element of maternal behavior became crystallized. In this respect, "an average expectable environment" (Hartmann, 1939) would be one in which such expectancies would be reached in an average chronology and for average points on the range. This concept of developmental relationships was delineated by Erikson (1950a, 1950b) in his formulation of a series of epigenetic stages determined by the points at which certain precursors of personality function come to their ascendancy, meet their crises, and find their lasting solution through decisive encounters with the environment. Deviations in timing and range of behavior in these encounters lead to the "asynchrony" referred to by Spitz (1959). In our evaluation of interactional material, for each time period of early ego development, we have worded an issue that concerns one especially prominent feature of interaction during that span of months.

Rather than define the issues in terms of whether or not a given feature of interaction will appear, we have framed them with respect to the degree or extent to which the feature will appear.

Our observational material of the first 18 months of life seemed to fall into five large time segments, each with a prominent feature that was encountered extensively in our data for that period.[1] The first period corresponds to the "undifferentiated phase" of early ego development (Hartmann, Kris, & Loewenstein, 1946), namely, the first 2½ months of life. Characteristics of the mother–child relationship at this time have been discussed by many students of early development (e.g., Escalona, 1952; A. Freud, 1936; Hartmann et al., 1946; Spitz, 1954, 1956). A central issue in these months concerns the degree of specific appropriateness the mother can maintain in her response to the cues the baby gives of his state and needs. The second period, from 2½ to 5 months, is the segment most thoroughly described by Spitz and Wolf (1946), in which smiling behavior is developing and coming to play a central role in the relationship. The degree to which truly reciprocal interchanges are established between infant and mother has been selected for evaluation. The third period, between 5 and 9 months, has interested us especially in regard to the way in which the mother responds to the baby's expression of initiative for social exchange and for various preferences. This formulation was suggested by Bowlby's (1958) conceptualization of the nature of the child's tie to his mother. The fourth period, between 9 and 12 or 13 months, has been delimited somewhat more arbitrarily. The feature of interaction that impressed us most forcibly during this phase concerned the intensity and insistence with which the child made demands on the mother and the manner in which she dealt with them. Descriptions of this focalization of demands on the mother have been made by Kris (1950) and A. Freud and Burlingham (1944). The fifth period, extending from the 12th to the 18th month, was described in detail by Erikson (1950a) in relation to the establishing of early autonomy. We have been especially interested in evaluating for each mother–child pair precisely how the self-assertion of the child is dealt with, particularly when it is in opposition to the mother's wishes.

By arranging the data according to these time segments, descriptive features of the observations can be compared in different subjects at roughly the same point in the life of the child. Individual variations in the chronology of significant interactions then become apparent.

DESCRIPTIVE CLINICAL MATERIAL

The remainder of this paper is devoted to describing in further detail the characteristics of mother–child interaction in each of the first five periods, illustrating the range of behaviors we have observed in our sample, and indicating the issues that have been extracted relating to these elements of the emerging relationship.

Period of Initial Adaptation (0–2½ Months)[2]

There seems general agreement that in the initial period of adaptation of the first 2½ months the primary adaptive task consists of a suitable meshing of mothering activities with the cues the baby gives of his state, necessary for him to live and thrive. This primary adaptation is usually achieved by the end of this period and is reflected in the child's adoption of some reasonably predictable rhythms of feeding, elimination, sleep, and wakefulness. If the environment is an "average expectable" one, there also emerges a capacity for discrimination, shown by the child in his responsivity to handling by the mother. He usually becomes more responsive, and quiets more readily for her than for others. A measure of the successful negotiation of the adaptive requirement may be seen as early as the third or fourth week in the mother's spontaneous comment that she now feels she "knows" her baby, which may be accompanied by a perceptible moderation of her anxieties about the baby's care.

This period is one that reveals a great many of the mother's insecurities and anxieties, and puts to test many of her attributes. The dimensions of the child's organization can remain unknown to her for a considerable time if she is not perceptive of the cues supplied in his behavioral feedback to her. Although variations of interaction in this earliest time have been extensively described, we found it a noteworthy experience to observe the striking contrasts revealed in our sample of a "normal" population: The range of adaptation achieved lies truly on a broad spectrum. The extent of adaptation ranged from the barest semblance of a behavioral synchrony between mother and child that was consistent with life[3] to a varied and harmonious interaction, specific in its accuracy of matching stimulus and response, infant need and maternal care. Such synchrony might occur in only one or in many sensorimotor channels. There is quite clearly a quantitative and a qualitative dimension to the specific appropriateness of maternal ministrations in respect to the baby's state. A measure of appropriate social stimulus initiated by the mother is included here as one of the infant's needs, and is observed, for example, in her efforts to produce a smiling response in her baby.

The degree to which mutuality will be established seems to depend, in part at least, on the balance the mother can maintain between her empathy with what she feels are the child's needs and her objectivity in viewing him as an individual apart from her own projections and displacements. A measure of objectivity is essential if the mother is to pick up the unique functional qualities an infant can show from birth. The balance a given mother can maintain between empathy and objectivity is characteristic for her and stems from her particular personality structure. This balance determines the unique combination of areas in which infant need may be met by appropriate response or further intensified by inappropriate stimulation or lack of response.

Thus the evaluation we make in this first period concerns the quantitative and qualitative aspects in the dimension of "specific appropriateness." The issue has been worded thus: "To what degree in the adaptation established between mother and child will the mother's behavior be specifically appropriate to the baby's state and to the cues he gives of it?"

For each pair, a rating on a 5-point scale was given, and the particular areas of inappropriate behavior were noted. In ensuing development the fate of these areas is watched and kept in mind in evaluating later unique aspects of behavioral style.[4]

The range of mother–child interaction that was encountered in our sample is illustrated in the following two examples.[5]

The interview with a Mrs. C. was held in the hospital after she had been shown her baby for the first time.

She was very pleased and enormously proud of her son. She said that the baby was crying intensely when he was brought to her, but when he was laid beside her, he immediately quieted and was quiet the whole time he was with her. She said she felt that her baby knew her because when the nurse came to take him again, he began crying again. She said she had stroked his cheek and he had smiled. When she had tried to feed him the water, he had known it was water as soon as it had touched his lips and he spit it out because he wanted milk.

Objectivity was at a minimum here. Her empathy with her newborn child hinged on the meanings she gave to his behavior. She viewed him to a great extent in a framework consisting chiefly of her projected feelings. The limitations of such a framework become evident when these feelings are highly ambivalent. The problem is compounded when the mother cannot decide when they match reality and when they do not.

The following is a report of a home visit with the same mother at 4 weeks. The baby was asleep in an adjacent room.

After about a half-hour there was a slight whimpering sound from the other room. Mrs. C. immediately alerted to this, although it was only the faintest sound and then said that she had better wait until he really cried as she half got out of her seat, then sat down again, and then immediately got up and went to the baby. I followed her into the bedroom to look at him. The infant was lying prone, head to the right, with some slight frown that did not seem like crying to me particularly. Mrs. C. turned him over and he lay quiet again. Again Mrs. C. said, looking at me questioningly, "I'd better wait until he really wakes up," and came back into the kitchen and sat down again. At another slight sound she got up again almost immediately, picked the baby up and brought him out, holding him first against her arm. He looked very sleepy and as though discomforted at being moved and he closed his eyes again. Mrs. C. then put him back in the bassinet; soon after this he began to cry, and she picked him up again. The whole sequence had a quality of a kind of disorganized indecision about it, as though Mrs. C. never once settled on any kind of action for more than a minute. Almost before she decided on one move, she was already reversing it.

Once it was definitely ascertained that the baby was awake, Mrs. C. took him into the kitchen and held him against her arm in a sitting position. As he quieted, she tapped his nose and chin: this seemed to be an irritant that set him off crying, and Mrs. C. now shifted him against her shoulder. He looked very cozy in this position, his legs drawn up under him so that he was curled up in a kind of little ball, and cuddled against his mother's shoulder, very quiet now.

As Mrs. C. had not given the baby his bath yet, she now decided to do this, taking him to a shelf by the sink and lying him down supine. Actually there were a few moments of indecision again as she thought that she would give him his bath, then looked at me questioningly, and then continued to hold him, and finally got up and made the actual decision to bathe him. The baby began to cry as she laid him down, and Mrs. C. shifted him about, tapped his chin and nose—all of this with a kind of uncertainty. It seemed to me that she made a great many small movements that gave me the sense of acute discomfort in watching and seemed to have a similar effect on the baby.

As the baby activated his arms, he seemed to try to get his hand to his mouth. He seemed not able to do this and cried briefly and then quieted. Mrs. C. spoke to him, tapped his nose and he again began to cry and Mrs. C., looking very distressed, pushed a pacifier into his mouth. She said that he was hungry and that he didn't like the pacifier, but the baby quieted again. As he yawned and stretched his arms a bit, the pacifier dropped out and Mrs. C. immediately put it back in. It would drop out again soon and the baby would seem to be yawning and stretching. But Mrs. C. seemed to take this as the beginning of a cry, although the baby looked quite content to me, and pushed the pacifier in his mouth again. This was repeated several times. Mrs. C. said to me, "I'll let you watch him and go finish my cigarette"; and indicated that she would like me to stand by him as she went toward the table. The pacifier very soon dropped out of the baby's mouth and I picked it up ready to put it in again; but, as he seemed to be yawning and not discomforted, I held it in my hand. Mrs. C. returned again very quickly and asked, "Doesn't he want it?," watched for a moment, and then decided that she would get the bath ready.

The second illustration provides a contrasting description of a mother–child interaction in a home-visit observation. Nancy, the baby, was 3 weeks of age.[5] Her mother was, in contrast to Mrs. C., at the other extreme of our personality grouping. Earlier in the visit, the mother had described how Nancy had indicated her preference for the prone position; she had told of a characteristic posture that the baby adopted before going to sleep. The mother also had been quick to pick up that her infant's wakening process was very slow. It took her daughter some time between her first whimpers of arousal until she was ready for her bottle; the mother had already learned to pace her feeding accordingly. During the visit, the baby had been sleeping until this time.

After Nancy had been sleeping for some time, she began to move about, though still asleep. She pulled her knees up under her and seemed to be stretching her arms and turning her head about on the pillow, her skin taking on a reddish tinge with the effort. Finally she made slight squealing sounds. Mrs. D. now turned Nancy over on her face, accomplishing this again with a quite easy but gentle movement. Nancy, as before, remained quiet for a few minutes, her eyes open, her mouth moving minimally; then she began moving her arms and legs about, finally putting her fingers to her mouth and then beginning to cry. As Nancy lay on her back, Mrs. D. stood beside Nancy chatting with us and holding Nancy's feet very lightly, touching rather than restraining, lifting the baby's nightgown to show how chubby Nancy was getting, and occasionally feeling the diaper to see if Nancy was wet.

Mrs. D. finally picked Nancy up, not letting her cry very long, and cradled her very comfortably and gently in her arms, looking down at her in a very warm, half-humorous, accepting expression. She held Nancy in this way for a while, pinching the infant's cheeks between her thumb and forefinger in a quick, repetitive gesture, then tapping her on the chin a few times playfully; and then, after a while, Mrs. D. put Nancy back on the couch on her stomach. At one point, while Mrs. D. was holding Nancy and the infant's fingers were going to her mouth, Mrs. D. commented, "I'd bet she'd suck my finger if I put it in her mouth." This time, as Mrs. D. placed the baby prone on the couch, Nancy's face came into contact with the pillow, and she lifted her head slightly, twisting about and kicking her legs, and seeming a little discomforted. Mrs. D. reached out her hand and patted Nancy with a gentle rhythm on her back, and the baby quieted very quickly. Mrs. D. said, "That has always worked." The infant began moving again after Mrs. D. stopped patting, and then the mother took the baby's feet in her hand, holding them very lightly as before, seeming to be establishing contact rather than restraining in any way.

We see here the mother's respect of the infant's gradual awakening and her reporting of her observations of the various idiosyncratic preferences of her child, her reaching out to contact the child, and demonstrate the baby to the visitor and to participate in its performance, she did not seem to carry this activity too far. She put the baby down. We see also the quality of her attention: She divided it between the visitor and the baby, and she maintained tactile contact with the baby after placing her in a prone position.

It is likely that the impact on these two infants of the experiences illustrated will be profoundly different. In our cases in which a mother failed to achieve appropriateness sufficiently specific for her child, the father often could establish it. He then became the one who could more successfully quiet the baby and the one who first elicited the smile.

Inasmuch as observations were recorded every 2 to 3 weeks, evaluations of the outcome of the issues were based on a review of a series of contacts.

This check, which is one of the strengths of longitudinal data, served to modify extreme impressions that a single contact might elicit. In general, mothers showed a high degree of consistency within any given period.

Period of Reciprocal Exchange (Approx. 2½–5 Months)

By the time of this second period, the mother had usually surmounted the anxieties of providing an environment adequate to sustain the life of her infant. One usually saw her now involved in the increasingly delightful experience of stimulating and responding to the emerging smiling behavior of her infant. It is one of the most pleasurable (and obvious) of the early interactional phases. We have attached importance to the crescendo quality occurring in the well-developed smiling play, in the way it spreads from the facial area to bring the whole body, including the voice, into a primitive organized effort. This extension of the response to its limits occurs as the smiling behavior of the infant is elicited in a series of repeated reciprocal activities on the part of the stimulator and the baby. A brief pause allows the infant his first response, then the mother's smiling face is brought closer, another pause for the infant to react again, another presentation of mother's face, each time with some new stimulus added— perhaps now an open mouth, or the touch of a finger, or a vocalization. The infant's initial localized facial response extends to involve arms, legs, trunk, and voice in an exuberant, wriggling, infectious, joyful display.

There were some mothers in our group who never reported, and were never observed entering into, this kind of interaction with their infants. There were others who engaged in it so intensely and over such a prolonged period that the child would break into crying, a response that would bring the mother to her senses and lead her to stop the stimulation. There is, therefore, a wide range in the experiences that an infant can have in respect to this element of interaction, one that is so often taken completely for granted. Other variations include the age at which a mother will first attempt to elicit a smile from her baby, as well as the amount of effort and attention she devotes to getting the smiling response started. There is a considerable variation in the age at which smiling behavior reaches its peak.

We have operationally defined reciprocal interaction as that showing the quality of alternation of stimulus–response, back and forth, between mother and child in the fashion just described. (Some mothers will stimulate their infants to smile, but the interaction is intended only to produce a reaction in the child, and not truly to begin a reciprocation with him. In others, the interaction may consist of reciprocity of vocal exchange rather than in the general area of smiling play.) The issue for this period has been worded then as follows: To what extent will the interaction between mother and child include reciprocal sequences of interchange between them, that is, back and forth, active–passive alternations of stimulus and response?

The following extract is taken from an observation during a home visit, which was made when the infant Helen S. was 3 months, 17 days old. If the mother's interaction with the child is compared in this example with the father's, the subtle differences in reciprocal quality of interaction become apparent. The observer writes:

Helen lay on her back in the bassinet, appearing pleased with the activity around. Her arms and legs moved about quite actively, and she smiled readily as Mrs. S. leaned over and spoke to her. Mrs. S. talked to Helen in a very animated, stimulating fashion, chucking her under the chin, calling her "Little Fatty." She moved her head toward Helen and back in rapid succession as she did this. Helen responded, looking at her mother with an expression of pleasure and moving arms and legs in excitement. As Mrs. S. discontinued this, the baby continued her excited movement for a bit, looking at her mother as though anticipating a return engagement. As it was not forthcoming, she quieted her movement and began to fuss minimally. She soon turned her attention to me, looking at me, breaking into a spontaneous smile as I spoke to her. Mrs. S. leaned forward and kissed Helen on the cheek in quick pleasure as she did this, seeming very delighted at the baby's display of responsiveness to me.

Mother and visitor became involved in conversation and Helen began to fuss as no attention was paid to her, making a series of separate little cries, her arms spread wide and up as though wanting to be picked up. After a while, Mrs. S. said, "I'll hold you for a while," picked Helen up, and held Helen on her lap against her left arm. The baby quieted immediately and sat looking at me for a moment, seeming very contented having reached her objective. She soon leaned well forward from her mother against the table and became interested in looking at something on the table; Mrs. S. talked to her asking, "What are you looking at? You looking at this?" She spoke in a very animated way, with Helen paying no attention, simply continuing to focus her gaze completely absorbed on something on the table. Mrs. S. said one could not distract Helen when she was interested in something. She had a mind of her own. Mrs. S. said the baby was very sensitive to know who would pick her up and who would not, implying that Helen differentiated between her father and mother in this respect. She spoke in a very definite way of her own imperviousness to the baby's "winding" (whining), implying that the infant knew who was the boss and of the uselessness of fussing.

Mr. S. came in after the mother had again placed Helen in the bassinet. He stood looking down at the infant, and she now turned to look up at her father, spreading her arms wide and a little upward as though appealing to him to pick her up, and she now began to fuss a bit again. Mr. S. made no move to pick her up, but after a while he leaned over and patted her on the stomach, moving her body back and forth very gently in a kind of quick awkward movement as though pulled to make some response to the infant's appeal. The baby made no response to this; she neither activated nor quieted, but waved her arms and legs as he spoke to her. Mr. S.

made no other approach to Helen, simply standing looking down at her as he made small conversation with me.

It is difficult to illustrate a mother–child pair in which the reverse situation is exemplified, inasmuch as the judgment of a relative lack of social reciprocity can be obtained only on a review of all our material. However, we have found that in those pairs in which the mother did not take advantage of the easy opportunity for this reciprocal exchange, the delightful readiness for response in the child nevertheless might be observed. The mother might be pleased and gratified as she watched her baby interact with others, or at the pleasure the baby showed at her approach, but she was not observed entering into the interchange herself. The following example is an illustration of this. It was taken from a home-visit observation of a mother whose personality showed strong obsessive-compulsive trends. She was restrained, gloomy, overanxious, and complaining. She had had an extremely anxious time in her initial period of adaptation. This observation was in the fourth month and the observer noted immediately that there was a lightening of the dark cloud of grave concern that had overhung the air before. The beginnings of interchange were evident, but no reciprocal play was noted. The observation reads:

> There seemed to be some quality of closeness between the mother and child which had been completely missing before. For example, at some point the baby lay staring at me and then turned to his mother to look at her as though for assurance, and Mrs. K. commented, "He's asking, is it all right, Mommy," in a quite pleased tone of voice. (She was not induced to play here with the child.) At other times the baby would smile at her and was very responsive when she picked him up or touched him, quieting almost immediately. Mrs. K. seemed to enjoy his responsiveness and to be pleased at his smiling at her or at her being able to quiet him. She even talked to him spontaneously *in response* to his smiling or looking at her, but her behavior was still limited pretty much to asking "What's the matter?" though in a much more conversational tone, and at one point she even ventured a "Goo."

We note here that it was the mother who was responding to her baby and not the baby who was being stimulated by the mother. We observed later that this child was of unusually serious demeanor and showed relatively little spontaneity. One could sense here a separateness between child and mother. She talked to the baby without spontaneous *exchange* with him.

We are interested in studying the extent to which a lack of specific appropriateness in the first period can be made up for by a satisfactory experience during this second phase. We are also interested in following the later outcome in children who do not experience an easy reciprocity with their mothers at this time or until some later age. We have examples in which this reciprocal feature has not really begun until speech is well enough developed to permit simple conversation. The mother–child relationship seems then to take on a new meaning and liveliness for both of them, and especially acquires a positive affective tone that has been missing before. In other pairs we have observed that reciprocal interaction almost disappears by the time speech is developing well in the baby. When this quality of interaction disappears from the relationship, the child appears unhappy and distressed; mother and child give the impression of having "lost" each other. It has been of interest to watch, as time moves on, the point at which reciprocal interchanges of smiling play begin to disappear from our observations; in many instances, this occurred by the eighth or ninth month.

We suspect that much of importance for the child's development hinges on the continuance of reciprocal exchanges in some other area of interaction. Whether it persists or not seems to depend a good deal on the mother's lead in continuing this quality of interaction in a new area such as vocalization and speech, or on her ability to play spontaneously on the level at which the baby may be in its development. This is illustrated in the following example during a home visit to a Mrs. Q., whose child was 10 months old. The observer writes:

> Although there was virtually no direct physical contact between Mrs. Q. and Ellen during my visit, Mrs. Q. did a lot of direct talking to Ellen, offering her a glass of milk and leaning over and whispering, in a somewhat tender and feeling way, various little unimportant statements. Ellen responded very nicely to these, paid close attention to her mother, and seemed to be very involved in their relationship.

Period of Early Directed Activity of the Infant (5–9 Months)

The social interchange between mother and child has been presented to this point largely in relation to the mother's initiative in eliciting and sustaining it. However, the baby's initiative in establishing social exchange with the mother begins to come into play as the smiling response reaches its height. The child attempts to reach out to the mother and stimulate her to respond to him. The manner in which the mother responds to the baby's initiative forms the basis for the third issue, which has been worded as follows: To what degree will the initiative of the infant be successful in establishing areas of reciprocity in the interchange with the mother? When this effort is successful in bringing the mother into smiling play, the infant learns to anticipate her response to him and can reproduce some of the joyful excitement of the experience by actions associated with this anticipation. The mother's ability to respond to the infant's initiative for social interchange is related to her general affective spontaneity, the gratification her child's pleasurable reaching out gives her, and the general level of interchange she shows in interpersonal relations. It seems also to be related to the priority given her child in the organization of her perceptual awareness.

Subtly and easily obscured are the tender beginnings of the child's directed activities in this period, as shown in the following example of Mrs. G.C. whose baby was 7½ months old:

> I remained a while longer as Mrs. G.C. began the feeding. She held the baby on her lap with his head resting against her arm as she spooned the food to him and although she had expected that he might refuse it since he had not been eating well the past few days, Douggie took the food quite readily, and the feeding went very smoothly. Once or twice during the feeding, Douggie would seem to want a brief respite from taking the mouthfuls of food and Mrs. G.C. would wait until he was ready. A couple of times when this occurred, he put his head back and looked directly up at his mother, completely engaging her in visual contact, and Mrs. G.C. seemed extremely delighted and, I thought, quite excited by this contact, returning his gaze and then seeming a bit embarrassed and pulling herself away and offering him the next spoonful.

We first paid attention to the baby's initiative in regard to its influence in starting social exchanges with the mother. However, it seemed obvious that the mother's response to the baby's initiative in general must be a large part of the issue at stake in this period. The baby is beginning to show preferences of all sorts, and is attempting actively to control the stimulations reaching him as well as those disappearing from him. Some of his efforts in the direction of his mother encounter a response in kind from the mother, a back and forthness, or a feedback of reciprocal quality, whereas some of his other efforts do not. We have assumed that those activities which the infant initiates and which lead to a reciprocal exchange with the mother must be clearly distinct in the infant's perception from those which do not. A dimension of anticipation must therefore be set up in the child's expectancies which reflects the balance of success or failure the child has experienced in establishing new areas of reciprocity with his mother. In our contrasting groups of maternal personalities, there was a wide variation in the respect the mother showed for early preferences stemming from the initiative of the baby, just as there was a wide variation in the mother's availability for reciprocal interactions.

The period from 6 to 9 months is a time that demands of the mother a certain keenness in reading and appreciating the cues of her child and further demands that she respond appropriately as in the initial period of adaptation. However, it has the flavor of a more passive response in adaptation on her part than the more active role she took in the first period. This difference is frequently observed as the mother begins the feeding of solids. The average mother who has negotiated the two earlier issues adapts so readily to the new pressures of the child's budding initiative that it is usually not readily apparent that an important issue is being settled. However, when we see an infant, who has progressed solidly through the first 4 or 5 months, meeting then an implacable barrier to his initiative, the picture is different.

The following example is taken from a tape-recorded interview with the mother whose son, Ned, was approximately 9 months old. Mother and child had experienced a satisfactory initial adaptation and a delightful early period of social smiling play. However, the battle[EN1] of initiative had shown its first beginnings in the area of motor activity when Ned was 4½ months old. At that time, he was able to pull himself to the edge of his carriage and was promptly harnessed because the mother feared he would fall out. The struggle extended in the following months until we felt entitled to label this period for this mother–child pair as "the battle of the high chair." Some weeks before the interview, the pediatrician had suggested that the mother could try again to introduce solid foods. The interviewer reported:

I.:   Well, to get back to Ned again. How is the feeding situation going?

M.:   It's picked up very good. He's got the idea that he's gonna gag. You know, he's always gagging on his vegetables.

I.:   Yeh.

M.:   And that's why he won't take it—and—or he didn't like the taste. If he didn't like the taste, he'd gag like, I'm disgusted. So last Friday, he was mad. He took a fit, he was mad. My husband was sitting there, and he was crying for my husband to pick him up, and I was feeding him and he was cross. I don't think he knows what I'm giving him—the mixed vegetables and the soup and his bottle.

I.:   Well, what was he—spitting it out?

M.:   He just quit taking them. I don't know what's wrong.

I.:   What do you mean?

M.:   He'll be happy and all. If you pick him up in the morning, he'll be so quiet and never say a word—up in his high chair. He'll just sit there and play. And we used to give him tea, a cup of tea or something. He'd be quiet, and then I'd feed him, and maybe he'd get cranky and be tired. But when I pick him up *now* and walk to the high chair [to feed him], he don't want that [makes crying sounds]. Sit down, sit down—he don't want that. He wants to go.

I.:   But when you do sit him down, then he—.

M.:   Then he goes, then he runs all—he pushes and he kicks and he bangs his head, and he'll just sit there. And look at him, he's crazy. I says I don't know. If he bumps his head enough times, he'll stop. Then he'll stop and he gets mad. Mm—mm—he'll start crying, and there's nothing to do but just let him cry.

I.:   Uh-huh.

M.:   If you keep on picking him up, you'll get nothing done and you won't accomplish anything. So, we leave him there. Then we give him a toy to shut up.

This baby, who had been one of our most attractive infants in his fourth and fifth months, lost all signs of spontaneous, pleasurable affect in the early part of his second year of life. He was completely defeated by his mother in this early struggle. This mother–child pair provided an instance in which the usual sequence of issues had not followed in order. The threat which the initiative of her infant posed for this mother was revealed by the fact that she suddenly went to work for 4 months beginning in the seventh month, leaving the baby in the care of her husband. She gave up this solution and returned to resume her control in the household because the husband was now yielding to the baby's demands to be picked up. She said, "That was the last straw." The outcome of the next two issues for this mother and child could have been easily predicted at this point. The self-assertion[EN2] usually seen in the early part of the second year of life submerged. In a recent follow-up at the age of 5½ years he showed a striking passivity and almost an avoidance of investment in the few activities he could begin himself.

Period of Focalization on Mother (9–15 Months)

The issue has been worded as: To what degree will the child succeed in his demands that the mother alone fulfill his needs? One of the roots of autonomy in the first year of life stems from the outcome the child experiences from the activities that he initiates. There are a series of steps by which this primordial autonomy widens its foothold vis-à-vis the outer world. Once Issue 3 is satisfactorily negotiated, the way is immediately opened in the relationship between child and mother for the next issue to come to the fore. This concerns the extension of initiative in the child to achieve something of a manipulation of the mother, especially a focalization on her as the person who meets his needs. During this period, there is a further discrimination of mother from other caretaking people. Whereas the child might have accepted a feeding before as easily from father as from mother, it is now only the mother who is clearly preferred for this activity. It is only the mother's lap that is sought for comfort or security. Such a process of focalizing interaction on the mother was termed *monotropy* by John Bowlby (1958). He considered it an innate characteristic of developmental behavior in the animal kingdom that the specific stimulus–response patterns become localized in one parent animal.

Although from the beginning the mother has been responding to her child's demands, these have gradually become more and more specific. Whereas the first demands of the child are diffuse expressions of discomfort, they now become directed efforts to possess and manipulate. It is one thing for a mother to come to the aid of the helpless infant, and quite another for her to yield to a clearly intended demand of her year-old baby. The demands of this period on the mother are intense and unremitting and involve the mother in the deepest threats to her integrity.[EN3] One could say that this period separates the women from the girls, those with flexibility from those without, those whose sense of identity as mothers is secure from those who are only partially committed. The smooth and satisfactory negotiation seems to depend on the mother's ability to yield or to compromise by keeping the baby in her awareness while she pursues her own interests. Her freedom to do so depends partly on her freedom to limit. Fear of strangers, strong at this time, is an additional factor serving to push the child toward the mother. The dangers from which a child in his beginning motor explorations must be protected are another factor binding the mother's attention to the child. On the other hand, the mother who is secure enough in herself and has confidence in the ultimate separateness and integrity of her child can enjoy and yield to this possession by him. When she does so, preserving areas of reciprocity with her child, she acts as a stable base of operations for him as his growing motility and inevitable curiosity carries him away from her.

The range of interactions that can be seen here was illustrated by one of our mothers whose principal preoccupation was to maintain her child's involvement with her. She welcomed any turn of the child toward her, and kept herself always available. The period was passed with little sign of the child's demand on her mother. On the contrary, notable efforts were made by the child to move away from the mother.

We have observed that by 9 months, the focus of the mother's attention is a percept that the child clearly has come to appreciate. The child struggles[EN4] for her attentive involvement. One of the consequences of the perception of attentive focus of the mother and its employment in the interaction is that such a simple signal can come to represent actual exchanges of considerable duration and complexity.

The capacity to find gratification in the outside world apart from the mother, to transfer the experience of gratification from interaction with her to interaction with the world is, we feel, related in part to a certain degree of success in negotiating this fourth period. Unless a satisfactory level of certainty of the mother's availability is established before the self-assertion that follows in the early months of the second year, the child is faced with an important asynchrony in respect to his mother: He is still seeking to assure himself of her while he already must begin to assert himself against her.

A single illustration will show the way the child exerts his possessive pressure in this fourth period. It is an excerpt from a tape-recorded interview with a mother whose child was 12 months of age.

M.:   But she gets into everything. She won't play by herself and she wants me to play with—and she won't stay out on the porch by herself. She likes to go out there, but she won't stay by herself.

I.:   She won't play by herself?

M.:   No, for a while she will, and then she always comes in to me, and she's either in the pantry or in the cabinet, or in the closet—and now she pushes the car bed away and gets into my closet.

This behavior continued as illustrated in the following example taken from a tape-recorded interview with the same mother when the child was 14 months:

I.:   Does she ever let you get away from her or—.

M.:   She bothers me all day. I can't do anything. I can't sit down to read a paper or do anything because she always tries to get up on me, and when I'm in the pantry, she's in the pantry; when I'm in the kitchen—if I'm sweeping, she's gotta sweep. No matter where I am she's gotta be. And she won't stay out on the porch, although she has been for the last couple of days playing at the door, but when the screen door closes, she doesn't like it. It's only a little porch. But when the door closes, she doesn't like it and she cries. And you know the bathroom has to be closed at all times.

Period of Self-Assertion (12–18 Months)

The clarity of this fifth issue and the timing of its onset follow on the outcome of the fourth issue. The fifth issue we have stated as: To what extent will the child establish self-assertion in the interaction with the mother? We might add, In what areas? At what cost? This period extends over the early part of the second year of life and corresponds to the well-known phase of negativism. This is the time of appearance of autonomy (Erikson, 1950b; Spitz, 1957), which emerges *pari passu* with the restriction of volition that is occurring. For example, Spitz (1957) wrote, "The jurisdiction of the fifteen-months-old eventually is limited practically to his own body." This factor has been described in relation to the struggle over toilet training in which the child may be pressed to retreat to a last fortress of assertion of volitional control, that is, in control of his body functions. In these present times, however, where the least well-educated of our mothers may have read when to begin toilet training and may not begin it until the close of the second year, toilet training itself may not enter so clearly into the picture. Yet, just as surely, the problem of self-assertion, the attempt to possess the initiative, results in conflict.

However, except in unusual instances in our material, we found, instead of a complete defeat of the child, that there are different areas in which self-assertion is achieved. Possible conflicts had been in evidence since the beginnings of self-assertion in the third phase, but now these reach an outspoken struggle. This represents the time of "decisive encounter" as Erikson (1950b) described it in his discussion of the emergence of autonomy. The areas of self-assertion achieved are of a wide variety, unique for the mother–child pair, and again reflect the particular character of the mother and her household. The following example is extreme for our population but not an unfamiliar picture to those acquainted with mothers who find it difficult to set limits. The description is taken from a home visit with Dora at 17 months:

> Dora runs the apartment and the family. Mrs. I. is unable to study for her examinations because she can't open a book when Dora is up. It has gotten to the point where Mrs. I. can hardly go down to the laundry in the basement with Dora because Dora runs around and gets into so much mischief, like opening the other washers and taking out the laundry, and so on. Dora's things are all over the apartment and the whole bedroom (only one bedroom in the apartment) belongs to Dora. Mrs. I. is constantly trying to anticipate Dora in the nicest possible way, but it is difficult for Mrs. I. and difficult for Dora. This home is almost too child-oriented. The walks outside are talked about as though it is Dora who determines where they should go. Mrs. I. is constantly at Dora's beck and call, although Dora does have trouble settling down to anything and really being satisfied with it.

The more usual state of affairs is better illustrated by the two following excerpts, which are taken from observations of a Mrs. D. and her child Nancy. The first is from a home visit when Nancy was 15 months, 23 days, about which the observer wrote:

> Mrs. D.'s handling of Nancy was warm and permissive. She was supporting, approving, and seemed to enjoy her very much. She wanted Nancy to "perform"—fold her arms, tap her nose, play peekaboo. She was not the least insistent or annoyed when Nancy wouldn't comply; said rather philosophically, "She never does things when you ask her to," quite accepting of Nancy's own will to comply or not. She relates that Nancy wants to do everything herself now; she refuses to be fed; she insists on holding her own spoon. Mother lets her, is not concerned with lower food intake when Nancy feeds herself. Lets her do as many things for herself as possible. Mrs. D. did not seem threatened by Nancy's quest for independence, but accepting of it and supportive. She made no mention of any troubles or mess resulting from this self-feeding; she only spoke of it in terms of what Nancy wanted and needed to do. Her eating habits are changing. She no longer wants baby food, but wants to (and does) try all adult food. Mrs. D. still tries to give her baby food for lunch, sometimes opens four to five cans to give her a choice, but Nancy turns them all down. "She really likes roast beef and steak," said Mrs. D. with a chuckle. She drinks very well from a cup. She rarely wants her bottle now, except for going to sleep. She is fed a little before the parents eat, then nibbles at their food during their dinner as well. Nancy no longer naps as long as she used to. She used to sleep for two hours in a blanket on the floor; now naps one hour at the most.

The second illustration at 16 months, 12 days shows how the degree of self-assertion possible becomes ascertained by the child. The observations were recorded while the mother was conversing with the pediatrician prior to the examination of the child:

> Then she looks up at camera, walks to mother's pocketbook on small table, pulls it off, vocalizing, takes it to mother. Sits on floor with it and proceeds to empty it. Takes out diaper first, then keys, at which point mother bends down and takes pocketbook. Nancy gets up and cries out in an angry squeal. Keeps crying while mother shakes keys in front of her to divert her, while continuing to talk to pediatrician. Nancy's cries become more urgent. Finally, mother gives her back the pocketbook. Nancy lets out a frustrated squeal. Mother bends down, I believe to open the pocketbook for her (here mother yields), Nancy quiets, proceeds as before. Takes out diaper, keeps rummaging inside the pocketbook. Real pleasure evident in this activity as it had been in moving screws on the table previously. Takes out box of Chiclet chewing gum, looks at it, holds it high in one hand, gives mother back pocketbook, keys, diaper. Holds chewing gum box, shakes it, and is just about to open box when mother takes it and puts it back into her pocketbook. Nancy screams loudly, inconsolably. Mother picks her up. Nancy holds arms into air, as if pulling on something, touches her hair, her ear. Angry, piercing screams as mother sets her on table. She quiets somewhat when the pediatrician hands her a roll of adhesive and scissors to play with. [This mother had always been quite concerned about the child's choking on small items, i.e., the gum, that she might put in her mouth.]

Such illustrations show the push and pull of forces between mother and child. The child wins the pocketbook and its entire contents except for the one item. Such equilibrium regarding limits is reached at a particular point on the range of possibilities for limits by each mother–child pair in an individual way. The process appears more complicated when the previous fourth issue has been unsatisfactorily negotiated. The asynchrony can be observed in the frantic efforts of such children to reestablish themselves with the mother after such a rupture, and the implications of frustration seem more total. The child is struggling for an adequate assurance of the availability of the mother, and at the same time he is struggling to assert himself against her. The possible relationship of developmental phases to levels of equilibria between infant and environment was suggested in Piaget's (1956) discussion of the part played by equilibration processes in the psychobiological development of the child. Assessment of the issues we have delineated will provide a means of exploring this concept.

The second 18 months have been divided more arbitrarily into three 6-month periods, from 18 to 24 months, 24 to 30 months, and 30 to 36 months. There are four issues being studied in reference to these periods. The first two are concerned with the destructive aspects of the child's aggression and the manner in which he directly challenges the mother's will and convictions. The other two involve the way the interaction with the mother includes the emerging secondary-process activities of the child and the preoccupations he develops with his body functions.

SUMMARY

We have presented here our modes of organizing the complex longitudinal descriptive data of early development in respect to one of its facets, namely, that of the mother–child interaction. The approach we are utilizing was conceived in response to the necessity of making cross-case comparisons of this detailed observational material in a sizable number of cases. It also stemmed from the challenge to examine new (i.e., behavioral or observational level) elements of the child's early object relations and to look for new relationships between those elements that appeared prominently in the material. We have developed a hypothetical schema, in which these elements can be studied in a phase-specific, epigenetic context. It provides a set of dimensions in respect to object relations that occupies an intermediate position between the levels of phenomenology and of the dynamic constructs by which meaningful information about object relationships is usually communicated. This intermediate position provides a bridge for us between prenatal appraisals of maternal character, observations in chronological sequence of maternal and infant behavior, and outcome in evaluations of later ego organization in the child. Exploration into the manner in which maternal character might exert influence on the early personality development of the child was one of the original interests in launching a naturalistic study of this type.

A method of analysis based on a hypothetical schema of course must itself be exploratory. A rough scaling of interaction has been devised on the basis of the concept that the adaptation between mother and child in a given period involves the settling of an issue. This assumption determines for the period the point of equilibrium that will be characteristic for a mother–child pair in respect to a particular element or dimension of interaction. Marked variations in the range of behaviors encountered in a "normal" population of mothers, such as ours, can be quite clearly delineated by this means and thus communicated more easily. These phase-related variations can then be correlated with evaluation of variables in later ego organization in the children. We hope that the effort to represent events occurring between mother and child in terms of the anticipatory function of the developing ego will open further avenues of study, as should our attempt to relate the epigenetic phase relationships of early development to a sequence of equilibrial positions of interaction between child and environment (mother in this case).

NOTES

This research was supported by U.S. Public Health Service Grants Nos. M.898, M.898 (C1-C4), M. 3325, M. 3325 (C1-C2).

Published in: *Journal of the American Academy of Child Psychiatry, 1,* 141–166 (1962).

1. It is obvious that a number of other interactions and issues might have been selected for a study. The prominence of these in our material may relate to the sample of subjects chosen and to our methods of observation and recording.
2. The time span ascribed to each period is that being used in the cross-case comparisons. It represents an approximation only, inasmuch as individuals may show considerable variation.
3. In one mother–child pair the mother was so preoccupied with the fear of her otherwise normal infant choking to death with feedings that she fed it a minimum amount. It had gained but a pound and a half over its birth weight by 3 months of life. We had real fears for its survival.
4. In one instance, the only outstandingly inappropriate maneuver of the mother in the first period was an extraordinary amount of tactile stimulation that she gave the child. A hair-clutching gesture of the infant's, which had already been observed in the neonatal period, came to be used by the infant at 7 months in response to excessive tactile stimulation. A few weeks later she began intense scratching of her own skin, and in the second year of life, the hair-clutching came to be recognized by the observers as a signal of distress.
5. The deliveries of both these babies were observed as a part of our routine. Resuscitation was uneventful in both. Lusty crying was established in the first minute and good color and muscle tone within the next 3 minutes.

EDITORS' NOTES

EN1 Sander's thinking often resorts to a semantic spectrum of terms, such as "battle," "conflict," "struggle," "victory," that intend to describe the strong dynamic in the negotiation between mother and child, and therefore assume a particular connotation in respect to their traditional use.

EN2 The basic theme of self-assertion will be resumed here (and subsequently in the following chapters): It is convenient to explain self-assertion as the collection of those prodromal behaviors that can then lead, more or less, to self-assertiveness.

EN3 Again, to understand the impact of this expression one must keep in mind Sander's particular use of certain terms (see the previous note), rich in narrative pathos, not to interpret it in psychoanalytic terms.

EN4 Again, one of the terms dear to Sander.

REFERENCES

Bowlby, J. (1958). The nature of the child's tie to his mother. *International Journal of Psychoanalysis, 39,* 89–97.

Erikson, E., II. (1950a). *Childhood and society.* New York: Norton.

Erikson, E., II. (1950b). Growth and crisis of the healthy personality. *Psychological Issues, 1,* 50–100.

Escalona, S. (1952), Emotional development in the first year of life. In M. E. J. Senn (Ed.), *Problems of infancy and childhood: Transactions of the Sixth Conference.* New York: Josiah Macy Jr. Foundation.

Freud, A. (1936). *The ego and the mechanisms of defense.* New York: International Universities Press.

Freud, A., & Burlingham, D. T. (1944). *Infants without families.* New York: International Universities Press.

Hartmann, H. (1939). *Ego psychology and the problem of adaptation.* New York: International Universities Press.

Hartmann, H., Kris, E., & Loewenstein, R. M. (1946). Comments on the formation of psychic structure. *The Psychoanalytic Study of the Child, 2,* 11–38.

Kris, E. (1950). Notes on the development and on some current problems of psychoanalytic child psychology. *The Psychoanalytic Study of the Child, 5,* 24–46.

Piaget, J. (1956). Reply to comments concerning the part played by equilibration processes in the psychobiological development of the child. *Discussions on Child Development, 4,* 77–83.

Spitz, R. A. (1954). Genèse des premières relations objectales. *Rev. Franç. Psychanal.,* 38. ("Development of first object relations", *French Psychoanalytic Review*).

Spitz, R. A. (1956). *Die Enistehung des ersten Objektbeziehungen: Direkte Beobachtungen an Säuglingen während des ersten Lebensjahres.* Stuttgart, Germany: Klett. The development of first object relationships: Direct observation of infants during their first years.

Spitz, R. A. (1957). *No and yes: On the genesis of human communication.* New York: International Universities Press.

Spitz, R. A. (1959). *A genetic field theory of ego formation.* New York: International Universities Press.

Spitz, R. A., & Wolf, K. M. (1946). The smiling response: A contribution to the ontogenesis of social relations. *Genetic Psychology Monographs, 34,* 57–125.

2

Adaptive Relationships in Early Mother–Child Interaction

Current research in the area of early personality development is turning toward the study of the nature of the interactions that take place between the infant and his environment. This focus is somewhat different from those investigations that center primarily on changes in the behavior and function of the infant or on the handling practices[EN1] and attitudes of the mother in relation to these changes; it involves rather a study of the phenomenology of the activity itself that takes place between the two.

This broad and complex task, only relatively recently undertaken,[EN2] has been approached already from such a variety of points of view and on so many levels of detail (Blauvelt & McKenna, 1959; Brody, 1956; Chess, Hertzig, Birch, & Thomas, 1962; Escalona, Leitch, et al., 1952; Levy, 1958) that it is difficult to construct a coherent sequential picture of the quality and changes in the interactions engaged in by a given child and his mother during the first year or two of life. In fact, it is even infrequent that systematically collected data are available from which a description could be assembled on one individual infant.

The longitudinal study of early mother–child relationships, which was carried out at Boston University Medical Center between 1954 and 1960, has provided naturalistic observational data on 30 mother–child pairs. This has made available a documentation of interactions month by month over the first years of life. In this paper I present an account of major interactional trends in two of the mother–child pairs in the first year of life. One of the difficulties in assembling complex descriptive detail is that of finding a framework within which the data can be placed and at the same time have their longitudinal coherence maintained. A second aim of the paper will be to illustrate the application we have made of the adaptational concept in constructing such a schema.

Perhaps because the task of evaluating events on a phenomenological level brings us closer to the problems of the naturalist, the concept of adaptation has provided a most useful point of departure in organizing interactional data. However, the concept of adaptation and the terms related to it have in general been used so loosely that I first summarize and define those aspects of the concept that we have used. The way we have applied them is briefly reviewed before presenting the interaction accounts.

For the purpose of defining the adaptational concept, we take a leaf directly from the biologist's notebook. I quote from a paper entitled "The Biological Basis of Adaptation" by Paul Weiss (1949), who wrote of adaptation:

> Right at the start we stumble over the word. Adaptation, in daily language, means "the state of being adapted" as well as the process of becoming adapted. To avoid confusion, let us confine the term "adaptation" to the adaptive process only and refer to the adapted state as "adaptedness." Also, while we are on preliminaries, it may be pointed out that the term "adapted" always refers to the relation of one entity to another. No system is adapted as such. It can only be adapted or conform to something else. If this conformance is achieved by direct interaction of the two, we shall speak of "adaptation," otherwise merely of "adaptedness." Adaptation, then, is the fitting and adaptedness the fitness, through which a system is harmonized with the conditions of its existence. Such harmony, or fitness, is the premise for the endurance of any circumscribed system in nature.

Three fundamental aspects of the adaptive process have especially impressed us. The first is that adaptation between two living systems is not a matter of passive toleration of proximity but involves an interplay of their "active affinities" (Weiss, 1947). The second emphasizes that adaptation is "primarily a reciprocal relationship between the organism and the environment" (Hartmann, 1939). The third, also central to the adaptive process, relates external aspects of adaptation to internal aspects of organization.

The interplay of active tendencies in infant and mother in reaching a reciprocal quality of relationship forms the unifying thread around which the interactional accounts will be organized. The reciprocal quality in interaction is an achievement that is marked by harmony. It represents a fit or fitting together of active tendencies in each partner. The framework that we have constructed from this stems from the fact that the active tendencies of the infant demand new levels of interaction as he grows older. Harmony in reciprocal interaction must be achieved for each new level. We have proposed five such levels in the first 18 months of life. In comparing the interactional course followed by one of our mother–child pairs as contrasted with another, evaluation is made of the degree to which harmonious coordination is achieved at each of the levels.

In Chapter 1, five levels of adaptive adjustment occurring in the first 18 months of life were derived and illustrated (see Table 2.1).

Erik Erikson, perhaps more than any other student of personality development, elaborated and applied the adaptive approach in a specific

TABLE 2.1
Levels of early adaptive adjustment between mother and infant

Issue	Title	Span of Months	Prominent Infant Behaviors That Became Coordinated With Maternal Activities
1	Initial Regulation	Months 1, 2, 3	Basic infant activities concerned with biological processes related to feeding, sleeping, elimination, postural maintenance, and so on, including stimulus needs for quieting and arousal.
2	Reciprocal Exchange	Months 4, 5, 6	Smiling behavior that extends to full motor and vocal involvement in sequences of affectively spontaneous back and forth exchanges. Activities of spoon feeding, dressing, and so on, become reciprocally coordinated.
3	Initiative	Months 7, 8, 9	Activities initiated by infant to secure a reciprocal social exchange with mother or to manipulate environment on his own selection.
4	Focalization	Months 10, 11, 12, 13	Activities by which infant determines the availability of mother on his specific initiative. Tends to focalize need-meeting demands on the mother.
5	Self-Assertion	Months 14–20	Activities in which infant widens the determination of his own behavior often in the face of maternal opposition.

schema. We have been influenced by his work and would like to quote certain of his recent formulations that express deftly and in enduring terms the elements in the adaptive concept to which we have been referring. We have spoken of the infant's activity involving various levels of interaction. Erikson (1962) refers to a primary activity of the infant as the very essence of the ego: "It is the ego's very essence to maintain an active state, not merely by way of compromises with reality but by a selective involvement in actualities."[1] The element of coordination in reciprocal interactions that we have traced he has previously termed "mutual regulation." The relationship by which active affinities reach harmonious coordination he brings together in the following formulation of mutual activation: "Mutual activation is the crux of the matter; for human ego strength, while employing all means of testing reality, depends, from stage to stage, upon a network of mutual influences within which the person *activates* others even as he is activated, and within which the person is inspired with active properties even as he so inspires others (1962)."

Given sufficient documentation, the operation of these principles can be traced directly in the longitudinal data. This material then can be related to an adaptational view of development with the help of the series of levels salient to major phenomenal characteristics of mother–child interaction.

THE TWO MOTHER–CHILD PAIRS

The descriptive accounts of the two mother–child pairs will be presented as a parallel paired comparison. The pairs have been chosen to illustrate the contrasts in adaptive tasks for both mother and child that come to light when the organization and expression of active tendencies on the part of the mothers vary widely.

The character structure of one mother, Mrs. S., centers about her actively expressed aggression, overcompensated independence, competitiveness, projection, and the enjoyment of her power to control her environment (a sadistic tendency). The second mother, Mrs. M., is highly repressive of her aggression, anxious, compliant, dependent, and secure mainly when pleasing and serving others (a masochistic tendency).

The understanding of the character structures of the two mothers and their socioeconomic and family frame was obtained from our extensive prenatal study and the subsequent close and frequent contact that was maintained with them.[2] Table 2.2 summarizes the schedule of contacts that was systematically followed with each. The clinical material to be presented will be limited largely to the first year of life, which concerns the first four of the adaptive levels.

A glance at the background data of the two mothers, illustrated in Table 2.3, indicates that there are few divergences that complicate the comparison.

The Developmental Course of These Two Mothers

In Mrs. S.'s development there had been striking early traumata. In the first 3 years of her life there were two prolonged hospitalizations of several months' duration each. One was consequent to pneumonia and the other to appendicitis. Repeated extensive separations from her mother characterized these experiences, which were associated with a developmental regression at the time. The ability to walk was lost in one hospitalization. Weaning from the bottle and toilet training were not accomplished until she reached 7. She was enuretic until 13. However, she became a "good" child in her relationship to her salty, directive mother, although the tie was a hostile, ambivalent one. Her adjustment in the home was in contrast to that of her younger sister who continued to be served by the mother and who was pictured as generally incapable, breaking the mother's heart by a premarital conception. Her marriage preceded that of Mrs. S. by 4 or 5 months. In her school years Mrs. S. directed her aggression outwardly in competitive sports and in

TABLE 2.2
Schedule of Contacts

Prenatal

Six to twelve tape-recorded interviews with the mother

Psychological testing of mother and formulation of her character structure

Interview with subject's own mother and/or husband

Home visit

Obstetrician's prenatal clinic record

Social service index

Screening conference and final prenatal conference with formulation of maternal character structure

Predictions of postnatal course of mother–child relationship

Delivery and Lying-in

Observation of delivery

Obstetrician's account of delivery

Immediate postdelivery observations of child

Daily observations, tests, and movies of child in lying-in period, including an 8-hour observation on fourth day

Daily report of visiting nurses' observations in first 14 days at home

Postnatal conference with assessment of endowment of child and further prediction at 6 weeks approximately

Postnatal to 18 months—a rotating schedule of

Home visit every 6 weeks

Tape-recorded interview with mother every 6 weeks

Well-baby clinic with pediatrician's examination report

Developmental testing (Gesell and Hetzer-Wolf Tests) at same well-baby clinic (both every 6 weeks)

Postnatal: 18 to 36 months

Pediatrician's well-baby clinic four times per year

Developmental tests (Merrill-Palmer or Gesell) four times per year

Tape-recorded interview with mother six times per year

Home visit six times per year

Play sessions with child six times per year

Two "intensive weeks" at 6-month intervals, beginning at 18 months, comprising three play sessions with child in a 10-day period plus a tape-recorded interview with mother

TABLE 2.3
Background Data of Mothers

	Mrs. S.	Mrs. M.
Age at first pregnancy	23	28
Study rating	3	3
Wechsler Adult Intelligence Scale	92	85
Socioeconomic status	Upper lower	Upper lower
Religion	Strong Roman-Catholic	Strong Roman-Catholic
Dwelling	Tenement, upper floor near parental apartment	Tenement, upper floor near parental apartment
Geographical stability	Stable (South End) Mixed racial district	Stable (North End) Predominantly Italian district
Work	Steady unskilled factory; group relationships with fellow workers gratifying	Steady unskilled factory; relationships outside of family of little significance
Parental home	Stable; tendency to matriarchal dominance	Stable; tendency to matriarchal dominance
Education	Graduated public high school at 18	Completed junior high school (9th grade) at 16
Lineage	Mgm: Nova Scotia (an orphan) Mgf: Irish Husband: Italian	Mgm: Italian Mgf: Italian Husband: Italian
Cultural factor	Weak, vague	Strong Italian
Sibling position of mother	Oldest of three	Fourth of eight
Husband's occupation	Unskilled factory	Skilled auto mechanic

fierce battles there and elsewhere to achieve her overdetermined independence. Her brother, who was seen by Mrs. S.'s mother as inevitably teetering on the brink of delinquency, was regarded with an air of condescending devaluation as was the blacksmith father, a taciturn, retiring man in the home, although a steady and respected worker in his job. The same attitude was held by Mrs. S. toward her husband, an unassuming boy who in school had lived for his intramural sports activities. They had known each other throughout their school careers in a relationship characterized largely by mutual teasing. Each had been the other's first and only date. Mrs. S. revealed her conflicted feminine identification in her description of herself as the "opposite from nature" in regard to her previous menstrual function and in her tendency to deny her pregnancy in the first few months.

In her prenatal period, Mrs. S. presented herself as a dark-haired, somewhat sharp-featured, strong, solidly built girl who appeared several years older than her 23 years. She had an air of vigor and determination about her and carried the interviews with her stream of rapid speech. Her remarks, delivered with a somewhat harsh voice and a certain push, were accompanied occasionally by a tense and explosive laugh. Her garrulousness often concealed a shift from circumstantiality to tangentiality in her associations, when she wished to avoid certain topics. She was eager to be a part of the study but consistently protected herself from counting on it. The interest we showed in her child was a source of important gratification to her in her environment of meager emotional satisfactions. She was always on her best behavior to be pleasant to us but easily expressed her feelings of frustration, tension, and exasperation in respect to her lot as mother of her firstborn son. Although well controlled, she was chagrined when her child performed poorly with us or reacted with shyness or anxiety to the staff, yet she clearly interfered when he began to establish a relationship with them. She then attempted to divert his involvement to herself. When mother and child were together in the clinic, she was always in complete control of the situation. She could make only a thinly veiled acknowledgment of any contrary position that might be timidly taken by her child.

In regard to the prominent factors in Mrs. M.'s development, a strong Italian family and cultural factor exerted consistent influence. There were three older and four younger siblings of Mrs. M. with little space between them. In this situation, Mrs. M. had an early childhood barren of special emotional nurturance in the relationship with her mother. She had been brought up to a large extent by her oldest sister. She was "nervous" as a child and afraid of all kinds of things. (After marriage, she was still afraid to be alone in the apartment by herself.) She had a history of car sickness and nausea as a child. As an adult, she still avoided bus rides. She was hospitalized for an elective appendectomy at 7 near the time of the arrival of her youngest sibling. Her oldest sister's first baby was delivered at home when Mrs. M. was 9. Later, at age 15, she was afraid to tend her sister's children for fear of hurting them while caring for them. She attributed her "nervousness" to anger. She used to get especially angry at her brother who dirtied things she had cleaned. She won her place with her mother finally as the one who cleaned and who served her siblings while they pursued their own interests without regard for her. She was always the "good" child, ingratiatingly eager to please, compliant to a marked degree in the face of authority, but dependent on the others for their support and encouragement while strongly inhibiting any sign of competitive hostility or envy of them. (Aggressive impulses were strongly indicated in her Rorschach, especially toward males.) Her meaningful relationships remained restricted to those of her own family circle. Her adolescence was strictly supervised, especially in respect to dating.

We considered Mrs. M. to have a more solid feminine identification than Mrs. S. She had a conscious longing for a baby and was married to a man whom she esteemed and who was a respected figure in the household. He was a skilled mechanic who has since risen to a position of responsibility in his shop. In the matriarchal organization of the two families, the husband not only remained strongly tied to his own mother but was importantly influenced in his marriage by his attachment to his mother-in-law to be.

In portraying Mrs. M.'s appearance at the Study Unit, we find that she, in contrast to Mrs. S., was a short, slender, and small-boned woman, who appeared somewhat younger than her 28 years. With her coal-black hair, dark eyes, attractive features, even teeth, and frequent smile, she seemed potentially a more attractive and feminine-appearing girl. However, her face was often set in an anxious, watchful expression. When talking with members of the staff or with others she considered to be either her judges or her advisors, her face assumed an almost childlike expression of wishing to please, with nervous bursts of laughter punctuating these efforts. Her smile became ingratiating and her voice strident. The interviewers felt that she often gave a response that reflected her compliance to her questioner's assumptions, or hewed closely to the acceptable and expected, rather than representing a real perception of her own. She was consistently concrete and unimaginative in her play with her son and seemed genuinely baffled and lost when he made sporadic attempts to involve her in some fantasy play.

Mrs. M. rarely appeared at the Unit without her mother. In the care of the baby, grandmother and mother functioned as a closely knit team, surrounding the infant with a blanket of solicitous vocal and tactile stimuli that they mustered indiscriminately at his least whimper.

Detailed attention has been devoted to the personalities of the two mothers to provide the background for an understanding of the tasks they each faced in achieving interactions with their offsprings of "conformance" and harmony through negotiation of the sequence of adaptive issues referred to earlier.

Many of the areas considered in a formulation of character may leave scarcely emphasized the salient differences in the organization of "active tendencies" such as characterize these two mothers. It could be said that both women had personalities that revealed prominent obsessive-compulsive characteristics. In each, evidence would point to a firm fixation at the anal level[EN3] of libidinal organization with a limited capacity for enjoyment or close relationships. Both had strong and quite rigid defenses, especially against aggressive components; both showed clear traits of excessive cleanliness, compulsive working, and rigid schedules; and both experienced strong superego demands on themselves with much guilt and ambivalence. Both showed constriction of interests, investments, and range of geographical mobility. The self-image was somewhat devalued in both, and self-confidence basically shaky. Both were talkative to the point of garrulousness. These women had sons as their firstborn and a strong need to control them. On the basis of these factors alone, it might have been expected that the course of the mother–child relationship in the first 3 years would proceed similarly in each. It turned out to be in striking contrast.

Pregnancy and Birth

Interactional coordination hinges also on the endowment and active capacities of the infant. In summary, the pregnancies of both mothers had been essentially uncomplicated, except that Mrs. M. delivered her 9 lb., 5 oz. son 4 weeks beyond her due date. Mrs. S. delivered at term a 7 lb., 10 oz. boy. Both were delivered by elective low forceps under nitrous oxide, oxygen, ether inhalation anesthesia with Demerol, Seconal, and scopolamine premedication. However, there were important differences in resuscitation and in our neonatal assessment shown in Table 2.4.

Although Ned S. presented more immediate neurological signs with severe AP molding, there was a spontaneous cry within 30 seconds and well-established respiration within the first minute. He gave the impression of a somewhat frail child with his marked irritability to almost any stimulus, spitting up, poorly differentiated sleep–wake cycle, poor and easily fatigued sucking, and pitiful cry. He turned away from all rooting or sucking stimuli. His gross motor activity, however, was vigorous. This impression of frailty remained over the first few months.

On the other hand, Benjamin M., who showed an entirely satisfactory examination and behavior in the neonatal period, had a definitely delayed onset of regular respiration. He showed no signs of postmaturity and was well coordinated and organized with strong gross motor and sucking activity. His performance over the first 2 years on our developmental test series showed all the characteristics that were revealed by the subgroup of our sample who also sustained perinatal anoxia (Stechler, 1962).

In turning now to the descriptions of the interactional courses followed by the two mother–child pairs, the reader is referred to the previous publication (Sander, 1962) for illustrations of interactions characteristic of more usual and harmonious mother–child relationships than these.[3]

Period 1: Primary Modulation (Months 1, 2, 3)

In the case of Mrs. S. and Ned, there was a clear difference between the first 6 weeks and the second 6 weeks of this first 3-month period. In the first 6 weeks Mrs. S. reduced all other demands on herself, subordinating them to the complete priority she gave to the infant. She seemed to feel entirely justified in this even to the neglect of her husband's needs. She was keenly perceptive and attentive to detail. Feeding observations repeatedly described her handling as smooth, warm, and comfortable. Feeding and sleeping schedules achieved a predictable regularity within days. However, the end of the first month marked a turning point in this picture and a disharmony appeared that was made clear at the 6-week well-baby clinic and was confirmed on the next home visit.

Ned S. began falling asleep regularly after taking 1/2 to 3/4 oz. of feedings, which appeared to observers to be comfortable, well-modulated

TABLE 2.4
Neonatal Assessment

Ned S.	Benjamin M.
A. Respiration	
Spontaneous cry in 30 seconds. Regular within 1 minute.	First gasp at 3 1/2 minutes. Second gasp at 6 1/2 minutes (both in response to strong skin stimulation). First cry at 13 1/2 minutes, becoming regular then. Abdominal respiration evident from 3 minutes.
B. Color	
Cyanotic to pink in 1 minute. Lax and limp for 3 minutes.	Pallor of feet, but trunk remained of good color.
C. Placenia	
Intact. Cord about neck once. Possible cord compression.	No evidence of overmaturity. Shows focal calcification, intervillous thrombosis, and infarction.
D. Appearance of baby	
Severe AP molding. 3 caput saccedaneum.	Shows no stigmata of postmaturity, but baby is heavily sedated.
E. Activity	
Gross motor—active and vigorous. Propels self in crib.	Gross motor—active and well coordinated. Propels self in crib.
First 4 Days of Life	
F. Neurological	
No grasp reflex at all. No distress on failure to rescue head from midposition. Marked irritability with any stimulation. Turns away from any tactile, rooting, or sucking stimuli. Cries when picked up.	Attractive, well organized. Well coordinated.
G. Sleep–Wake Cycle	
At no time was there deep repose. Sleep–wake differentiation clearer after fourth day with general improvement in feeding.	Sleep–wake differentiation. Crying preceded feedings and relaxed sleep followed them.
H. Sucking	
Sucking was "not strong," easily fatigued. Spitting up frequent.	Sucked well. Sucked on own finger with vigor.

ones. He would awaken again in 1 or 2 hours, hungry and crying. For a number of weeks the mother strove heroically to maintain a demand-feeding schedule. Finally, the irregularity so disrupted her characteristic way of coping with her compulsive needs that it threw her into increasing distress, anxiety, and finally some depression after 2½ months, when she felt she simply could no longer neglect her husband's needs and the demands of her house cleaning. Her decision was indicated by her subsequent description: "He doesn't interfere—the thing is I don't pick him up … like he cries or something like that. I never made it a habit to pick him up. I let him get used to playing by himself, see." In addition, she began enforced separations. She placed Ned across the street in the carriage for 1 or more hours where she could see him from the window, or in another room where he could cry it out, while she completed her housework. She described spells in which he "screamed to exhaustion." By the end of the 3-month period Ned began to scream whenever the mother left him in the crib. He would awaken from his nap screaming, as his mother described it, "as if something was gone."

The first step in this inharmonious turn seemed to begin with Ned's falling asleep at the bottle, with resultant loss of feeding regularity. Although Mrs. S. mobilized at first to maintain demand feeding (really an infant-initiated or infant-centered interaction) at all costs, it did not restore harmony. A closer look reveals complex interference in several areas in which mutually shared adjustments might have occurred.

Mrs. S. relied heavily on the bottle as a means of responding to Ned and avoided picking him up or letting anyone else pick him up during the day "so he won't get spoiled." She allowed it only in the hour or two after supper when her husband was home and her mother and friends visited. Only later did we become aware of how important it was for this mother that her baby sleep, so that she could have time of her "own." She did not balance sleep periods with stimulus experiences in wakeful periods or actively counter his tendency to fall asleep. In all our contacts up to the fifth month Mrs. S. was never observed to contact her baby specifically to arouse him or to get him to respond to her. She reported that she used the feeding time to watch television as she held the baby and bottle. Finally, in attempting to help the mother in the third month to achieve some regularity in the feedings, the pediatrician discovered that the mother had not changed the amount of the feeding in spite of the increase in weight and size of the baby. She was still using a 4 oz. bottle and was not letting the infant finish the bottle at a feeding. She was keeping out some, as she explained it, so that she would have it handy in case she needed it between feedings to quiet him. When it was suggested that she use an 8 oz. bottle and allow the child to take as much of it as he wanted, improvement followed at once and a 4-hourly schedule was finally reached. The reader may recall that in the first days of life Ned had already showed an outstanding withdrawal reaction to stimuli, even to those usually gratifying to an infant. He had also showed at that time an easily fatigued sucking reflex. This tendency had disappeared by the second week of life, only to reappear by the 6-week contact.

The description of the initial adaptation between Mrs. M. and Benjamin involved a similar increase in difficulty in the second 6 weeks, but the situation was in many respects the reverse of the situation between Mrs. S. and Ned.

In the first 4 weeks of Benjamin's life Mrs. M. also was described repeatedly by the team as handling her baby gently, competently, and with a sense of sureness and pride, although she was overanxious about his physical condition. She overresponded, as did the maternal grandmother, to the baby's least whimper with an all-out effort to quiet him. The mother said she could not bear to hear him cry, fearing a hernia might develop. As did Mrs. S., she relied early on the bottle to quiet Benjamin, although we observed that he would also quiet well to her holding only. If the bottle was not effective, she would pick him up, rock him in her arms, while walking up and down, talking to him and patting him all at the same time. We called this a "barrage" of stimulation. Often it would be augmented by vocal, tactile, and visual contributions by the maternal grandmother.

At the 6-week well-baby clinic visit it was evident that a marked change had taken place from the observations 2 weeks before. Mrs. M. described herself as having become completely "tired out" from the prolonged holding, that she did not know what her baby wanted or what to do with him when he fussed. Benjamin had become quite clearly overweight (at 6 weeks his weight was 12½ lbs.; at 12 weeks 15½ lbs., and at 4 months 17 lbs.). He had become strikingly lethargic, apathetic, and unresponsive to the point that he was considered untestable in his developmental examination. (Retardation in the motor and general developmental areas continued until the end of the first year.) The mother's overreaction to the slightest symptom had become almost one of panic, and she was constantly concerned with quieting him. With this turn of events, the adaptive struggle was interrupted when the mother developed an infection on her thumb for which she was hospitalized a few days with antibiotic treatment. Although her condition did not demand it, she turned over the entire care of her son to her mother for a period of nearly 4 weeks. In this circumstance, being relieved of the necessity to respond, she seemed to be able to enjoy her baby more.

It is clear here that the excessive reliance on the bottle was associated with the infant's excessive intake and with the mother's investment in the procedure. She summed the matter up saying, "The more I feed him the better I think he is satisfied." At the same time the indiscriminate mobilization of the "barrage" of stimulation appeared more and more inappropriate and not in any timed relationship to the baby's cues. In fact, as the mother became concerned at the end of the first 3 months by his apathy and unresponsiveness, the "barrage" was used to arouse and get a response from the infant just as it was used the next moment to quiet him when he fussed.

Thus although there was infant centeredness here to an excess in the environment, there was, in areas other than feeding, a clear lack of reciprocal interactions developing in channels through which fine modulation could occur.

The usual picture in this first 3-month period is that the primary adaptation is reached by the end of the first 6 weeks with increasing harmony in the second half of the period. In certain of our mothers with prominent obsessive-compulsive character traits and who bottle fed, the picture has been one of smoothness, warmth, and apparent easy fitting together for the first 4 to 6 weeks with increasing difficulty in the second 6 weeks. The observations suggest that the adaptive task of achieving a widening range of coordinated activities is not being met. It is evident at once when certain of the multiple channels in which this is possible are not included in modulated sequences, as with Mrs. M. We have considered that, in the face of such adaptive difficulty, particular proclivities of infant endowment may come into play. Ned, for example, shows the reappearance of withdrawal and easily fatigued sucking that had been identified in the lying-in observations. Withdrawal became established as a characteristic response in later adaptive difficulties. Although Benjamin's neonatal study showed no immediate sequelae of his initial anoxia, we have been impressed with the possibility that this experience may occasion a lowered capacity in the infant for establishing coordinated reciprocal exchanges with the mother. This was suggested by H. F. R. Prechtl (1961) in a study of mother and infant interaction in a series of anoxic babies. A much greater accuracy of fitting her response to his cue would thus be demanded of the mother than otherwise.

We have also considered that after the first 4 to 6 weeks modulations must be increasingly consequent to variations introduced by the baby. Mrs. S. could show excellent mutual coordination with her baby during observation, but it was in the longer time span of the day that difficulty arose in maintaining reciprocal interaction. Adaptation of the mother at this point would thus be to the increasingly active role of the infant in manifesting his unique need variations. This seems to represent what Erikson (1950) spoke of in referring to the strength of the infant vis-à-vis his world: "It must be added that the smallest baby's weakness gives him power; ... a baby's presence exerts a consistent and persistent domination over the outer and inner lives of every member of a household. Because these members must reorient themselves to accommodate his presence, they must also grow as individuals and as a group." When this is not the case, the adaptedness of the infant is jeopardized.

Period 2: Social-Affective Modulation (Months 4, 5, 6)

The issue for this second period, which we initially termed reciprocity and have since referred to as that of social-affective modulation, concerns important changes in degree of expression of infant activity (manifested in preferences such as are shown, e.g., in the taking of solid food, resistance to postural change in dressing, etc.). The infant's capacity to sustain active sequences of reciprocal social smiling and play emerges. It is the full development of the latter, incorporating spontaneous exuberant reciprocity of joyful affect, that marks harmony in this period.

Ned's smiling response emerged rapidly between 2½ and 3 months of age. However, there were no observations during the entire period up to 6 months in which the mother was seen stimulating her child in order to elicit a smile from him. Sequences of reciprocal smiling play in which a crescendo of mounting joy or exuberance emerged were never reported or observed between mother and child.

However, the charm and readiness of Ned's smile and his early use of it even by 12 weeks to initiate an engaging social interaction was outstanding. One could not easily escape if he caught one's eye. He was much more the initiator in this than the average child. Repeated observations indicated that his smiling response would interrupt his sucking during a feeding.

The mother gradually succumbed to this irresistible influence, at first interacting with Ned by voice and eye at a distance. Finally, in the fifth month, she not only allowed herself to be involved by him but spontaneously picked him up and held him or reached out to initiate play with him herself. This play was in the form of little games rather than direct smiling. Their relationship gradually became more harmonious and activation more mutual. There was achieved a reciprocal, nicely modulated body positioning as mother held her baby, which appeared to be gratifying to both. Reciprocal vocalization was also described and observed. The mother referred to this as a secret language that only she and her baby understood. Toward the end of the period, certain reciprocal games, such as peek-a-boo, were reported by the mother to us. By the fifth month, therefore, it was considered that a good reciprocal quality was present in much of their interaction and in many areas of routine care, furnishing delight and satisfaction to the mother. The issue was judged as negotiated at this point, although the mother's affect, unmistakably revealing pleasure, pride, happiness, and gratification in her baby, never showed the qualities of expressed joy or exuberance. The overall impression was of a prevailing matter-of-fact atmosphere.

There remained, however, the same prominent ambivalent split in respect to his demands that had been reported in the first period. She complained in the 6-month interview that Ned was "draining me dry" by his bids for social involvement with its consequent complete disruption of her housework schedule. She said at this time that she had gotten so that she avoided looking at him, so that she would not get "stuck with him" in an involvement. She continued enforcing periods of separation. She kept Ned in a highchair or in a carriage outside for periods of 1 to 3 hours. He was now restrained in the carriage by a harness. Mrs. S. reported at 5 months that he "cried himself sick" in tantrums on separation from her. She also told us that he had cut himself with the straps in his struggles against the harness.

The father developed a very important and exciting reciprocal play relation with Ned by 6 months. The mother was sensitive to the gratification evident in this playing with father and felt that he "likes his father better than me." She complained that after a weekend of playing with father Ned gave her "trouble" because he whined and fussed more when she was alone with him.

In the second 3-month period, Benjamin's interactional experience was almost exactly opposite to that of Ned. In contrast to Ned's alert and charming initiative for social interaction, Benjamin continued his profound motor retardation and was consistently described by observers as bland, bored, lethargic, and generally unresponsive. Although Mrs. M. was now using her "barrage" of stimulation, much of it often inappropriate, to elicit a smile from him, the interaction distinctly lacked the reciprocal quality. Reaching out with arms toward the mother was not described. A home visitor reports the mother's efforts to get a response from the baby: "She went into his room and played peek-a-boo through the door. She called to him, she clapped her hands, and before he had had a chance to assimilate and respond to one kind of stimulus, she was piling on a variety of others. During this period the baby did not respond at all, except that he looked at his mother and grunted or vocalized in her direction. He didn't smile and his face maintained a very impassive quality." Another time when the grandmother, the mother, and one of the mother's sisters responded to Benjamin's fussiness, they all talked at him at once, moved, danced in front of him, and so on. His response to this was as follows: "He looks from one to the other with the expression that, had he been older, could only be described as bored indifference and then fixated on the fruit on the plastic tablecloth, ignoring all the activity around him." The record during this period revealed not one observed instance of a sequence of a back-and-forth reciprocal smiling play in which mother and child exchanged a series of alternations of stimulation and reception. The vocal channel was most employed in reciprocal exchange. This experience was reflected in his developmental test in which his vocal ability stood out in contrast to the poorer showings in other test items. Mutual coordination between mother and infant had not been well established by 3 months, except in the one modality of feeding, nor had social reciprocity by 6 months.

Period 3: Initiative (Months 7, 8, 9)

It is during these months that the adaptive struggle shifts from the increasingly vigorous but more quantitative modulations of the first two periods to a more qualitative dimension of conformance. In this period the curiosity and manipulative activity of the infant makes itself felt in the family as a unique set of new interests. It becomes possible for the infant to begin to turn passive experience to self-initiated activity. Of special significance in our evaluation is the infant's ability now to *elicit* a socially reciprocal response from others if they are attending to such an opportunity to respond.[4]

It was in regard to infant-initiated activity that the divergence between the interactional courses of the two pairs was most obvious. With Ned S. there was decisive failure in these intended activities to secure a reciprocal response from his mother.

The smoldering conflict of Mrs. S. about her responding to Ned erupted at 6½ months when she abruptly decided to return to factory work on a 4 p.m. to 11 p.m. shift. This freed her from the problem raised by the evening relationship and by bedtime, inasmuch as this was now left to the father. Concurrent with the increased absence of the mother, Ned's reaction to separation became exquisite and intense. When he was sitting in the highchair and she turned her back to move away, he would begin screaming. Tantrum behavior was frequent and he refused to go to sleep. Faced with the virtual impossibility under these circumstances of resolving the issue in reciprocal adjustments, the mother oscillated in her attempted solutions. She would lie down with him until he fell asleep as a means of managing the screaming that arose when he was put down for a morning nap. On the other hand, when he exhibited tantrum behavior on being put in the now-restrictive highchair, she resorted to slapping him.

During these months the relationship between Ned and his father continued to blossom in their reciprocal, exciting, and mutually satisfying play. The mother repeated her conviction that Ned now preferred his father. An alliance emerged between father and son in which the bedtime struggle with Ned was solved when the father allowed him to fall asleep on the couch in the living room. After Ned had fallen asleep, the father would put him in his bed. This apparently had gone on for some little time before the mother discovered it. At the discovery she abruptly gave up her work (when Ned was about 9½ months) and returned home. She explained to us that when she found that the father was allowing him to get away with falling asleep in the living room, she could no longer remain out of the situation. She expressed her reaction about it later, saying, "To me this was the end." She returned home and resumed control.

An interview with the father toward the end of this period indicated that he had stepped down in the face of his wife's control. He revealed in the interview his own sense of deep personal inadequacy. He corroborated the mother's picture of the struggle and expressed his sympathies with Ned, but concluded that in the house "she" is the boss. He added, "It has to be."

Her image of her boy emerged as she described his play with a baby girl of the same age: "He's so strong. He's so big. He really hurts her. He grabs her and he's bit her." By 10 months, however, the mother first began reporting his acquiescence, that is, he would "give up." These are the exact words she had used prenatally to describe herself when she could not master a situation: "Then I give up." She confessed that his acquiescence pleased her. As she summed it up: "Ned has to learn that *he* doesn't win—that *we* win."

The study of interaction, when pursued in the light of its total context, shows how interaction becomes a final common path of the influences that make up this context. Here, in a single moment, experiences of crucial quality for the infant can summate the influence exerted by (a) a mother of a certain character; (b) a father of a particular character, each with established modes of interacting; and (c) by the particular equilibrium in which they exist. This is illustrated in the following excerpt of a tape-recorded interview with the mother when Ned was 9½ months old. She first reveals clearly the kind of change that can be observed happening at this age. She has just stated he had no special toys but then adds, "Just now he's starting to … and one toy he really squeezes the living life out of it. Before, you could squeeze it like that, making a noise, and he wouldn't bother squeezing it." Then on being asked how she now felt about him, she began by comparing her feelings to those of the maternal grandmother: "My mother always says to him, 'Poor Ned.' What's so poor about him? … 'But he's a kinda tiny thing.' I said, 'I know that, Mama, but there are some things that can't be perfect.' … but she says, 'The poor little thing, they can't tell you… .' If he was sick, I'd feel the same way, but he's happy. I give him something and he's happy. But when they're small, there's really no life in them as far as I'm concerned. I don't like them until they're about 6 months old. My husband says: 'He's 6 months old, do you like him now?' I say, 'Yeh, because he's more the human being, you know.' Because now he's taking these little fits, I call them. But I just don't pick him up. [As though to husband:] '*You* have him.' [As though to baby:] 'I'm not making you cry. You're making yourself cry.' I feel as though if I make a big thing of it, he might feel that's the only way he can get something out of us. He'll try. My husband will sit in the chair and he'll beg for my husband to pick him up, beg for him and touch him and hang all over him and my husband will just sit there and he'll say, 'Ned, I'm here,' and just sit there. And he'll scream, even yell. Sometimes I have to laugh and he'll even laugh too, because he makes a big scene about it, you know. But my husband will just sit there close to him and it's really … anybody would say, 'The poor thing.' But we didn't do a thing to him and he shuts up as fast [i.e., if they don't respond] as if we did pick him up and give him a toy or something. Or, if he gets real mad, we push it away and say, 'The heck with him.'"

It was evident to us, especially on a perusal of the total record, that mother and father did not lack what *they* knew as affection for and pride in their child, nor a genuine desire for the best for him. What is inevitable, however, is that they employ the behaviors by which their particular organization of affection is expressed in the final common path of interaction. The reader will recall that it was teasing that mediated the affectional bond between Mr. and Mrs. S. However, it is a devastating experience at this period for the infant to suffer consistent failure to establish, as predictable, the reciprocal, social response that he wishes to initiate. Our record reveals here that 2 or 3 months later Ned ceases to try and begins to withdraw.

We turn now to the contrasting experience that was encountered by Benjamin as he and his mother struggled to reach an adapted state in the third 3-month period. It was toward the end of the third period (7–9 months) before Benjamin's success in securing his mother's response by his active means began to contrast with Ned's failure. His flabby, inactive unresponsiveness remained his chief characteristic until the latter part of this third period. Mrs. M., by this time, showed a consistent need to contact him by her poorly timed, inappropriate means, which were mostly unproductive of reciprocal exchange. However, there were isolated indications of the long-delayed interactions appearing: his first reaching out for objects in the seventh month, an episode of reciprocal laughing exchange with the mother reported in the eighth month, the mother's first expression to us of her satisfaction with him. In spite of the minimal initiative that Benjamin showed in this period, her immediate responsiveness to him had already established the mother as predictably available. Her description vividly illustrates: "He's a little lazy. The bottle—he won't hold his own bottle. He wants you to push it in his mouth [but] he likes to play with the bottle. He bangs himself with it. If it's a cookie, I have to hold it for him. He won't eat it himself. I bought him those baby teething biscuits. He holds them for a little while, then he throws them on the floor. Sometimes I would rather hold it for him because he throws so many away."

In his developmental tests at 7½ months, Benjamin showed a failure to grasp objects or to mouth, actually dropping any item placed in his palm as if it were a hot potato. In contrast to the mother's availability to respond to his need to be fed, we found that she was slapping his hands whenever he reached out for objects, calling him "fresh." In a number of the mothers of our sample we have observed in this period such a split in the fate they accord the infant's initiative. Here we see a wide divergence between the reinforcement by reciprocal response for any move that secures the mother's personal ministrations and yet an interference with any activity by which the infant seeks on his own to explore his world motorically. As has been mentioned, this interest of the baby's tends to be regarded as aggressive.

It was instructive for us to trace again the confluence of multiple influences on the final common path of interaction, in this instance mother's interference with Benjamin's grasping and manipulating of objects. This stemmed not only from her characteristic anxieties, but reflected her submissive position vis-à-vis her husband and indirectly the influence of the father's character. First, her own words graphically illustrate her own fears: "I have to stay there though a lot of time is wasted for me. I have to stay with him that way instead of going on with my work. If you leave toys or something, he might put them in his mouth. I don't give him anything that would like come off. Those plastic eyes. He might eventually pull those every day. So, you're always worried anyway. Yuh, he might put something in his mouth. That's what I'm afraid of."

In addition, she felt the pressure of her husband's concern. "He's worse than me—oh yuh. He'd kill me first. That's why I gotta have my eyes open. He says, 'Make sure you're careful. Watch him all the time. Watch him every minute of the day.'"

Looking further we found that the control of the "fresh" boy had played a big role in the father's earlier life. He had been the eldest sibling and especially responsible for a younger brother. As Mrs. M. told us: "There was one brother that used to drive his mother crazy. Oh, he got into more mischief. T. [Mr. M.] was always after that one there, trying to keep him good. He was always the fresh one. The mother couldn't do anything with him. He was awful fresh. They say keep Benjamin—watch out for him. Don't let him be fresh. Yuh, what am I gonna do? If he's a fresh boy, what am I gonna do? Be good, Benjie—yuh!"

Period 4: Focalization (Months 10, 11, 12, 13, 14)

In our evaluation of Ned's record, we considered that the fourth issue, which is concerned with the extension of the infant's manipulation of his mother to the point of focalizing on her as the one to meet his needs, could not be opened in the interaction. The course over these and succeeding months was characterized by an increasing tightening of her control and increased plasticity[EN4] in Ned. He developed a wan listlessness and clear withdrawal of interest from efforts to involve him. This we have viewed as a possible return,[EN5] in the face of new maladaptation, to a solution in withdrawal established in the maladaptation of the first period. Associated with this was an increasing frequency of colds, bouts of diarrhea, and finally, in the 21st month, a nocturnal choking spell. This so frightened the mother that she began to allow him certain freedoms to play as he wished. For the first time she recognized that his tantrum behavior was his "way of telling me what he wants." The effect of this change in mother's handling of Ned's behavior was a dramatic renewal of his manipulative interest and involvement (reopening and negotiation of issue 3) and by 24 months a clear self-assertion (issue 5) in opposition to his mother, with a "No" that his mother now respected. However, the experience of successful "focalization" (issue 4) remained absent.

It will come to the reader as no surprise by this time to learn that we found, in contrast, that Mrs. M. yielded in the issue of focalization to a son who during this period had become somewhat imperious in his demands.

Toward the end of the ninth month rapid change in Benjamin's capacity to express his initiative appeared, to the extent that the father referred to it as "the change." He described Benjamin as beginning to recognize people, "say" things, reach out for and "play" with things, and so on.[5]

With the appearance of this surge of expressed initiative, the mother's complaints rose sharply. She began to sound much like Mrs. S. in her interviews as she described her struggle to cope with both house and infant. At about 10 months she pleaded with her husband for relief, just to get away for a few days. At this critical point, in one decisive moment, the complex influences that determine the particular equilibrium that exists between parents exerted their telling effect. The father was adamant: "Wherever we go, Benjamin goes." In a similar position, Mrs. S. had been free to resort to old-established defenses, but Mrs. M. was forced to remain and continue to struggle for an adaptation between herself and her son.

Whereas he had previously developed the behavior of whining and pointing to what he wanted, Benjamin now began commanding with an emphatic "eh-eh-eh" sound, to which his mother responded. At 12 months she described the situation as follows. The interviewer asked her when Benjamin began this pointing and commanding her with the "eh-eh-eh" sound. She replied, "Quite a while now. Everything he points—eh-eh-eh—and if you don't get it, Oh! Oh! He wants it, he demands it, like." Interviewer asks: "What does he do if you don't get it?" Mrs. M. replies that he "gets mad," clenches his fists, and finally cries. "He cries. Then after you get it for him, you calm him down. I usually get it for him."

Although Benjamin could consistently secure his mother's response in this period, their interaction lacked the reciprocal flavor that the more harmonious of our mother–child pairs have achieved by the fourth period. This was true of her responses to him (except for feeding) as well as in her social stimulation of him or play with him. At the same time the father's play had achieved a highly reciprocal, exciting quality. Mrs. M. described ball-rolling play between father and Benjamin at 12 months as follows: "He's more attached to the father. I mean I play with him. Even though I scold him, he comes to me after, but he's more attached to the father—like if he's sitting with me, he wants to go to his Daddy. His toys, he'll take them over to the Daddy. Yuh, his Daddy was playing ball with him today in the room and he was going to town, he was getting all excited. He gets excited too quick. I get nervous but not excited."

In numerous contacts, observations bore out the mother's report. They illustrated that coordinated, affectively reciprocal interactions between mother and child had not yet been achieved by the end of the first year. This was so in spite of the fact that Benjamin's activity obtained immediate response in the person of the mother. This latter experience constitutes perhaps the most striking contrast between Ned's experience and Benjamin's at this age.

The following observations, taken from the staff visitor's original notes of a home visit with Mrs. M. and Benjamin at 14 months, illustrate the problem with coordination and yet the mother's immediate responsivity. Mrs. M. had begun to talk about Benjamin's progress in learning to walk and stand. To demonstrate this:

> She held him by his arms and at a point at which his feet were on the ground, she let go his arms and he fell quite heavily and bumped his head against the table. He immediately began to howl. She blushed and was obviously anxious about this. She snatched him up, took him to the sink

and began in a very distracted way to give him a sip of water, constantly talking to him: "Here, have a drink of water, little chicken, drink some water. It'll be alright." She seemed completely unable to tolerate his crying. She then ran to get him a graham cracker which she gave to him and he quieted down. (It seemed to me that obviously her first impulse on signs of any distress in this child was to feed him.) We again sat down for coffee with Benjamin on mother's lap and again he wriggled off her lap and went over to the cabinet on the other side of the kitchen and began to reach up and pull at the knob. It seemed to me that it was difficult for Mrs. M. to allow him to get very far away from her or to do any independent investigation of his own because she would immediately pull him away and say, "No, no, don't do that." In order to distract him, she began to bounce the ball toward him and bounced it so that it hit him on the head. This time he did not actually wail but suddenly became absolutely still with a very startled expression on his face and stayed that way for quite a period of time. Mrs. M. again was profuse in her apology. She snatched him up and began to kiss him in this engulfing sort of way and call him her little chicken and other endearing terms. She took him on her lap and he stayed on her lap for the remainder of the visit.

In certain respects the interactional courses taken by the two pairs were like mirror images. Their over-all longitudinal courses can be summarized in biographs by means of the evaluations we have made for each period. The height of the bar represents the evaluation on a 5-point scale of the degree to which coordination was achieved in each of the five adaptive tasks (numbered I, II, III, IV, V). The evaluations for each period (represented by the height of the bar) are based on data from the time segment assigned to the corresponding period. However, the bars have been placed at points on the chronological scale at which it was judged that this degree of coordination had been reached. This may be delayed or early, as comparison with the Schematic Ideal indicates. This chart depicts what the situation would tend toward in an ideal, harmoniously developing mother–child relationship.

The upper part of Figure 2.1 indicates that Mrs. S. and Ned achieved in adaptive issue 2 a degree of harmonious coordination approximating that of the average of our sample (3 on a 5-point scale). However, the failure of Ned's active tendencies to establish a maternal need-meeting response predictable for him is depicted by the omission of a bar representing adaptive issue 4. Mrs. S. did not develop her capacity or role as elicitor of reciprocal response from her child and frequently avoided participation. In the period between 15 and 20 months the reciprocal relationship broke down. It was reestablished only when some of Ned's active preferences were again responded to by the mother with mutuality and with the eventual negotiation of issue 3 at a very tardy 21 months.

With Mrs. M. and Benjamin the reverse was true in respect to the opportunity Benjamin's active tendencies found to establish a certain predictability of response from his mother. This constitutes a basic distinction

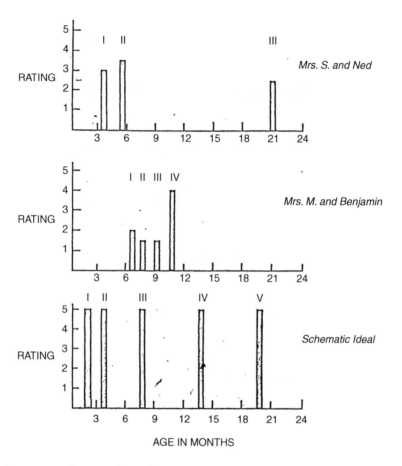

FIGURE 2.1 Evaluation of coordination achieved by two mother-child pairs on five adaptive tasks.

between the experiences encountered by the two boys. It is evident as a persistent trend from the second 6-week period onward. Reciprocal coordination, however, especially affectively modulated, did not advance apace. In the third period reciprocality appeared chiefly as an alternation between Benjamin's control of his mother's response and her control of his motility.

DISCUSSION

In choosing an interactional focus as our point of departure for organizing the data of our longitudinal study, we have utilized the adaptive framework. We have started with the biological concept of adaptation as a process by which the active affinities or active tendencies of two systems reach harmonious coordination by means of reciprocal interactions. Erikson's concept of "mutual activation," in which the infant's "active selective ego" finds new avenues of reciprocal involvement, expresses this relationship. It has been possible, through a focus on the evaluation of interactional qualities, to trace and describe these two elements of the adaptive process separately.

We have illustrated the difficulties that the infant experiences in achieving an adapted state when he encounters either premature assault on his "active tendencies" or a maternal partner unable to reciprocate on one or more of the phase-related levels of activity. Erikson neatly characterized development in terms of a series of selective involvements by the term "developmental actuality."[6] Although limited to the first 18 months of life, our framework of adaptive issues appears to illustrate Erikson's model. It provides a means of breaking up the complexity inherent in an interactional approach, allowing particular trends to be traced out. For example, the contribution of special features of endowment or deficit of the infant to the adaptive process can be followed, as well as particular characteristics of maternal personality. Given sufficient documentation, the manner and degree of success in the achievement of interactional coordination can be evaluated in each of the five proposed levels. Such separate appraisals show quite different patterns when they can be compared across the sample of mother–child pairs. Such an overview illuminates the manner in which mother–child mutuality, which keeps pace with the infant's growth, involves a continuous modification. In this the functional experience gained by the infant at each point can be seen to provide essential ingredients for the achievement of the next level of coordination.

It will be recalled here that the longitudinal picture of developing reciprocal coordination between Mrs. M. and Benjamin revealed a relative lack of clear, reciprocal (back-and-forth) social experiences in the *second* 3-month period. Thus Mrs. M.'s response to her son's more directed activities of the *third* 3-month period had to be forthcoming without an active coordination already having been established between them. The intensity and directedness of the stimulus aspect of each partner's activity, which can be included in reciprocal interactions between them, usually shows a gradual increase over the first year of life. In this way, the task of maintaining interactional coordination is facilitated by the opportunity for each to adjust by small increments to the element of activity in the other. A resource in the accumulation of a harmonious behavioral repertoire of coordination is thus established by the time (in the third period) that the infant's activity becomes sharpened by the development of his intention. It cannot be regarded as only fortuitous that the infant happens to be endowed with a smiling response. Through this he becomes *able to reciprocate* with a directed social stimulus of the mother's and so establish such a behavioral relationship.[7] In the third period, when a new reciprocal interaction must now be achieved in respect to directed activities initiated by the infant, the burden of fitting together seems again to be borne more by the mother (as it was in the first 3-month period). The still highly pleasurable social exchanges of the second period can afford a behavioral background supporting a smooth transition to interactional coordination with the more uniquely individual aspects of the infant's initiative. In fact, in our optimally functioning pairs who show well-developed smiling play in the second period, the transition to a new level of adaptation based on the thrust of infant-initiated activities is so smooth, one would not be aware that an adaptation was being effected. The observations made on the pairs, such as Mrs. S. and Mrs. M., in which difficulties have been encountered in reaching an adapted state, are the ones that have suggested the issues and their timing.

It follows logically that the opportunity for the infant to organize his world of experience through the operation of his own activity on it would vary in the third period with opportunities for him to establish predictable reciprocations. At this time, as well, an opportunity exists for the mother to learn to meet the challenge to interactional coordination posed by the emerging split in the interests of her infant, that is, toward and away from involvement with the mother. We have seen with Mrs. M. that the wide split in her responses already in the third period left her little harmonious experience to draw on in adapting to Benjamin's more intensely expressed directional duality of the fourth period. One of our aims in evaluating interactional qualities lies in studying the relationship of these particular types of experience to individual characteristics of the child's subsequent behavioral organization.

The briefest glimpse of the behavioral outcome at 6 years of age gives the perspective in which this early experience of the two boys may be viewed. Ned, in our evaluation during his first school year, showed himself to be capable of profound social withdrawal, strikingly negativistic to attempts to involve him. Both of these characteristics were utilized to incense his teacher to the very limit of her toleration. Benjamin, on the other hand, in spite of the trauma of major surgery at 26 months, emerged in his first school year pervasively compliant, skilled in pleasing, yet not functioning in unison with his class. He organized his productive efforts quite egocentrically. He emerged from a long period of extreme separation anxiety in respect to his mother, flaunting, to her dismay, his ability not to yield to affectionate behavior with her, though he demonstrated it to her sisters without their solicitation. He was ensconced in an obvious identification with his father.

The relationship of early experience to later characteristics could be formulated in the usual way. However, when studied on the phenomenal level, the possibility exists to study the third of the three elements of adaptation mentioned in the introduction, namely, fitting together. This concerns the relationship between organization and adaptation, which again has a biological foundation. This relationship was expressed by a profound student of the subject of adaptation: "From the biological point of view, organization is inseparable from adaptation: they are two complementary processes of a single mechanism, the first being the internal aspect of the cycle of which adaptation constitutes the external aspect" (Piaget, 1936).

Nearly 25 years ago Hartmann (1939), in the concept of the synthetic, integrative function of the ego, clarified this dual relationship as it applies to the psychological realm. He spoke of it as "a special case of the broader biological concept of fitting together." In this he related the external aspect of adaptation with an interdependent internal aspect of fitting together in "the lawful correlation of the organism's individual parts," or biologically speaking, "the organization of the organism."

With exploratory naturalistic data one is limited to documenting and illustrating theoretical formulations. Nevertheless, from these attempts more specific testable hypotheses can emerge, bearing out Hartmann's (1939) observation that "familiar processes often, though naturally not always, appear in a new light when they are considered from the point of view of adaptation."

NOTES

Published in *Journal of the American Academy of Child Psychiatry*, 3, 231–264 (1964).

1. Erikson (1962) defined actuality as "The world of participation, shared with a minimum of defensive maneuvers and a maximum of mutual activation." In distinction to this, he termed reality "The world of phenomenal experience perceived with a minimum of idiosyncratic distortion and with a maximum of joint validation."

2. The longitudinal study itself, from which this material is drawn, was organized by investigators with a clinical background primarily to meet the needs of clinicians. It was felt that the retrospective view of the emergence of the early mother–child relationship, which is the usual one available from anamnestic material, urgently needed to be augmented by a direct observational study. The investigation therefore was planned to fill in the longitudinal characteristics of the changing mother–child interaction from a descriptive naturalistic viewpoint. The clinician's orientation in his work is toward an awareness of the total situation from which he can assemble the cogent relationships. The view of the mother–child interaction that was desired in the research was a multifaceted, multidisciplinary one, concerned with an appreciation of the interplay of at least the major influences associated with this interaction.

3. It must be kept in mind that the mothers of our sample are all primiparae from a distinct population. Generalizations to other populations and to multiparae should not be made.

   A word of warning is in order as well for the reader accustomed to assimilating clinical material on the basis of the more familiar psychodynamic formulations. These add an interpretive light that becomes the means by which coherence is achieved. Such an interpretive structure is of a next level of inference. If the factual approach preserves the detail and the apparent contradictions of the observation, a primary organization on this level serves as a bridge to the more usual theoretical organizations.

4. There is a tendency for certain mothers of our population to interpret the child's initiative between 6 and 9 months as intentionally aggressive, justifying restriction. This also marks the onset in certain mothers of a marked dichotomy in their response toward those actions in which the child attempts to involve them as opposed to those he uses to turn to the world around him and away from them.

5. In the seventh month of the serial developmental tests our infants who had experienced perinatal anoxia reached their maximum deviation from the rest of the sample. In the months following this there was a gradual return to more expected test patterns, which was achieved somewhere near the 24th month (Stechler, 1962).

6. Erikson (1962) formulated "developmental actuality" as follows: "Ego strength at any level is relative to a number of necessities: previous stages must not have left a paralyzing deficit; the stage itself must occur under conditions favorable to its potentials; and maturing capacities must evoke in others cooperative responses necessary for joint (ego) survival. This, then, is *developmental actuality*; it depends at every stage on the active, the selective ego being in charge, and being enabled to be in charge by an *mwelt* which grants a human being the conditions it needs—and this includes the condition of being needed."

7. Ned's striking lead in this was most unusual for our sample.

EDITORS' NOTES

EN1 *Handling* is typically a Winnicottian term that does not imply "managing" the child, but entering and remaining in physical contact with him, which meant for Winnicott prototypical "caring" for the child and holding him (Winnicott, 1987, p.34).

EN2 Remember that the article was written in 1964.

EN3 Here is evidence of the theory apparatus' dating, today considered obsolete.

EN4 In the negative sense.

EN5 That must be understood as recurring to previously adopted solutions to relational problems, rather than regression to former stages.

REFERENCES

Blauvelt, H., & McKenna, J. (1959). Neonate interaction: Capacity of the human newborn for orientation. In B. M. Foss (Ed.), *Determinants of infant behavior* (Proceedings of a Tavistook study group on mother–infant interaction) (pp. 3–29). New York: Wiley.

Brody, S. (1956). *Patterns of mothering*. New York: International Universities Press.

Chess, S., Hertzig, M., Birch, H. G., & Thomas, A. (1962). Methodology of a study of adaptive functions of the preschool child. *This Journal, 1,* 236–245.

Erikson, E. H. (1950). Growth and crisis of the healthy personality. *Psychological Issues, 1,* 50–100.

Erikson, E. H. (1962). Reality and actuality. *Journal of the American Psychoanalytical Association, 10,* 451–475.

Escalona, S., Leitch, M., et al. (1952). Early phases of personality development: A non-normative study of infant behavior. Monographs of the *Society for Research in Child Develpment, 17.*

Hartmann, H. (1939). *Ego psychology and the problem of adaptation.* New York: International Universities Press.

Levy, D. M. (1958). *Behavioral analysis: Analysis of clinical observations of behavior as applied to mother–newborn relationships.* Springfield, IL: Thomas.

Piaget, J. (1936). *The origins of intelligence in children.* New York: International Universities Press.

Prechtl, H. F. R. (1961). *The mother–child interaction in babies with minimal brain damage: A follow-up study.* Paper presented at Tavistook Study Group on Child-Mother Interaction, London.

Sander, L. W. (1962). Issues in early mother–child interaction. *This Journal, 1,* 141–160.

Stechler, G. (1962). *A longitudinal follow-up of neonatal apnea.* Unpublished manuscript.

Weiss, P. (1947). The problem of specificity in growth and development. *Yale Journal of Biology & Medicine, 19,* 234–278.

Weiss, P. (1949). The biological basis of adaptation. In J. Romano (Ed.), *Adaptation.* Ithaca, NY: Cornell University Press.

3

The Longitudinal Course of Early Mother–Child Interaction
Cross-Case Comparison in a Sample of Mother–Child Pairs

The major content of this presentation will be devoted to three descriptions of the longitudinal course of interaction between mother and child pairs over the first 18 months of life. These three pairs are part of a sample of 22 mother–child pairs whose records are being analyzed as part of a naturalistic longitudinal study that has been going on at Boston University Medical Center since 1954. As research intensifies in the area of early mother–infant interaction, there is the opportunity to focus minutely on relatively small behavioral units. At the same time, there is a need to view these smaller units in their relation to broader interactional trends operating over longer spans of time. Empirical data of this latter sort is less frequently reported.

The descriptions that follow will not be a matter of three case histories of early development but will represent a particular approach to the study of interaction between mother and infant. They will illustrate a method of comparing certain sequences and trends in observational material across the sample of subjects. Both the approach and the method stemmed from our attempt to organize empirical data in the longitudinal study concerning the characteristics of the mother, the endowment of the infant at the neonatal level, the interactions between the two over the years of the study, and the systematic assessments of infant development and outcome. In assembling these facets from the ground up, so to speak, we have had to deal with concepts about organization and the processes that mediate it. To do so we have turned to models from the biological sciences. This appeared to be an appropriate aspect of the work to mention at this conference, as it was Dr Bowlby's formulation of the nature of the child's tie to its mother that so vigorously stimulated the search for biological models that could be applied to early development. A further aim of this chapter will be to illustrate the use we have made of ideas from biology.

THE INTERACTIONAL DATA: THE METHOD OF LONGITUDINAL COURSE COMPARISON

Approach, method, and models have emerged together as we grappled with the task of data analysis posed by the longitudinal study. This was an exploratory, naturalistic, yet an intensive, systematic multidisciplinary investigation. It was launched by Dr Eleanor Pavenstedt, the founder of our Child Development Unit, for the purpose of providing clinicians with a clearer picture of the emergence of normal mother–child relationships. The clinician's view, on which so much work in Child Guidance Clinics depends, is usually based on anamnestic material furnished largely by the mother herself. The study was not designed to discover the causes of developing personality organization, but to describe systematically the ontogenesis of the infant's interpersonal relationships. It was a comprehensively detailed look, however, at a reasonably large sample of some 30 primiparous mothers and their families.

The problem of how to proceed with this complex order to make a cross-case comparison of interaction and to communicate what had been encountered lay first in selecting the most salient interactional variables to focus on in each pair. Although the longitudinal study was based on and launched with a framework of psychoanalytic considerations, the attempt to apply this orientation directly in defining initial categories for analysis led to classifications of primary data that often required a high level of inference. There was also a tendency for a certain circularity of reasoning, in which the variables that we wished to study as outcome were being used to interpret the primary data.

The notion of a way to proceed arose from the experience of interviewing the study mothers in a systematic way every 6 weeks while we were, at the same time, studying the development of their infants. Times of stress tended to be followed by times of harmony. After following 10 or 15 of the pairs one could begin to anticipate the time of appearance of some of the important concerns the mother would express, or, on the other hand, feel relieved about. This gave the impression that we were watching a sequence of adaptations, common to all the different mother–infant pairs, although acted out somewhat differently by each. Each advancing level of activity, which the child became capable of manifesting, demanded a new adjustment in the mother–child relationship. A new equilibrium had to be reached. The problem was that there appeared to be a certain time scale on which these changes could be placed. If a pair had difficulty getting coordinated on one particular level, they presently were already struggling with the next before they had comfortably adjusted to the first. One could begin to appreciate, too, the difficulties this imposed in reaching the second adaptation. We became aware that we were looking at the substance of epigenesis in terms of interaction, that synchrony or asynchrony in this process was a highly important phenomenon.

This germinal idea has been gradually refined into a systematic way of studying our data of early mother–child interaction. The first step was to identify and define the sequence of adaptations. This effort was first published in a paper entitled "Issues in Early Mother–Child Interaction" (Sander, 1962). In this, five levels of adjustment were identified in the first 18 months of life in the order of the temporal epochs that were appropriate to their negotiation. See Table 3.1.

The next task was to identify component behaviors that could be teased out of the data in relation to the particular interactions of each epoch and which bore on the adjustment being made. These categories constituted the evidence for or against the adaptation and degree of harmony that had been reached.

As one follows the mother–infant pair from the beginning, one can represent the degree of harmonious coordination that will be reached in any of the epochs as a particular open-ended question, that is, an issue, which is in the process of being settled for each individual pair. For the guidance of the data analysts, who were extracting and evaluating the material, these issues were worded as questions. They are listed in Appendix 3A, along with some of the observational and interactional categories. All evidence that could be discovered in the record, both for and against, was extracted for each category to provide a base from which the pre-

TABLE 3.1
The five levels of adjustment over the first 18 months of life and their component behaviors

Period Name	Time Segment	Prominent Infant Behaviors That Become Coordinated in the Interaction
1 Primary modulation	Months 1, 2, 3	Basic reflex activities of infant concerned with biological needs of feeding, postural maintenance, and so on, or stimulus needs in quieting and arousal.
2 Social-affective modulation	Months 4, 5, 6	Smiling behavior that extends to full motor and vocal involvement in sequences of back-and-forth smiling play.
3 Initiative	Months 7, 8, 9	Activities initiated by infant to secure a reciprocal social exchange with mother or to manipulate environment.
4 Focalization	Months 10, 11, 12, 13, 14	Activities by which infant focalizes need-meeting demands on the mother.
5 Self-assertion	Months 15, 16, 17, 18, 19, 20	Activities in which infant widens the determination of his own activity; often in the face of maternal opposition.

dominant trends for each span of months could be evaluated. As can be seen, these periods ranged from 3 months in duration to 6 months. Agreement between analysts on evaluations of trends, when taken in these large blocks and based on extensive and repeated documentation, is not impossibly difficult.[1]

This is a feature of the longitudinal study that is one of its greatest strengths, namely, that repeated observations at different times and under a variety of circumstances can reveal the redundant and consistent. In the same way, any deviation, once a trend has become established, shows up strikingly. The data collection schedule that was followed systematically for each pair is illustrated in Appendix B. The contacts were spaced at regular intervals every 3 to 4 weeks for the 3 to 4 years of most intensive sequential data collection. Besides the *variety* of contacts and their regular repetition, on which we relied to give us a fair picture of the child in different situations and environments, objectivity was enhanced by (a) the use of tape-recorded interviews, which followed an associative anamnesis in the first half-hour and a standard sequence of items in the second; (b) standard situations of observations in the Well Baby Clinic, in the Developmental Tests, and in the Play Interviews; (c) for these observations we employed multiple observers (at certain observations, one for mother, one for child, and one for running sequence); (d) observers were guided by preestablished observational categories; and (e) regularly repeated developmental tests.

This schedule has given the opportunity for unusual richness of actual experience with each subject, which provides a certain solidity to the *interactional picture*. Documentation is comparable in detail and completeness on 22 subjects through the third year of life.

A further feature of the material collected was that the study was designed to provide as wide a range of maternal character as could be found in the normal population of our prenatal clinic. The plan was that this selection would, in turn, spawn as wide a range and as gross a contrast in mother–child interaction as existed in this "normal" population. It was anticipated also that this would make it easier to identify and to follow longitudinally unique individual idiosyncrasies. By following such variants to an outcome point, important factors in the developmental process could come to light. Indeed, it was probably largely because of this spectrum of subjects in the sample that our method of cross-case comparison had any usefulness.

One could ask what the expected longitudinal interactional course is in a normal population when analyzed in the framework of this sequence of issues. One needs a basis—some yardstick—for evaluating the variations that can be found between any two pairs. If, indeed, the average mother–child pair is negotiating five adaptations in the first 18 months of life, the behavioral appearance of this sequence of achievements should look something like the usual course of events. In this sense, the usual course of events would be part of the "average expectable environment"

(Hartman, 1939). We have used the following version as just such a yard-stick in our data analysis. It is a picture that will be recognized easily, as will be deviations from it.

First Issue

In the first 3 months of life, a stable regulation of such basic biological processes as feeding, sleeping, and elimination is usually achieved. Usually by 4 to 6 weeks the primiparous mother has recovered from the delivery, has learned to read the important cues of her infant and respond to them in such a way that things settle down to a certain predictable routine. She begins to feel a confidence that she *knows* the baby's needs and can specifically meet them, while not jeopardizing her own needs and the remaining activities of her day. There is usually some sign of baby's preferential responsivity to mother or her ministrations by the end of this period. A positive and pleasant affect begins to pervade their interactions, especially with the appearance of the smiling response. (We have termed this first period that of initial adaptation or initial regulation).

Second Issue

In the second 3 months, 4th, 5th, and 6th, the mother develops active reciprocations with her infant around the spontaneous development of smiling play. Both come to participate in this with delight and mounting expressions of exuberance as the period wears on. At the same time the principle activities of caretaking, such as diapering, dressing, or beginning of spoon feeding, are being accomplished more and more through a reciprocal coordination of the actions of each. Anyone who has tried to feed a 5-month-old his cereal knows the coordination it involves—and the effort needed by each to achieve it. We have called this the period of "reciprocal activation" or "establishing reciprocal exchanges."

Third Issue

The third 3 months, 7th, 8th, and 9th, find the infant beginning more vigorously to express his initiative in bids for attention, for social exchange, for motor, exploratory or manipulative activities, or to indicate his own special preferences. The mother attends to, reads, and responds to these activities with a certain respect for the specific and individually unique quality they are beginning to signify. As she does so, she makes it possible for the infant to experience success—or an interference—in achieving a result in line with that which he has specifically initiated. The adjustment of the mother to the child's increasingly precise and specifically intended activities may be scarcely discernible when an adequate level of reciprocity has been achieved in prior issues. However, in other instances, varying degrees of maternal ambivalence in respect to these new capacities leads to idiosyncratic patterns of interference mixed with reinforcement. For example, activities that are directed away from mother or independent of her wishes may tend to get blocked and those directed toward her be fostered or vice versa. We have especially examined interactions during this time in terms of initiations for social exchange and their success or failure to result in a reciprocal level of response. This period has been termed simply "initiative" or "period of early directed activity."

Fourth Issue

In the fourth period, months 10, 11, 12, and 13, the advent of locomotion and the extension of the capacity to direct one's own activity and express specific intentions by it, sets up the opportunity for the child to settle the extent to which mother is available to him. This is an availability specific to the child's bid—not just for care in general. This is a time when needs are recognized in great measure by the context of the situation in which they are expressed. For example, the simple knowledge of a mother that her child is still subject to stranger reaction will greatly facilitate her appreciation of her child's behavior at a time of distress, and suggest to her an appropriate response for it. In a sense, in this period the level of reciprocation depends on information, which exists in the adapted mother–child system, already having been built up through earlier achievements of reciprocity. This information of "context" is an addition to the earlier individual characteristics of mother or infant on which reciprocation has been dependent so largely in prior issues. It is this specificity of familiar sequences and their context that is lost with separation from mother at this time.

One mother will be gratified by this special knowledge of her baby's needs and her capacity to act specifically on them. Another mother experiences the child's directed and more specific demands at this time as exceedingly threatening—something to be escaped from—or defended against. Ambivalent availability of mother, which may have been subtly evidenced earlier, may now be dramatized openly as limits begin to be set. If her limits are consistent and constructive, we find the mother has a certain confidence that if she yields to her child, still he will eventually turn away from her to wider horizons of his own. The pressure the child exerts at this time varies with the ambivalence of the mother in responding to him. If her availability is certain, he can turn to greater novelties; if she tries to run away, he is demanding; if she reacts to threat by aggression, his demand may provoke her attack or her surrender. We have termed this period from the 10th to 14th months "focalization."

The successful negotiation of a reasonable set of conditions for, and of limits to, a predictable availability of the mother has appeared from the study of our material to be closely associated with a preservation of the same basic affect of delight that has marked interpersonal "fitting together" since issue 2. Depending on adequate negotiation of the issue of focalization, the same affect becomes available for the next in sequence, namely the turning of investment and attention to widening mastery of the world beyond the mother.

Fifth Issue

In the 14- to 20-month period there emerges a new capacity of the child to organize his world actively, to assert himself, and to widen his initiative to determine and select his own direction of activity. The child's aim at this time often seems to be to possess the initiative for its own sake. When his directions tend to run counter to the mother's wishes or the household rules, the issue is raised of the degree to which or the areas in which this assertion will be successful. There appears to be a shift in the content of the toddler's awareness during this time, and he becomes more sensitive to various visual and auditory stimuli and to events within his own body. Spitz (1957) proposed that during this period the toddler has a heightened awareness of his own intentions; at the same time his wishes are being restricted as part of the imposition of rules and the constraints of socializations. Spitz associates this process with the emergence of the "I" experience.

The child's initiative, obviously, is not *all* in a direction away from or contrary to the mother but is balanced by bids for reciprocation with *her.* The probability of success for the latter he has been determining in the previous issue, a probability that now provides the context in which he can pursue his own inner intentions and the independent plan of action stemming from them. This pursuit extends the bifurcation of direction of investment toward and away from the mother begun in issue 3. The heretofore relatively coherent progression of adaptations based on the differentiation of new levels of coordination with the mother through the reinforcement of matching reciprocations with her is now complicated by gratification and reinforcement arising from the successful realization of the toddler's own inner idiosyncratic intention, goals, and plans of action. It will be seen at once that if the previous reinforcement and gratification have been connected with the achievement of a reciprocal exchange with the mother, we are now encountering a new phenomenon. The appearance of success and gratification begins to become evident as the infant maintains his own inner aims even if they are in opposition to rather than in reciprocation with the mother. In other words, guidance of behavior on the basis of the pleasure of realizing inner aims can take precedence at times over the more familiar (pleasurable) reinforcement of finding a coordination with the parental caretaker. Whereas before this period the child has reacted to separation as an upsetting event, now he himself initiates separation, both physical and psychological. The importance of a stable basic regulation has to do with a context in which the child can begin dimly to recognize his own role in determining action; that is, that he is pursuing his *own* intention rather than reacting to a lead. The emergence of autonomy as here proposed is based on the further differentiation of awareness—especially that of inner perception, which sets the stage for the "disjoin" of the self-regulatory core. The description of the next two issues[EN1] is given in Chapter 4.

It is evident from this descriptive picture that we are focusing on certain broader "formal" features of interaction for the evaluation of trend. These are features that can be represented in progressively more differentiated behaviors from the first to the fifth issue. They might be summarized in three words: initiation, reciprocation, and regulation. The emphasis is in distinguishing the level at which the infant is initiating his activity, the degree of reciprocal coordination achieved in the interaction with the caretaking activity, and the stability of regulatory harmony that prevails. In an observation in which the levels of activity are widely disparate between infant and environment, the question of who initiates is usually clear.[2] Equally clear to the observer of the mother–child interaction are the failures of the pair to achieve harmonious coordination or regulatory stability. On the other hand, behaviors that are smoothly mutual do not strike the observer with the same impact unless he has been following them from their more awkward beginnings. They can be easily taken for granted. Furthermore as one watches longitudinally the activities initiated by the infant, he can note the progression in the level of these activities, which become coordinated with the mother in reciprocal interactions. In this way interactions can be viewed as the arena of differentiation. Those activities initiated by the infant that become incorporated into this reciprocal coordination become differentiated from those that do not. That this should be so becomes even more reasonable as it is appreciated that stability of regulation for the infant, as the months pass, depends on this increasingly differentiated reciprocal exchange. The advanced levels include newly coordinated elements as well as features of old behaviors whose coordination has already been established at an earlier level. To put the same thing into the language of adaptation, as new capacities for activity appear in the infant's behavior, as he advances chronologically, fitting together or adaptation is reachieved between infant and mother at each new level. The harmony or disharmony that prevails over time gives indication of the stability of this coordination. Under "initiation," therefore, we describe not only *who* is initiating, but *what* is initiated, and the variety, vigor, directedness, and timing of the acts. "Reciprocation" likewise implies attention to its specificity, spontaneity, duration, and affective qualities. "Regulation" includes the full 24 hours of the day and is evidenced in the basic functions of arousal and quiescence, and the evenness in maintaining or changing sleeping, feeding, and eliminative behaviors, as well as the prevailing signs of distress or comfort that characterize them.

In the usual course of events, the transitions from one period to the next are so smooth that one is scarcely aware of the introduction of the new active capacities of the infant. In our particular population, which had its own special sociocultural features and wide range of maturity in maternal character (Pavenstedt, 1965), these transitions were often abrupt and marked by considerable turmoil. The possibility of handling such variations systematically from epoch to epoch and giving them even crude evaluative assessments provides a means of exploring the relation of an individual child's adaptive experience to variables of later behavioral organization.

We can turn now to the description of the interactional course followed by the first of the three pairs. It will illustrate an actual instance in which our yardstick of the usual course of events is closely approximated. It also illustrates the problem of assessing a prevailing trend in interactional data, in which behavior may vary from contact to contact often within considerable range. Evidence from systematic and frequent contacts under a variety of circumstances is one way of coping with this problem.

FIRST PAIR (ELLEN AND MRS. Q.)

Issue 1 (Months 1, 2, 3): Initial Regulation

It did take the first 6 weeks for this mother to get over the physical effects of the delivery and to establish with her baby a smooth and regular routine in which the mother could be confident. In the first 6 weeks there had been a mild depressive reaction and major concern of the mother about damage to her own body. She had had excessive postnatal abdominal cramps and bleeding. She showed a curious concern with "gassiness" in the baby by which she accounted for the baby's crying and alternately good and bad nights of sleeping. In the first weeks she left the baby at the breast for up to 2 hours at a stretch and soon developed painful nipples. However, after the obstetrician stopped the breast feeding at 6 weeks as a means of relieving the abdominal cramps and bleeding, which it did, there appeared consistent pleasure and contentment in the mother with the baby. The baby's sleeping became regular, smiling appeared, and reciprocal play with mother began to emerge. In direct observations mother was reported as deft, sure, and quick with the baby. She referred to the baby as a "good baby," one who cried little, and was little bother, and showed little discomfort. One could see a steady improvement in harmony from the first to the last of the period.

Issue 2 (Months 4, 5, 6): Reciprocal Exchange

In the second period (4–6 months) this pair showed, outstandingly, a high level of mutual enjoyment in reciprocally coordinated interactions involving smiling, vocalization, and back-and-forth play. Father and especially mother-in-law contributed important additional amounts of play. On the incoordination side of the ledger during these 3 months, mother's consistent efforts to block mouthing of objects and finger sucking was the principle incoordination. The child was reported briefly as "cranky" between 4 and 5 months, during a period when mother was working a few hours a day in a family business. At this time, Ellen's demand for social contact and play began and became clearly expressed. Mother readily let her housework go to enjoy holding and playing with the baby.

Issue 3 (Months 7, 8, 9): Initiative

The third issue began early in this pair, therefore (i.e., at 4 rather than 6 months), and was highly successful of affective reciprocation. In the 7th, 8th, and 9th months, it was impossible to say in our observations who predominantly initiated interaction between mother and child, so evenly balanced was this. It became even more enjoyable for the mother to reciprocate with these now more direct bids of Ellen for interaction with her. There was no pair in our sample that showed a more mutual exchange or a more spontaneous enjoyment. In addition, Ellen's increasing skill in object manipulation and motor development was a delight to the mother, who often reinforced her vigorous bangings. Already at 9 months mother repeatedly described her as having a "mind of her own." But it was with pride that mother described her as insisting on holding her cup and feeding herself, refusing help, and so on. Mother was described, during this time, as talking a great deal to her baby, with reciprocal vocal imitations between them, and with the employment of mutual attention to distance communication. The variation in our sample of this dimension involving perception of focus of attention is quite distinct and of importance to assess in this third period because it plays so vital a role in the negotiation of succeeding issues. It is indeed an interactional bridge between the all-or-nothing world of direct contact and the coming interactional world of representation by language and symbol.

Mother often dwelt in her interview on the question of the one to whom the child went most. It seemed important for her to be the preferred one. On the negative side of the ledger, concerning the interferences or disharmonies, there was some excessive concern of mother to control biting by her infant, which we never could substantiate as more than occasional.

Issue 4 (Months 10, 11, 12, 13): Focalization

As has been stated, the fourth issue concerns the degree of availability of the mother to child-initiated bids. Ellen and her mother achieved the highest coordination in this respect. The following original notes of a home visit characterize the consistent picture:

> There was much contact between baby and mother, visual, bodily, and verbal. Initiative seemed mutual. Mother did not hover over the baby yet was always available when the baby would make the slightest gesture or noise which indicated to the mother that she wanted her. These indications were always quite direct. She would look at her mother, make a sound, and could say some words clearly. … The tone of the child's voice or the direction of her look seemed to give the mother her cues.

On the dissonant side of the ledger, there were continuations of over-concern with the child's biting or hitting out in anger when frustrated by mother. When the child became angry or hit out, mother angrily yelled and the child yelled back again angrily. Reciprocation existed even here. This frustration appeared often to be a part of a new kind of teasing interference by mother. The teasing was mostly centered about mother's interfering with an object the child was engrossed in manipulating, that is, an involvement independent of the mother. Again in the overall picture this held a very mild and tempered place and was not a major obstacle that countered the mainstream of initiative in this instance as it did in the next pair to be described. Mother seemed both pleased, and yet somewhat threatened, by the child's autonomy. It seemed to tie in with mother's sensitivity in regard to whom the child preferred. She preferred mother when tired or at bedtime but stayed easily with others. When she obviously enjoyed being held by the visitors on a home visit, mother would test out whether Ellen would leave them and come to her. If not, mother would pretend to leave the apartment or actually go away to the neighborhood store for a bit during the visit, or threaten to give the child to the visitor. When she did leave the child alone with home visitors at 14 months, there was no protest or distress on the part of the child, who continued to play with the visitor. Mother attributed this to the fact that she had not put on her coat as she left, for if she had, she maintained, the child would have protested. That is, the usual signal for separation was not present. One could also suggest that it was not necessary for this child to test mother's availability by this time in this context, that it had been already established by mother's response to a large number of trials over previous months. The ability to tolerate separation did not reflect here a lack of attachment but a predictable stability of regulation. The importance to the mother of a preferential one-to-one relationship was obvious. It was as though mother tested during this period as we might have expected the child to have tested.

It was at the end of the fourth period, near 14 months, as the child achieved walking and was showing an ability to be apart from mother with a strong investment in her own independent course of action, that the mother became pregnant again.

Issue 5 (Months 14–20): Self-Assertion

The course of the fifth period between 14 and 20 months was colored by the mother's pregnancy. The predominant trend in the material confirmed mother's ability to allow Ellen autonomy and to regard her new capabilities with pride. In the developmental test situation Ellen showed this independence and self-assertion with the tester, insisting on manipulating the items in her own way rather than as suggested by the tester. She also showed her ability to work on her own task persistently and with intense involvement, without turning to mother for help and without being overwhelmed by frustration in the face of obstacles. As a matter of fact, Ellen had repeatedly excluded the mother in her attempts from time to time during the test to get Ellen's attention. The assertion of the child was evidenced in such observations. It was also evident in the clashes stemming from activities the child initiated and which the mother interfered with, such as Ellen's grabbing for the visitor's pocketbook, or insisting on peeling wrappers off the crayons in the Clinic. In the latter instance the child refused to yield her crayon to mother's active efforts to wrest it from her. In the subsequent observations of crayon situations, peeling was returned to by Ellen and accomplished now without further attempts of her mother to block it.

On the incoordination side of the ledger were continued examples of mother's teasing intrusions into Ellen's play and a period of irritability when mother was depressed. This was between the 3rd and 5th months of this second pregnancy, when Ellen was 17 to 19 months of age. Mother began again to bleed intermittently, gave evidence of concern whether she would be able to carry the baby, was unable to do her housework, and left the child for longer periods restrained in her feeding chair or carriage. There was one report from the mother, during these weeks of depression, that Ellen was not wanting the mother to leave, and was demanding to be held and played with. The mother, in a way that was unusual for her, said she now was not in the mood for this. Our social worker, who visited the mother at this time to get her to keep her clinic appointments necessitated by the bleeding, found the mother just sitting on the front steps with Ellen strapped in the carriage at one side. Both looked disheveled and solemn. Mother said she had just been sitting there for hours. However, depression was a matter of a few weeks and as a consistent trend this behavior was not borne out in repeated contacts. An example of the mother's unusual irritability at the time of depression occurred during a home visit. It shows, however, the strength with which Ellen tended to maintain what she initiated. The child was in her feeding chair and the visitor was conversing with mother, who was apparently paying little attention to Ellen at the moment. Ellen was exploring the chair for crumbs and mother suddenly got up and angrily demanded, and wanted to remove from Ellen's mouth, a crumb that she had just picked up. Ellen yelled in rage and mother yelled back and then said to the visitor, "That's what she does when she doesn't get what she wants ... that's when I have to hit her"—but she didn't and Ellen kept her crumb. Taken alone, this example would miss the more numerous observations of Ellen's usual success in initiating interactions with her mother in which the same highly sensitive reciprocity and pleasure was present as had been customary in previous issues.

The reason such material has been included is not to introduce confusion into the picture, but to illustrate as fairly possible the kind of thing one runs into when a detailed account of an actual life history is available. Contradictory and ambivalent behavior is simply what the infant is so often confronted with in his encounters with real caretakers. It is one of the reasons why we have been interested in data over longer periods for evaluation and have tried to stay with the complexity of the material, while attempting to estimate predominating trends. We have attempted to estimate the degree to which an enduring coordination is achieved in respect to particular levels of activity that the infant can initiate. This is something that is also essential for the infant to do. If his behavior is to be organized on the basis of a predictable feedback to the activities he initiates, then the pressures the toddler exercises by his assertions in the fifth period, and in the months that follow, may go a long way toward clarifying for him the extent of his mother's earlier and more subtle contradictions.

In summary, Ellen's interactional profile showed the achievement of a stable and harmonious regulation in the first period, after an initial period of difficulty; a high level of affectively mutual reciprocal exchange in the second period and a very evenly matched initiative for social contact with a high degree of maternal availability in the third and fourth periods; and finally the appearance of independent directions of interest and investment, which could be maintained in the face of the mother's opposition.

As we move on now to the descriptive accounts for the second and third pairs, two contrasting variations from the yardstick of a "usual course of events" are illustrated. Further illustrated also is the way trends are compared between pairs in terms of the evaluations of success or failure in the negotiation of the five issues.

A paired comparison of interactional course can carry a step further the exploration of the emergence of organization through the interactional process. As we compare, in these two pairs, the interplay of initiation, reciprocation, and regulation, we will be following the progress of the infants as they struggle to differentiate[3] their repertoire of adaptive behaviors.

The relation of organization of behavior to mother–infant interaction can be illustrated by experiments on the development of behavior in animals. There is an interesting parallel that exists between the sequence followed in our five issues and the steps in the longitudinal course of suckling behavior in mother cat–kitten interaction as described by Rosenblatt et al. (1961). When the initiative taken by kitten or mother in achieving feeding coordination is traced, initiative passes from mother cat to the kitten after a period of mutuality or reciprocal coordination. In Harlow's (1963) account of the maternal affectional system in monkeys, coordination was described in terms of maternal activities in a contrived cage situation. This shift in the mother's role was identified in three steps as attachment, ambivalence, and separation. In humans, the initiation of activity in the interaction between mother and child in our adaptive issues, whether or not the interaction accomplishes a fitting together by reciprocal coordination, ordinarily rests in the first two issues with the mother predominantly. It is more a 50–50 proposition in issues 3 and 4, and becomes highly related to the child's initiative in the fifth and later periods. At this point it is a matter of selection for the infant whether he turns toward the mother or away from her. It was possible with the kittens in the experiment by Rosenblatt et al. to study the effects of separating the kittens from the mother at various points in this transition and to see the steplike progression of experiences necessary for the normal organization of kitten behavior in the feeding situation. If the repertoire of interactional adaptive behaviors between individuals in the various animal species is built through the experience the infant has in achieving coordination with the mother during a sequence of stages of shifting initiative, then it should be possible to study the organization of interpersonal behavior from the same point of view. In the human, however, being unable to manipulate the interaction at different points in the chronology as in animal experimentation, we must wait for naturally occurring experiments to reveal relevant relationships. These can come to light in paired comparisons when there is a systematic framework for comparison that includes chronological sequence.

The comparison of the second and third pair in respect to our yardstick of the usual course of events illustrates variations in the dimensions we have been discussing: initiation, reciprocation, and regulation.

SECOND PAIR (NED S. AND HIS MOTHER)[4]

The adaptive task for this pair concerned the problem of fitting together encountered by a vigorous, aggressive, garrulous mother who was a compulsive housekeeper, and an infant, who although he showed good spontaneous motor activity in the first 4 days of life, also gave the appearance of a certain frailty particularly in irritability to stimuli. As a neonate he tended to turn away from tactile rooting and sucking stimuli, cried when he was picked up, and showed an easily fatigued sucking with frequent spitting up. These difficulties seemed to clear after the first 4 days.

Issue 1 (Months 1, 2, 3): Initial Regulation

The first period showed the reverse of the expected increase in coordination between infant and mother over the first 3 months. Things appeared to go most smoothly in the first 6 weeks, with increasing difficulties after that time. The mother had habitually managed her anxieties by controlling her environment. This was easy for her in the first 6 weeks when Ned was sleeping for long stretches and she could count on sufficient time to get her housework done as well as time to respond to him. She was reported to be keenly perceptive of the infant and attentive to detail. Feeding observations repeatedly described her handling as smooth, warm, and comfortable. This is an illustration, I think, of the problem in trying to assess adaptation by examining only small segments of time. Adaptation and regulation imply a stability over the full span of time. Difficulties began at the end of the first month, when Ned began falling asleep regularly after taking ½ to ¾ ounces of feedings, which appeared to observers to be comfortable, well-modulated ones. He would awaken again in 1 or 2 hours, hungry and crying. For a number of weeks the mother strove heroically to maintain a demand-feeding schedule, which was evidence of her basic devotion. However, the irregularity so disrupted her characteristic way of coping with her compulsive needs that it threw her into increasing distress, anxiety, and finally some depression after 2½ months. At this time she felt she simply could no longer neglect her husband's needs, and the demands of her house to meet Ned's schedule of discomforts. Ostensibly to decrease his dependency she began to avoid picking Ned up and enforced separation for one to several hours per day while she completed her housework. She often placed him across the street in the carriage where she could see him from the window, or would put him in another room where he could cry it out. She described spells in which he "screamed to exhaustion." By the end of the 3-month period Ned began to scream whenever the mother left him in the crib. He would awaken from his nap screaming, as his mother described it, "as if something was gone." Thus separation can exist even when mother is present and separation behavior can be interpreted as having another meaning than strength of attachment.

The mother's principal aim in interaction was to quiet the baby and one could see her plan to try to train him out of his demands. Mother relied heavily on the bottle as a means of responding to Ned and she was never observed during this first period to stimulate the baby to arouse him or to get him to respond to her. There were none of the little early reciprocations evident between Ellen and her mother. Only later did we become aware of how important it was for this mother that her baby sleep so that she could have time of her own, and that her initiative be not compromised by his. She reported later that she had used the feeding period to watch television as she held baby and bottle. Finally, while attempting to help the mother in the third month to achieve some regularity in the feedings, the pediatrician discovered that the mother had not changed the amount of the feeding in spite of the increase in weight and size of the baby. She was still using a 4-ounce bottle and was not letting the infant finish the bottle at a feeding. She was keeping out some, as she explained it, so that she would have it handy in case she needed it between feedings to quiet him. When it was suggested that she use an 8-ounce bottle and allow the child to take as much of it as he wanted, improvement followed at once and a predictable 4-hourly schedule was finally reached in the fourth month, a month behind our schedule. This illustrates the longer time spans in adaptive regulation that may not come to light when viewing interaction more microscopically.

Issue 2 (Months 4, 5, 6): Reciprocal Exchange

In respect to the second period, Ned's smiling response emerged rapidly at 2½ months of age. The charm of his smile and his readiness to respond delightfully to a social interaction even by 12 weeks was outstanding. Over the next 2 months Mrs. S. gradually succumbed to this irresistible influence, at first interacting with Ned by voice and eye at a distance. Finally, in the fifth month, she not only allowed herself to be involved by him, but spontaneously picked him up and held him or reached out to initiate play with him herself. This play was in the form of little games rather than direct smiling. Their relationship gradually became more harmonious and activation more mutual. There was achieved a reciprocal, nicely modulated body positioning as mother held her baby, which appeared to be gratifying to both. Reciprocal vocalization was also described and observed. The mother referred to this as a secret language that only she and her baby understood. Toward the end of the period, certain reciprocal games such as peek-a-boo were reported and a good reciprocal quality was present in much of the routine care interactions, furnishing delight and satisfaction to the mother. The issue was judged as negotiated at this point, although the mother's affect, unmistakably revealing pleasure, pride, happiness, and gratification in her baby, never showed the qualities of expressed joy or exuberance. The overall impression was of a prevailing matter-of-fact atmosphere.

There remained, as an undercurrent, however, the same prominent ambivalence, in respect to demands, that had been reported in the first period. Mother complained in her 6-month interview that Ned was "draining me dry" by his bids for social involvement, with subsequent complete disruption of her housework schedule. She said at this time that she had gotten so that she avoided looking at him when she went by his playpen so that she would not "get stuck with him" in an involvement. Periods of enforced separation continued and he was now restrained in the carriage outside by a harness. Mother reported, at 5 months, that he "cried himself sick" in tantrums on separation from her, and had cut himself with the straps in his struggle against the harness. During this time the child developed outstanding social responsiveness and an excellent reciprocal interaction with the father. This remained excellent for the most part throughout, and is an important part of the wider view of his interactions.

Issue 3 (Months 7, 8, 9): Initiative

At the end of the sixth month as the third period was opening, the mother suddenly decided to solve the problem of Ned's demands for involvement with her as well as a new problem—his refusal to go to sleep alone—by beginning to work outside the home on a 3 p.m. to 11 p.m. shift. Concurrent with the increased absence of the mother, Ned's reaction to separation became exquisite and intense. Tantrum behavior was frequent and he even refused to go to sleep for his morning nap. Faced with the virtual impossibility, under these circumstances, of resolving the issue in reciprocal adjustments, the mother oscillated: As a means of managing the screaming that arose when he was put down for the morning nap, she would lie down with him until he fell asleep; on the other hand, when he had a tantrum on being put in the now restrictive highchair, she resorted to slapping him. Here is another level of ambivalence—a gross one.

After she had been at work some weeks, having left the major task of getting Ned down for the night to her husband, she suddenly gave up the job to take full charge again in the home. This occurred after she found her husband was handling the matter by letting Ned fall asleep on the couch in the den, while he watched television. She felt Ned was being allowed to get away with it: "To me that was the end," she said. Mother won the violent struggle over restraint in these months and clearly indicated her avowed intention in this matter to win, saying, "Ned has to learn that *he* doesn't win, that *we* win." The defeat of his initiative to get his mother to respond to his bids was unquestioned. Interestingly enough, in the times during this period that she set aside to be with him as part of *her* plans, such as to bring him to the clinic for an afternoon of observation, there was much of the same comfortable mutual relationship that had developed before in the fifth month, but it was on *her* terms and time, not *his*. In the evaluation of issue 3 in this instance, definitely less than the usual degree of success attended the efforts Ned initiated.

Issue 4 (Months 10, 11, 12, 13): Focalization

In respect to the fourth issue, the mother remained clearly determined not to yield to Ned's demands and her compulsive schedule retained its priority. An observation in the home at 12 months reported the mother and child as having "lost contact" with each other. Reciprocal interactions and communications had largely disappeared from the observations by the 14th month, as had the child's once charming affect; he began to show the listless withdrawal that dominated the next 6 months. The mother's complete control of her own availability was never in question, although there was never, at the same time, any further physical separation. There was a clear failure in this pair then to negotiate issue 4, either during this period of 10 to 13 months or later.

Issue 5 (Months 14–21): Self-Assertion

In the fifth period there was an increasing tightening of the mother's control and an increased plasticity in Ned. The mother was pleased that his demands were lessening and at first seemed not to notice the development of a wan listlessness and an affect of persistent sadness and whining. She didn't mind lying down with him now to put him to sleep, or the rituals at mealtime before he would eat. At about 18 months, after mother punitively inhibited his masturbation, which had been increasing rapidly, he developed a remarkable spontaneous withdrawal of investment whenever anyone became successful in securing his involvement to manipulate an object. Later in this period his mother was observed frequently trying to initiate play with him by stimulating him in contrast to her usual aim to quiet him. She even went so far, during a home visit, as to run a bat up his pant leg to his genital area while he was lying in his usual withdrawn way, stretched out on the floor at her feet. Nevertheless, she remained unsuccessful in achieving an exchange with him.

Tantrum behavior, frequent before 14 months, gradually disappeared and there was an eating inhibition, certain eating rituals, and a persistent sleep disturbance, increasing frequency of colds, bouts of diarrhea, and finally in the 21st month a nocturnal choking spell for which he was rushed to the hospital.

Here we see a situation in which, in the first period, there were major difficulties in basic regulation, and early affective reciprocation was not fostered by the mother, although it finally emerged in the second period, in the presence of a highly responsive, almost irresistible child. Even this threatened the mother's sense of being the one to determine her own involvements. Mutually shared initiation of contact was not achieved in the third period, nor was her availability determined by him in the fourth period. This was part of mother's clearly conscious intention and we see him in the fifth period withdrawing from an active effort to organize his world, and developing increasing physical symptoms.

I think it is important to bring out here that this mother loved her child. She was not out to destroy him as *her* child—to this day she refers to him as she must have wished him to be—"my Ned."

THIRD PAIR (BUD AND MRS. E.)

We can now turn to the pair with whom we shall contrast Ned's course. The mother in this instance was a conscientious, attractive-appearing girl, but quiet, shy, and reserved, almost to the point of somberness. She kept herself well in control in anxiety-provoking situations and showed a capacity to endure without complaint. If there is a role for the so-called normal feminine masochism in childrearing, its usefulness may become evident in this instance.

Mrs. E. was a very effective housekeeper, in the sense that she kept a neat and well-organized home, but, in contrast to Ned's mother, did this with one hand, so to speak, without the slightest complaint or sign of burden. She refused our offers of home nursing help after the delivery and her time seemed unusually free to attend to her baby.

The infant, Bud, had sustained a clear perinatal anoxia as a complication of the delivery. He required some 15 minutes to establish a regular breathing pattern and showed in the neonatal exam a general hypertonicity of the legs and an occasional limb tremor, both of which persisted well into his first year of life.

Issue 1 (Months 1, 2, 3): Initial Regulation

There were two chief sources of anxiety in the first 3 months for his mother. The paramount problem was in respect to his poor feeding behavior and the second was his developmental retardation, which became evident by 8 weeks. In this latter, he showed a developmental course that was consistent with our 8 other subjects who had sustained perinatal anoxia (Stechler, 1964). The feeding problem had started almost from birth and was manifested by his taking very small quantities at a given feeding, rapidly going to sleep on the bottle, and reawakening after a short period of time hungry for more food, the same situation grossly as with Ned. However, between Bud and his mother, coordination and regulation steadily improved over the 3-month period. After the first 10 days, in which mother had tried to increase his intake by stimulating him and felt nervous and concerned about his low intake, she spontaneously recognized her anxiety and decided that she might be adding to the problem by her tension during the feeding. She decided that these frequent small feedings were characteristic for him and that she should accept it and make the feedings as relaxed and happy as she could. From then on things steadily improved. It was 3 weeks before he slept for a 3-hour stretch at night. At 1 month of life he was taking about 3 ounces at a feeding and by 2 months he could sleep for a 5½-hour stretch and take 5 ounces at a feeding. Although in our observations at 6 and 12 weeks, he was described as tense and fussy, and was reported by his mother to have a fussy period of 2 to 3 hours per day, mostly around dinner time, mother always described him as a good baby, not colicky, and not difficult to care for. In our observations during this time, mother seemed to want to be in constant visual contact with him when he was awake. She always held him so that she could look at him, engaged in extensive gentle talking to him, and put him to sleep by rocking him. She felt confident she knew his different cues, knew when he was "faking," and also that he knew her and would quiet for her. We felt she was highly predictable as to the kind of response she would offer him in respect to his various state changes.

The developmental retardation, which was the second problem, became evident in the later part of the first period. It was the source of an increasing anxiety in the mother after the feeding difficulty abated. The retardation consisted chiefly of delayed social perceptual responses and delayed adaptive development in response to, and in approach to, materials.

Issue 2 (Months 4, 5, 6): Reciprocal Exchange

In respect to the second issue, the appearance of the smile was late, at 8 weeks. It was not obtained first by mother, but by father and aunt, who used somewhat stronger stimuli than mother. However, Bud at this time was not a very alert or perceptually organized baby, and his developmental difficulties were becoming more apparent to Mrs. E. In the undercurrent of concern that often popped through to the surface, mother seemed to be torn between a basic capacity for a warm, easy-going relationship with her child and a need to deal with him in such a way as to foster development, particularly fine motor development. She was quite accurate in her perception of his difficulties and worked very hard to overcome these deficits by imposing a kind of training on him, endlessly encouraging and urging him to reach for, grasp, and manipulate objects. In the 6-month developmental test the tester made the following observation:

> If left alone, he was tense and rigid, whether moving or still. If he was still, the tension was manifest in his muscle tone, with rigid, extended limbs. During periods of movement, the total arm and wrist movements were sharp, jerky, abrupt, and uncontrolled, and were unsuccessful in achieving the object, a small red cube, that was quite obviously the goal of his activity. One could tell that this was the goal of his activity by the intense visual concentration upon the object and the sudden activation of his limbs and the movement and struggle of his entire body towards that object. (The observer generalizes): I doubt if I have ever seen a baby in whom there was such a wide discrepancy between his desire to achieve a particular goal, such as securing an object, and his total inability to do so.

The hypertonicity of his legs gave him advanced scores on some of the items such as pull to standing, so that the total test picture was irregular. When his difficulties began to clear up in the 7th month a much lighter mood prevailed. Nevertheless, during the 4th, 5th, and 6th month period mother developed many ways to play with Bud and establish a back-and-forth exchange. Mrs. E. is not an articulate woman, but she gave a spontaneous description of interaction with him, illustrating her appreciation of what we refer to as reciprocal, or back-and-forth exchange from a tape recording: "Well, he'll go uh-uh—and I'll talk to him. I'll say, 'What are you telling me? A story?'—something like that. If you screech to him, he goes ah—like that and I'll do it and then he'll do it. Then I'll do it and we'll keep on going back and forth. And when Ralph comes home, I said, 'See, he can do it! And after I do it, he'll do it.'—but he wouldn't do it." Bud's mother reported to us how she employed reciprocal play to capture his attention to manage him while changing or dressing him. At about 3 months after the feeding difficulty was largely resolved and mother was confident about his nourishment, she began propping his bottle. He was very slow in accepting solid feedings and did not give up his night bottle until the 7th month, but mother, in sensing his cues and pacing herself, did not try to hurry this progress. There was no evidence that she was compelled to be with the baby at all times. From very early she had gone out for an evening with her husband, leaving the baby despite the fact that he did not always respond well to this. In fact she seemed to note with some pleasure that he didn't do as well without her. However, when she was with him, she seemed always observant and attentive to him, perhaps overly so. He was in addition much involved with reciprocal play with father and aunt over these months.

Issue 3 (Months 7, 8, 9): Initiative

During the third period, mother's need to "train" abated, when Bud developed initiative to reach, grab, manipulate, and secure a social response from her. His development on tests remained about 1 month retarded during this period. As part of her eagerness to promote his reaching out, she was completely permissive to the activities he initiated during these months, facilitating them whenever she could. She continued to be active in involving him in a great many reciprocal games. In repeated observations it became difficult to tell who initiated contact with whom, so mutual was it. There was no evidence in the record of failures of one to reach and involve the other. The baby was, at this time, now a predominantly visually organized baby and, as with Ellen, the third period saw a well-developed distance responsivity and the use of distance reciprocation by voice and facial cue. For example, during the developmental examination at 9 months, mother sat as usual where she could see him, and frequently tried to make contact with him. The observer writes, "A few seconds later, they caught each other's gaze again and she played a little game with him, nodding her head and talking in a tender way."

However, he was not a very appealing baby, appearing pale, flabby, and heavy jowled, with clumsy, awkward stiffness and serious mien. Stranger reaction, which began at 7 months, was unequivocal, but mild. His first separation anxiety began at 7½ months with protest on his mother's leaving the room. Her effort was to minimize this experience or separation for him whenever she could.

Issue 4 (Months 10, 11, 12, 13): Focalization

Mother's strong desire to gratify Bud and to facilitate his motor development, coupled with her alertness and sensitivity to his cues, contributed to the completeness of her availability to him during the fourth period, and the negotiation of the issue of "focalization" in our interactional sequence. Mrs. E. never appeared disturbed or upset by Bud's demands during this period but seemed unambivalently to feel that it was her role to respond to them to give him what he wanted. She did this in a gentle and giving, although at times in a teaching and controlling manner. Most of the interaction from mother and child was of the visual and social-verbal level, with relatively little physical contact. This mother was able to maintain a certain continuity of reciprocal interaction with him by means of this well-developed distance channel and because of this she was capable of dividing her attention. For example, while engaged in conversation with the visitor, she was constantly aware of his activity and could maintain contact with him. Here is a new level of interaction important to the negotiation of this issue. On this level, mother's availability can be mediated by the child's perception of the mother's focus of attention on him.

Although Bud experienced a high degree of frustration in mastering standing and walking, which we saw as a sequel to his early neurological findings, mother did not attempt to minimize his task. She often responded to his plight by some vigorous stimulating play that further heightened his effort by adding a new twist to his interest or anticipation. As he became able to creep and walk, he vigorously launched himself into exploration in directions away from his mother, moving into issue 5 in a very charming and playful way.

Issue 5 (Months 14–20): Self-Assertion

He developed distinct self-assertiveness in the 14- to 20-month period, especially in the home situation where he had pretty much the run of the place, getting into the pantry, breaking knick-knacks, and climbing over the furniture. He insisted on feeding himself. In the clinic he showed less vigor of exploration of materials, being chiefly preoccupied with the observers and not particularly eager to invest in the materials. However, in time, he was observed in a certain single-track testing of limits as he would repeatedly run down the hall against the express wish of the mother, continuing what he had begun, in direct opposition to her "No." During this span of time, his mother's position pretty much was that he was too young to understand and be limited and that she was not the kind of person prone to struggles, preferring to avoid them unless absolutely necessary. In other words, Bud determined to a degree where the limits would be.

The interpretation of the material during this period was, to some degree, complicated by the birth of a sister when he was 18½ months old. After this, some of his demanding control of mother increased, in which he reasserted her availability to him at his expressed wish. There is the observation, during a feeding of the new baby, in which he completely displaced the baby from the mother's lap and gained sole possession of it himself. This may have been, in part, a regression and, in part, have reflected her lessened ability, at this time, to deal as effectively with his demands. But it certainly describes his assertion with her. It is only toward the very end of the fifth period that the mother became concerned over his continued victories, expressing apologetically that it was her inability to limit him that was at fault. Only at about 21 months did he develop temper tantrums as his aims were frustrated. At this time he was beginning to show intense pressure to have things his own way, which, for the first time, began to be evocative of an expression of anger in the mother. This is, however, ushering in the next period during which we look particularly at data concerning intentional and provocative expression of aggression vis-à-vis the mother. This is the reverse of attachment behavior and although this is a vital phase in the total picture, it is one that we shall not be examining in this chapter. By 20 months the outcome of the issue of self-assertion remained clear in Bud's data, as did the relatively mild degree of tension this behavior elicited in the family.

There are two levels of *outcome* in respect to which these interactional evaluations are being studied. The first concerns the course in each child of the intentional acts of aggression and defiance toward mother in the 18- to 36-month period and the manner in which this clash abates. These events will not be taken up here, but they culminate often in dramatic episodes, the picture of emerging regulation. Spelled out here are ambivalent undercurrents that may have revealed themselves by only subtle clues in the earlier interactions.

A second outcome assessment has been obtained on these subjects during their first year at school. Although designed around a separate research problem, the data furnish a careful description of classroom behavior. The data collection has been carried out by a new team under the direction of Dr. Eleanor Pavenstedt and includes a 2- or 3-day period of classroom observations in the fall and in the spring, interviews with teacher and with mother, a home visit, and psychological testing. Data collection was completed at the end of the spring term 1965 and analysis of it is still underway.

Many questions are raised at once as to which classroom variables should be studied in relation to the interactional evaluations of the first 18 months.

The summaries that follow, of our three children, are based on documentation from all the school outcome data. They were prepared by a data analyst[5] who has been working independently with this material over the past 2 years. He did not participate in the data collection of the longitudinal study and was unfamiliar with the earlier material on the subjects. The descriptive accounts are based on his detailed analysis of the organization of the child's *attentive* behavior as recorded in the classroom observational data.

With respect to Bud's behavior in the classroom, he wrote:

Most striking is his intense interest and involvement in work and mastery of tasks. His attention is strikingly on his work. Attention to teachers with lack of attention to peers are both related to the primary focus on work. The attention to the teacher is not very personal but rather is that he understands that she is teaching and explaining and his attention is to the task of mastery. He is very alert to what is going on and comprehends easily, and as a result is very conforming. Physically he seems well-coordinated, though perhaps over-controlled and not showing a free-flowing grace. There is a great capacity for control and surprisingly little evidence that this costs anything in terms of decreased function in any other area. He seems greatly relaxed. Motor behavior is controlled and directed in the service of work. The time when it is least controlled is the way he stands up out of his seat when raising his hand eagerly. He shifts from one activity to another while manifesting the ability to attend more than one thing at a time and to be finishing one thing while already starting on another. He is very much an achiever, constantly striving for mastery as well as for approval and recognition. He attacks things with intensity. There seems to be relatively little competitive element in his motivation and his need for mastery is not based on competition with peers. He is appropriately independent of the teacher and even his intense involvement in subject-matter seems, by the time we saw him, independent of stimulation by her. He maintains an appropriate distance from her, as she does from the class. In all the rankings which have been obtained thus far on the study children in respect to overall adaptation, attention deployment, and learning in the classroom, he has been given top ranking.

Ned, on the other hand, is described in the summary of his classroom behavior as a

[P]assive withdrawn boy who maintains a barrier between himself and the teacher. One function of this may be to protect himself, but another, by his mute unresponsiveness to the teacher's efforts to reach and motivate him, is to aggravate her to the limit of her tolerance. When the teacher is near or talking to him or the class he avoids her eye and when she does get and hold his attention he responds with frozen impassivity. Sometimes when he should be working and she is at a distance he will watch her as if to keep track of her whereabouts. In spite of this he still seems able to comprehend most of what she says, but his learning is secondarily hampered by the immense tension he is under which expresses itself as a constant distraction by internal stimuli, resulting in wiggling, hand-mouth stimulation, and generally prevents him from concentrating on anything. He shows a very short attention span and high distractibility at all times. He spends much of his time being distracted from work, although there are longer periods of staring and day dreaming. He brings home Fs in most of his subjects, just doesn't do his work in school. He dawdles over it at home, but is not *ever* aggressive about this refusal.

Ellen turned out to be one of the most flexibly adapted of all the children in the school situation. She was described in her summary as follows:

She shows more spontaneity and affect than most first graders, which gives her the appearance of lively intelligence. She loves interaction of any kind, getting much pleasure from her many peer interactions, but loving praise from the teacher as well. She has the most difficulty in following requests to be quiet and to talk less with peers. Otherwise, she adjusts well to limits. She knows easily and clearly what is expected and what she can get away with. As her desire to adhere to the teacher's demands increase over the year she exerts more conscious effort and becomes less spontaneous. There is always a striking inner directed or inner motivated quality to her behavior. She is very interested in her work and is not dependent on the teacher, but enjoys interaction with her and is stimulated to learn by her. Her attention in class is usually task-oriented, though motor discharge is at high level. It is controlled, in nature and direction, so as to be permissible, but there is much body twisting, scratching, and occasional mouthing and finger sucking. She pays good attention when *she* is interested and especially when it offers an opportunity to interact. She can be easily distracted by external stimulation, but she controls this and can then return to work easily and can at times concentrate without interruption. She seems only to really strive for achievement when she is interested in what is going on. Her skills are good though not top. She does not get upset about failure and is not competitive with her peers but is interested in what they are doing.

In as much as developmental testing was carried out on all subjects at regular intervals from 6 weeks of age, the trends in the test scores of our three children have been included. These are graphed in Figure 3.1.

The questions we are asking concern the *process* by which these strikingly different patterns of behavioral organization came to be established. The way we are proceeding to study these questions is by having a framework for cross-case comparison, comparable longitudinal observational accounts for evaluation, and naturally occurring experiments arising from the range of subjects selected for the sample. We also need new models of developmental organization that will bring more precise focus on the variables and the relationships between variables that are the most salient.

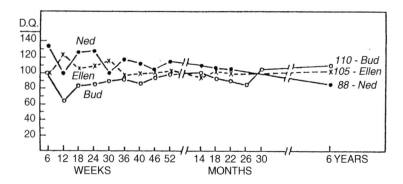

FIGURE 3.1. Scores represent Gesell test results at ages specified in the abscissa for our three subjects. The score at 6 years is a WISC IQ. The Gesell results are described in detail in a publication by Stechler (1964).

DISCUSSION

There have been several aims in presenting these three accounts of the longitudinal interactional picture over the first 18 months of life. The first was to provide empirical data that would constitute a broader interactional context for the smaller and more localized components of behavior that are being studied in the mother–infant interaction.

A second aim was to stimulate a consideration of the methodological problems involved in defining and evaluating longer trends in directly observable interactional data encountered in early life.

A third aim has been to convey some of the thinking that has been stimulated in this attempt to investigate process in interaction and to explore relations between early interactional experience and later consistencies in function.

It was mentioned at the beginning of this chapter that research approach, methods, and models have developed together as we have proceeded and that conceptualizations from basic biological sciences have been most helpful. A few words in conclusion about some of these useful ideas may serve to bring coherence to the presentation.

New modes are needed if one is to focus attention on interactional phenomena and specify the salient dimensions. The interactional sequence depicted by the five issues can be conceptualized as the interplay of two basic models. One concerns adaptation and the other concerns information processing. At the level of the more primitive living systems, these two models may operate as one and the same, but at the level of postnatal ontogenesis in the human infant, it is more useful to apply them as an interplay of two models. The interplay centers about the relations of each to "regulation," a pivotal consideration in the maintenance of living systems.

The first of these two, namely adaptation, has been frequently referred to in the body of the chapter. Because, however, the term adaptation is used loosely and often carries more than one meaning, certain essential points should be clarified. Adaptation has been used here as the concept in its evolutionary sense. As such, it has been formulated concisely and lucidly and its application to ontogenesis detailed in a paper by Weiss (1949).[6] Drawing on his extensive investigations of embryo genesis, especially of the nervous system, Weiss depicted the processes of adaptation taking place between tissue components as they are differentiating. In this formulation one is looking not just at the individual component, but is considering a field or system that is maintained by the interactions or exchanges between component subsystems. The active tendencies of each of these components are emphasized and given a central role.[EN2]

The reciprocal coordination or fitting together of these active tendencies is achieved by the adaptive process through modifications in the tissue components participating in the interaction. These modifications stem from their "clastic" and "plastic" properties.[7] Weiss pointed out that in ontogenesis the necessary modifications are chiefly quantitative ones, and relatively small in degree. They give great precision to the fit and are effected through direct "on-the-spot" interplay of the active tendencies in question. The rough prefit between components, which provides the approximation in which these finer adjustments can occur, derives from phylogenetic evolution.

The adapted state is reached in the system when reciprocally coordinated interactions of "active tendencies" can endure over time and when they are "harmonious with the conditions for existence" of the participants. These conditions include influences vital to stability of regulation. Endurance over time in evolutionary adaptation represents a span of stability long enough to complete the reproductive cycle. In ontogenesis enduring stability in the adaptive field between two elementary tissue organizations establishes them in a new unit of the next order, for example, an organ system. Such stable systems can then interact in this adaptive process to provide a next level of integration, for example, an organism. Thus hierarchical order as well as articulation of elements entails these basic aspects of adaptation. Organization and adaptation are inextricably related.[8] This is a relationship made clear in Piaget's (1936) introduction to his sensory-motor theory of intelligence (1936), in which he concisely summarizes the matter as follows: "From the biological point of view organization is inseparable from adaptation. They are two complementary processes of the same mechanism, the first being the internal aspect of the cycle of which adaptation concerns the external aspect."

The external aspect of the cycle concerning the nature of interactions involved in adaptation has been elucidated to some extent by Weiss's formulation. The internal or organizational aspect has been in a similar way illuminated by the information processing model.[9] Piaget anticipated many of the essential features of the information processing model, for example in his conceptualization of schemata, their emergence, and modification by new experience.

This is a model that has been widely applied to the organization of functions in biological systems and especially to their regulation. It is not within the scope of this chapter nor the competence of the author to take up this body of concepts in any detail. Inasmuch as it has been of great help to us in appreciating the crucial relationship of regulation to the emergence and organization of behavior it should be touched on briefly.

One of the features provided by a successful reachievement of regulatory stability on advancing levels is to maintain smaller degrees of variation or mismatch in the interaction. Information processing can be more optimally carried out under such circumstances by the manipulative activities of the infant organism. The larger increments of stressful excitation that go with interactional asynchrony and dissonance tend to promote protective withdrawal and defensive reactions in the infant rather than his active manipulative approach. Furthermore it is essential that the initiative of the infant be free to manipulate selectively the very interaction itself with the mother. In the information processing view, through this manipulative process, the variations that are experienced in the interaction would tend to be brought into some predictable relation to the actions that the infant determined. Reciprocal coordination in this view would involve a particular feedback to a particular configuration of activity initiated; that is, specificity would be a critical feature.

In a context of stability of regulation, one can assume an option, on the part of the infant, to exercise selectivity in initiating new variations of manipulative activities in reducing the error signal occasioned by the small degrees of variation and novelty that would characterize a regulated system. In a context of regulatory instability this option would be lost in the necessity to restore or maintain basic regulation. The smaller degrees of novelty could not be attended. The extent to which reciprocal coordination is achieved at each level would determine both the task of regulation that is imposed on the system and the selectivity optimal for new organizations of activity to be tried out or integrated.

From the point of view of the information processing model, the infant's selective initiative to employ advancing capacities for activity in manipulating his environment provides him with an increasing repertoire of schemata or TOTEs. Eventually these will include those interactions with the mother necessary to mediate his own regulation.

It is in issue 1 that the mother comes to "know" her baby as she initiates variations of her own in her caretaking procedures to determine what works and what doesn't in stabilizing the baby's regulation.

It is in issue 3, on the other hand, that the child himself must begin to experience reciprocation as produced specifically at his own initiative and at the time he designates. It is precisely the freedom of the infant to initiate exploratory and manipulative variations that can be so sensitively interfered with or facilitated during this period.

It is in issue 2, in the period of "establishing reciprocal exchanges" that we see the affective display of delight and joy in both participants of the interaction when a back-and-forth specific reciprocal exchange has been achieved. This extends from smiling play to a host of little back-and-forth games in which one learns to match the other's actions. The specificity of this match becomes familiar to both. Joyful affect may come to operate as an indicator of specificity of fitting together. This is suggested also by the next step in the child's organization of his behavior. In the 6- to 9-month period the same effect of delight begins to mark the child's success in manipulating objects to fit what he has intended to reproduce. It is possible that this affect later becomes a signifier of reciprocal fit in interpersonal interactions.

From the investigation with kittens mentioned earlier it was suggested that we are looking at a shifting equilibrium of initiative in the interaction through which the kitten is organizing its behavior step by step in ever more independent degrees. One thing is certain: Such a shift can be compromised by the human in many more ways than the animal perhaps can even imagine with the more stereotyped set of caretaking behaviors available to it.

There is only so much that can be usefully dealt with under the general rubric of the organization of behavior. It should be obvious that we have limited ourselves here to interactions of the first 18 months of life and have discussed them on the level of the organization of behavior. The events of the second 18 months of life must be considered with respect to a next level of organization, namely, that of personality. Although it is built on the foundations of the first 18 months and can be approached via the same interactional principles, mother–child interaction in the second 18 months involves important new and additional capacities in the child. When these are followed in our longitudinal material and ordered in terms of the concepts we have presented, we suspect that bridges to more familiar personality theory can be outlined. This must be left for future work to determine.

APPENDIX 3.A: EXAMPLES OF CATEGORIES GUIDING EXTRACTION OF DATA FROM RECORDS

Issue 1: Initial Adaptation (Months 1, 2, 3)

To what degree in the interaction between mother and child will the cues of the infant and/or his state be met by a specifically appropriate response on the part of the mother?[EN3]

Categories

1. Examples of appropriate and inappropriate interaction with respect to specificity, timing, modality, intensity, appropriateness, consistency.
2. Sequence: That is, whether infant or mother has priority in initiation; nature of interaction initiated.

3. Regulation: Extent and duration of comfort or distress in infant and mother (achievement predictable schedule of feeding, sleeping, elimination).
4. Evidence for preferential responsivity of infant.

Issue 2: Establishing Reciprocal Exchanges (Months 4, 5, 6)

To what extent will the interaction between mother and child include reciprocal sequences of interchange between them, that is, back and forth alternations of activity and response?
Categories

1. Examples of sequences of affectively reciprocal back-and-forth smiling play; frequency; vigor.
2. Reciprocal coordination in other activities (and with other people): Extent to which reciprocation characterizes interaction? Non-reciprocation?
3. Regulation: Extent and duration of comfort or distress in infant feeding, sleeping, and elimination.
4. Amount and quality of separation.

Issue 3: Infant's Initiative to Direct His Activity (Months 7, 8, 9)

To what degree will the initiative of the infant be successful in establishing social contact with the mother, especially in the form of a reciprocal interchange with her?
Categories

1. Examples (success and failure): Initiation of social contact with mothers, especially reciprocal sequences.
2. Facilitation or interference with child's initiative (respect shown his specific preferences).
3. Reciprocation of attentive and distance signals.
4. Motor manipulation and coordination.
5. Amount and quality of separation.

Issue 4: Availability of Mother on Infant Initiative (Months 10, 11, 12, 13)

To what degree will the infant succeed in his demands that the mother herself fulfill his needs?
Categories

1. Extent of infant demands *for* maternal response, extent of activity directed *away* from mother.
2. Extent of maternal response (availability) frequency, specificity, and affect.

3. Use of attentive and distance signals for maintaining availability.
4. Special devices used by child to secure maternal availability.
5. Child's preference for mother in presence of others.
6. Amount and quality of separation.

Issue 5: Self-Assertion of Infant (Months 14–21)

To what extent will the child establish self-assertion in the interaction with mother?
Categories

1. Extension and vigor of motor and manipulative exploration.
2. Vigor of child in consummating his own intentions against interference; extent of child's yielding.
3. Attitude of mother to child's self-assertion and to his victory; extent of parental yielding.
4. Behaviors of negativism, possessiveness, exhibitionism, and temper tantrums.
5. Progress of toilet training.
6. Progress in ability to separate from mother; through own activity.

APPENDIX 3.B: SCHEDULE OF CONTACTS

Prenatal

Six to 12 tape-recorded interviews with the mother.
Psychological testing of mother and formulation of her character structure.
Interview with subject's own mother and/or husband.
Home visit.
Obstetrician's prenatal clinic record.
Social Service index.
Screening conference and final prenatal conference with formulation of maternal character structure.
Predictions of postnatal course of mother–child relationship.

Delivery and Lying in

Observation of delivery.
Obstetrician's account of delivery.
Immediate postdelivery observations of child.
Daily observations, tests, and movies of child in lying-in period, including an 8-hour observation on fourth day.

Daily report of visiting nurses' observations in first 14 days at home.
Postnatal conference with assessment of endowment of child and further prediction at approximately 6 weeks.

Postnatal to 18 months

A rotating schedule of home visit every 6 weeks.
Tape-recorded interview with mother every 6 weeks.
Well-baby clinic with pediatrician's examination report.
Developmental testing (Gesell and Hetzer–Wolf Tests) at same well-baby clinic (both every 6 weeks).

Postnatal: 18 to 36 months

Pediatrician's well-baby clinic four times per year.
Developmental tests (Merrill–Palmer or Gesell) four times per year.
Tape-recorded interview with mother six times per year.
Home visit six times per year.
Play sessions with child six times per year.

Two "intensive weeks" at 6-month intervals, beginning at 18 months, comprising three play sessions with child in a 10-day period plus a tape-recorded interview with mother.

APPENDIX 3.C: INTERANALYST RELIABILITY OF DESCRIPTIVE
AND INFERENTIAL STATEMENTS OF ISSUES

	++	+	0	−	− −	
Issue 1	10	4	1	0	0	15
2	11	2	1	0	0	14
3	5	2	0	0	0	7
4	8	6	2	0	0	16
5	7	5	0	0	3	15
Total	41	19	4	0	3	67

Note. Frequency of statements judged to be of high (++) and moderate (+) agreement, and those judged to be of high (− −) and moderate (−) disagreement. 0 refers to those statements in which comparison was not possible.

NOTES

This work was through supported USPHS Grants M898C$_1$, C$_2$; M-3325 (C$_1$), (Formerly M-3923), M-3325 (C$_2$); K3-MH-20-505; and NAMH 1-925-00-561.

Acknowledgment is made to the research associates whose teamwork made the longitudinal study possible. The data collection and analysis on the three subjects presented was particularly contributed to by Manon McGinnis, MSW; Ann Ross, Ph.D.; Ilse Mattick, B.A.; Gerald Stechler, Ph.D.; and Abraham Fineman, M.D.

Published in B. M. Foss (Ed.), *Determinants of Infant Behavior* (Vol. 4, pp. 189–227) London: Methuen.

1. To test the repeatability of extracting and evaluating these items from the same protocol, two teams, working independently, made separate complete sets of evaluations. Agreement and disagreement on 67 items was judged independently with the results given in Appendix 3C.
2. Spitz (1965) described this disparity of levels between mother and infant. In introducing the concept of development as a process of differentiation from an undifferentiated beginning he wrote the following:

   An equally peculiar and perhaps unique aspect of the mother–child relation is that the psychic structure of the mother is fundamentally different from that of her child. The relation between such conspicuously unequal partners cannot be anything but asymmetric; accordingly the contribution of each of them to the mutual relationship will be dissimilar. Aside from the somewhat comparable relation of a human being with a domesticated animal (a pet, for instance) such a high degree of disparity in two as closely associated and interdependant individuals is not found anywhere else in our social organization. (p. 12)

3. For those who regard personality development from the approach and point of view of the embryologist (i.e., in terms of emergent organization), the problem of the process by which differentiation takes place occupies a key position. The formulation of this point of view in the study of personality development has been represented in the orthogenetic principle of Heinz Werner (1947). Here development is portrayed as proceeding from the less differentiated to the more differentiated—the differentiated units becoming articulated and hierarchically integrated. Our question concerns the process by which differentiation takes place and by which articulation and hierarchic integration are effected. Interactional phenomena should indicate, even mediate this process, and so provide an avenue of access for investigation. Detailed paired comparison between individual records offers a method of study in addition to the correlation of outcome variables with interactional trend evaluations.
4. Some of the interactional material for this pair was described in a previous publication (Sander, 1964) in which a particular focus was brought to bear on the interplay of maternal character evaluation and infant endowment in understanding the adaptive course that follows in the issues.
5. Dr. Padraic Burns, who participated in the school follow-up study as a Special Research Fellow in the Boston University Division of Psychiatry.

6. In a previous publication (Sander, 1964) this view has been applied in a paired comparison of two mothers, with contrasting character organizations in respect to aggression, as they negotiate the five issues.

7. A similar notion appears in other formulations of developmental process, for example, the yielding and resisting properties of tissues subjected to shearing forces as conceptualized by D'Arcy Thompson and described by S. Escalona (1959, pp. 8–13) in explaining some of the background for her developmental views. The modification of behavior via the "invariants" of assimilation-accommodation (Piaget, 1936) might be another example.

8. One of the difficulties with our usual concept of psychological organization is that we tend to think of it in terms of the individual. The essential feature of the biological view is that organization is a characteristic of a system and cannot be considered as a property that can be maintained separately. These points are dealt with in general systems theory (Von Bertalanffy, 1952) and the organismic approach (Goldstein, 1939).

9. References to the information processing model are widely represented in the literature of a number of disciplines. Most influential in this study have been discussions of concepts by D. MacKay (1955, 1956); of concepts and neurophysiological applications by Miller et al. (1960) and Pribram (1963); application to physiological controls and regulation by Yamamoto and Brobeck (1965); and the review by J. McV. Hunt (1961).

EDITORS' NOTES

EN1 See the reported description in chapter 4.

EN2 These arguments will be continued and elaborated on in successive chapters.

EN3 It is important to note that, to understand *question* in Sander's sense of the term, it is necessary to refer to a question pertaining to the measure in which the inquiry was negotiated.

REFERENCES

Bertalanffy, L. Von (1952). *The Problem of Life*. New York: Harper.

Escalona, S. and Heider, G. M. (1959). *Prediction and Outcome: Meninger Clinic Monograph Series, 14*. London: Image.

Goldstein, K. (1939). *The Organism*. Boston: Beacon Press.

Harlow, H. F. (1963). The maternal affection system. In B. M. Foss (Ed.), *Determinants of Infant Behavior, II*. New York: Wiley, 3–34.

Hartman, H. (1939). *Ego Psychology and the Problem of Adaptation*. New York: International University Press.

Hunt, J. McV. (1961). *Intelligence and Experience*. New York: Ronald Press.

Mackay, D. M. (1955). The epistemological problem for automata. In C. E. Shannon and J. McCarthy (Eds.), *Automata Studies*. Princeton: Princeton University Press, 235–51.

Mackay, D. M. (1956). Towards an information-flow model of cerebral organization. *Symposium on Cerebral Activity: Advancement of Science*, 42, 392. New York: Henry Holt.

Pavenstedt, E. (1965). A comparison of the child rearing environment of upper-lower and very low-lower class families. *American Journal of Orthopsychiatry*, 35.1, 89–98.

Piaget, J. (1936). *The Origins of Intelligence in Children*. New York: International University Press.

Pribram, K. (1963). Reinforcement revisited: A structural view. In M. R. Jones (Ed.), *Nebraska Symposium on Motivation*. Lincoln: University of Nebraska Press.

Rosenblatt, J. S., Turkewitz, G., and Scheirla, T. C. (1961). Early socialization in the domestic cat as based on feeding and other relationships between female and young. In B. M. Foss (Ed.), *Determinants of Infant Behavior*. New York: Wiley.

Sander, L. W. (1962). Issues in early mother-child interaction. *Journal of the American Academy of Child Psychiatry*, 1, 141–67.

Sander, L. W. (1964). Adaptive relationships in early mother-child interaction. *Journal of the American Academy of Child Psychiatry*, 3, 231–64.

Speigel, L. A. (1959). *No and Yes: On the Genesis of Human Communication*. New York: International University Press.

Spitz, R. A. (1957). *The First Year of Life*. New York: International University Press.

Stechler, G. (1964). A longitudinal follow-up of neonatal apnea. *Child Development*, 35, 333–48.

Weiss, P. (1949). The biological basis of adaptation. In J. Romano (Ed.), *Adaptation*. Ithaca: Cornell University Press.

Werner, H. (1947). *Comparative Psychology of Mental Development*. New York: International University Press.

Yamamoto, W. S., and Brobeck, J. R. (1965). *Physiological Controls and Regulations*. Philadelphia: W. B. Saunders.

4

Infant and Caretaking Environment
Investigation and Conceptualization of Adaptive Behavior in a System of Increasing Complexity[EN1]

INTRODUCTION

The assignment of bringing together one's "research perspective, research philosophy, methods, and findings" in one autobiographical account presents some rather obvious and many more subtle difficulties. It is obvious that such a contribution cannot be in the usual format of a scientific paper. And it is difficult to generate a personal synthesis and at the same time offer it as a research contribution. It has seemed feasible for me only to try to organize and communicate in some reasonably concrete way the course that my work and thought have taken over the last score of years. During that score of years my career in clinical child psychiatry has become largely a commitment to certain problems of early developmental research in particular, a concern with the question of organization itself in personality development.

A RED THREAD

The opportunity that research in child psychiatry presented to me was of gaining at least some perspective of a dismayingly complex universe, one that is rapidly becoming more complex as the knowledge of every aspect of the biological process widens. From my original dismay has emerged the conviction that what it is essential to understand is the way coherence, integration, or "unity of the organism" can be achieved and maintained in an individual engaged in interactions with surroundings of great and apparently increasing complexity.

I assume that the synthesis Dr. Anthony has asked for concerns those gaps between the more formal and objective communications of my scientific publications. These gaps contain the personal information, influences, and rationalizations referred to by Polanyi (1959) as the "personal coefficient of knowledge." In his discussion of Polanyi's position, Wallerstein (1973) described this aspect of the world of natural science as related to "realities created by acts of perspective and interpretation." He went even further to propose that "even the world of natural science is a man-created reality, a particular way of looking at and giving meaning to the facts of nature" (p. 18).

In fact, the recent address given by Robert Wallerstein as outgoing president of the American Psychoanalytic Association provides a most fortuitous frame of reference for an essay intended, as I have assumed, largely for an audience of psychiatric professionals. In his paper Wallerstein pursued the relatively neglected problem of the construction of the world of outer reality as itself a "psychic instance," pointing to the necessity of going beyond the notion of an outer reality as an "average expectable environment" in conceptualizing psychic organization. He argued that it is insufficient now to make such a generalizing assumption in formulating the role of the ego as mediating among an id, a superego, and an *outer reality*. Wallerstein concluded that

> until recently, cultures, no matter how different, each contained a conservative tradition: that children reared within the reality of each, could expect to complete their days within that system of demands—the basis for the conception of the stable and the average expectable. It is in our generation that our life task has become fundamentally different: to survive successfully within a reality matrix in which the *adaptive requirements* are being radically and varyingly transformed within the lifetime of each of us as individuals, rather than slowly over the many generational history of a people. In maintaining our *psychic integration* under such circumstances, we need all the understanding that psychoanalytic study of all the interacting pressures upon us can give. (pp. 31–32)

For such an understanding are needed new, more detailed, and more explicit conceptualizations of the adaptive process in relation to personality development, especially conceptualizations that can account for psychic integration in the face of an increasing complexity, both within the individual and in his encounter with his environment. Just as information-processing models, introducing cybernetic control in regulation, have replaced hydrostatic models of behavior organization, so also relatively simpler biological models of adaptation such as those based on the use of an "average expectable environment" may have to be replaced by more inclusive formulations.

Biologists long have been thinking about the problem of organization of behavior, extending the framework provided by a concept of adaptation. A wealth of leads has been offered from this source for students of interpersonal adaptation, such as those given by Mason[1] (1968) or Ashby (1952). Psychopathology can be viewed as a failure of integrative mechanisms just as easily as it can be viewed as a consequence of conflict. However, as Mason pointed out, just as in biological research relatively less attention has been paid to problems of synthesis than to those of analysis, so in psychiatric research less attention is given to understanding the genesis of ego strength than is given to the genesis of conflict.

When one views the empirical data of human interpersonal behavior, he finds disturbingly paradoxical functions that must be accounted for in the same individual. Both integration and differentiation must be accounted for by the same model. Can factors introducing complexity also provide mechanisms for synthesis and simplification? Can more sophisticated models of adaptive behavior representing processes of basic regulation also suggest more adequate models for the so-called "higher functions" of the human, functions such as cognition, self-awareness, or "inner perception?"[2] In fact, polarity in the arrangement of the forces with which the adapting organism must cope are so ubiquitous in the natural world (e.g., night and day, heat and cold, activity and rest, input and output) that it would not be surprising if a key to the comprehension of adaptive mechanics in development could be found in the organism's confrontation with and resolution of oscillating or opposing tendencies.

For me, the traditional training and concerns of clinical psychiatry initiated the guiding questions and provided research direction.[EN2] The primary concern of the psychiatric clinician is with "the person"—an essential coherence synthesizing components interacting in the greatest complexity. In the therapeutic encounter, if the sensing of and the attention to the facilitation of essential coherence is neglected in favor of any one element over others, the therapeutic process soon becomes compromised or obstructed. The central question arises almost at once: How are the events in an interpersonal interaction to be related to the generation of changes in the organization of a personality, especially to improvement of the integration of its component parts—its coherence?

In the early 1950s the way the organization of a child's character became established was attributed largely to the effect of the maternal character on the actual caretaking interactions of a mother with her child. The preceding question, stimulated by speculations about the therapeutic process, could be as easily asked about the developmental process: How do the events in the rearing interaction influence the organization or coherence of the child's personality in the first place? Might there be basic processes by which interpersonal interaction influences organizing functions in the human that are common to both levels of inquiry? Much theory revolves around the role of "object relationships" in this process, and synthesizing conceptualizations[3] have outlined the major steps in the development of object relationships, not at all a simple concept in itself. However, in the early 1950s few had looked in any systematic way at any appreciable sample of individuals for the actual course of events taking place between mother and infant over the first few years.

A LONGITUDINAL NATURALISTIC PERSPECTIVE OF INTERACTION BETWEEN INFANT AND MOTHER

It seems now purely a stroke of good fortune that shortly after I had completed training in child psychiatry at the Judge Baker Guidance Center and the J. J. Putnam Children's Center, Dr. Eleanor Pavenstedt invited me to join her group as a research psychiatrist. The opportunity to participate in a detailed naturalistic study of the early mother–child relationship was a most fortunate beginning for my experience in developmental research and is only part of the larger debt that I owe to Dr. Pavenstedt. It was in 1954, some time after she had founded the Boston University Child Guidance Clinic, that the longitudinal study entitled, "The Effect of Maternal Maturity and Immaturity on Child Development" (Pavenstedt et al., 1954) was launched under her direction. The aim of the project was primarily to contribute to clinical child psychiatry. Its hypotheses reflected an awareness of and a commitment to holistic issues in a conceptualization of organization in developing personality. For example, one of the hypotheses of the project proposed "that the degree to which a mother perceives and interacts with her child as an *'individual in its own right'* will correlate directly with the level of *maturity* of her personality and with the level of *maturity* reached by her child at six" (each of these clusters being defined in terms of variables described on the observational level).

The effort to document such a proposal one way or the other gives evidence of the clinician's confidence that he can make inferences from a synthesis of clinical material, as well as evidence of a certain aplomb in confronting the many levels of inference involved. This effort also illustrates again the essential place of synthesis in the attitude of the clinical-therapeutic approach to the psychiatric enterprise. Synthesis, after all, may not be a pitfall to be skirted in the name of science but the very essence of that which we seek to understand in early developmental research.

A brief description of this initial naturalistic longitudinal project is given here as a background for discussion of the work that led from it:

Beyond the documentation of a natural history, the groundwork of a body of data was laid, which made it possible to ask specific questions of the role of developing object relationship in the ensuing organization of the child's personality. The design of subject groups, the systematic schedule of observations, tests, and interviews, and the guiding hypotheses made this possible. The subjects consisted of 30 primiparous mothers, meeting basic criteria for normality. They were selected during their second and third trimesters of pregnancy from a general hospital prenatal clinic over a three-year period. The selection was on the basis of closeness of agreement of a detailed characterologic assessment of each with one of three maternal character profiles which had been drawn up to represent the most mature, the most immature, and a middle group. It was expected that the contrasting behaviors exhibited in child-rearing by these three different groups of mothers would provide an empirical basis for studying the relationships between events experienced by a child and features of his or her character at an outcome point, namely, the first year at school or the sixth year of life. It was considered that *outcome* in the development of a personality organization in the child could not be judged from empirical data before such organization had sufficiently consolidated. Therefore, the guiding hypotheses of the study, which related maternal character variables, interactional variables, and variables defined for the child's characterological development at six, were proposed *only* in terms of an outcome to be assessed during the child's first year at school. The application of hypotheses to the data depended on detailed definition of both maternal and child character variables in terms of empirical criteria derived from behavioral observation and clinical experience.

As has been pointed out, the investigation of relationships by this method is a type of clinical research, depending on the synthesis of evidence and depending on a level of inference by which psychoanalytic concepts can be applied in categorizing and assembling empirical data. A feature of a longitudinal study such as this, which is one of its greatest strengths, is that its repeated observations at different times and under a variety of circumstances can provide the data from which such inference reasonably can be drawn. The redundant and consistent becomes apparent, as does any deviation, once a trend has become established in the data.

A most intensive schedule of data collection was carried out[EN3] with remarkably little missing data, by a multidisciplinary team, which numbered as many as 15 at one point. Although it had been designed and initiated as a 10-year investigation with hypotheses relevant only to an outcome at age six, the entire project was terminated approximately at its midpoint, when necessary further funding could not be obtained. Completed data had been collected on some 22 subjects over the first 36 to 40 months of life with consistent data on the remaining 8 only through the first 1½ to 2½ years of life. Needless to say, the transcription of all tape-recorded interviews, dictated observations, home visits, testings, examinations, play interviews, etc. resulted in voluminous data on each pair, which although remarkably encompassing became equally difficult to organize, reduce, analyze, and communicate. The problem remaining in 1959, then, was to analyze these data without the hypotheses, part of the design, or any of the outcome data. Nevertheless the struggle with this problem provided most of the incentive for the research that has followed. Although we could not know at the time, by dint of the rather enormous personal effort of Dr. Pavenstedt and her colleagues, later on a detailed outcome observation[4] was carried out anyway over the first year at school for the 22 subjects having the most complete early data.

In salvaging the extraordinarily rich documentation of interaction and development over the first 3 years of life, we felt we should at least communicate something of the striking range of behaviors we had encountered in the rearing observed in our three subject groups. In making comparisons we wanted to stay at the level of observed behavior in mother–infant interaction. But short of 30 case histories, how could these essential differences be defined and compared systematically from one mother–infant pair to the other over a 3-year span? What were the salient variables and how were they to be related over time?

As a solution at least for communicating the essential clinical differences between the courses followed by the different infant–mother pairs, we formulated an epigenetic sequence of the adaptive issues negotiated over the first 3 years in the interactions between each mother and infant. The sequence was common to all pairs, but the actual behaviors, through which the adaptive adjustments were carried out, were idiosyncratic (Sander, 1962, 1964).

The sequence and its rationale represented the interweaving of ideas about the adaptive process from a wide variety of sources—from the work of others and from our own experience of interviewing mothers and observing their interactions with their babies. The basic perspective was the biological viewpoint of the living organism: from the cell upward, living organisms are actively self-regulating and, at the same time, of necessity exist in a continuous intimate exchange with essential support factors provided by the surround. There is an obvious polarity inherent in this view: attention to either cannot be given at the expense of the other. There are mechanisms of active self-regulation and there are essential factors whose source is provided by a surround. The content of behavior must be accounted for in a specific context.

A most useful resolution of this polarity rests on cybernetic theory. The information-processing model is applied to the adaptation between the self-organizing components—the infant and the mother—and the adapted state then consists of a relatively harmonious coordination between them, consistent with the conditions for existence of each. With one component, the infant, rapidly growing and consequently rapidly changing, new qualities and quantities of infant behavior are constantly being introduced into the content of interaction. The regulation of infant functions, based on behaviors that have become harmoniously coordinated between mother and infant, will become perturbed with the advent of each new, and usually more specifically focused and intentionally initiated, activity of the growing infant. Thus adaptation or mutual modification on a new level is required. Because the behavioral innovations by the infant are often aimed at a progressive assumption of control of situations as a part of the widening of his scope of self-regulation vis-à-vis the environment (i.e., he becomes more vigorously alloplastic), these changes impinge critically on the mother's long-established strategies of self-regulation (i.e., especially strategies for the control of extrinsic variables as a means of regulating her own intrinsic variables). The interactional picture is best organized in terms of the epigenetic sequence in which this progression of relative coordinations is achieved.

The levels that represent this sequence on the basis of empirical data were selected from the experience of interviewing the mothers regularly and systematically over the first 3 years of their participation in the longitudinal study. It became apparent that each mother was experiencing times of relatively greater worry and stress, which were then followed by times of relatively greater harmony in her role as a mother. After we had followed 10 or 15 of the mothers, we could even begin to predict, for a given age, the area of stress or the area of success the mother might report. A perspective emerged, and a relatively simple sequence of the usual course of interactional events[5] could be consolidated. The sequence is listed in Table 4.1 with the time span in the longitudinal course over which it was most usual for the adaptation to occur.

For evaluation of the data collected, each of the adaptive levels listed was worded as an open-ended question, an "issue"[6] to be negotiated between infant and caretaker, which represented the degree to which harmonious coordination was reached by the pair in relation to the interactional behaviors designated for that level and over the time span indicated.

Since the first five issues in Table 4.1 were described in detail in previous chapters, we will bridge to a discussion of issues 6 and 7 with a brief description again of some of the features of issue 5—the issue of "self-assertion"—that also emerges between 14 and 20 months of the infant's life as a new capacity of the child to assert himself and to widen his initiative to determine and select his directions of activity.

ISSUE 5: SELF-ASSERTION

In turning then to "wider horizons of his own" in the 14- to 20-month period, there emerges a new capacity of the child to assert himself and when these directions tend to run counter to mother's wishes and household rules the issue of the degree to which this assertion will be successful is raised. In the usual instance in this span of months, these tender ventures are regarded with a certain affectionate condescension, often with a yielding for a time of a limit just drawn by the parent. The child's initiative, obviously, is not all in a direction away from, or contrary to the mother, but is balanced by bids for reciprocation with her. The probability of success for the latter, he has been determining in the previous issue.

TABLE 4.1
Adaptive Issues Negotiated in Interaction Between Infant and Caretaker

Issue	Title	Span of Months	Prominent Infant Behavior That Became Coordinated With Maternal Activities
I	Initial regulation	Months 1–3	Basic infant activities concerned with biological processes related to feeding, sleeping, elimination, postural maintenance, and so on, including stimulus needs for quieting and arousal.
II	Reciprocal exchange	Months 4–6	Smiling behavior that extends to full motor and vocal involvement in sequences of affectively spontaneous back-and-forth exchanges. Activities of spoon feeding, dressing, and so on, become reciprocally coordinated.
III	Initiative	Months 7–9	Activities initiated by infant to secure a reciprocal social exchange with mother or to manipulate environment on his own selection.
IV	Focalization	Months 10–13	Activities by which infant determines the availability of mother on his specific initiative. Tends to focalize need-meeting demands on the mother.
V	Self-assertion	Months 14–20	Activities in which infant widens the determination of his own behavior, often in the face of maternal opposition.
VI	Recognition	Months 18–36	Activities (including language) that express perceptions of own state, intentions, and thought content.
VII	Continuity (conservation of self as active organizer)	Months 18–36	Activities rupturing and restoring coordination on an intentional level. (Intended and directed aggressive behavior in equilibrium with directed initiations aimed at facilitating restoration of interactional concordance.)

Now this probability provides the context in terms of which he pursues his own inner intentions, and the independent plan of action stemming from them.

It will be seen at once, that, if heretofore reinforcement and gratification have been connected with the achievement of a reciprocal exchange with mother, we are now encountering a new phenomenon. The appearance of success and gratification begins to become evident as the infant maintains his own aims even if they are in opposition to rather than in reciprocation with the mother. Whereas separation before this period is reacted to as an upsetting event, now separation both physical and psychological begins to be produced at the initiative of the infant, or so we expect if all has followed the "usual course of events."

ISSUE 6: RECOGNITION

At the beginning of the second year of life and over approximately the same time span as the previous step, the other side of the bifurcation becomes evident as the rapid development of secondary process functions heralds a new level of increasingly differentiated communication between infant and mother. Speech and the child's capability of predictably communicating inner experience and intentions so they can be read by the empathetic mother make possible a confirmation for the child of his inner perceptions in an actual exchange. This is communication based on a new level of inner awareness rather than the sensorimotor level of physical objects or of direct encounter. The development of speech is a necessary condition for interactions that can now idiosyncratically and specifically convey the child's experience of his own feelings, his fantasies, his play objectives, and so on.[7]

The issue here is how much the mother and child will develop and broaden their reciprocal coordinations on this level, especially in the face of the disharmony consequent to this issue of self-assertion and the subsequent related behaviors of directed aggression, which are described in the following step. The stimulus to develop a new level of communication may arise in part from its success in maintaining reinforcement through reciprocity with the mother on a new level of symbolic representation and language, whereas the older, sensorimotor avenues of interaction now become involved in the disruptive encounters.

The label we have given to this aspect of the sequence of adaptive coordinations in the progression of mother–infant interactions is *recognition*. It gives ascendancy to a new level of awareness in negotiating adaptation for both mother and toddler. The experience of coordination (here matching of a particular communication between partners) must constitute a first level in the experience of self-recognition, namely, realization that another can be aware of what one is aware of within oneself, that is, a shared awareness. It is assumed that this level marks the beginning potential for awareness of a self-organizing core within—actually a core that from the outset has been operative in the service of regulation at the more biological level but is now in a position to be accorded a new priority in the guidance of behavior. Thus, although the progression of interactions can be looked on as belonging to an ontogeny of regulation, it involves and even may in part rest on an ontogeny of awareness. Negotiation of this issue sets the stage for the establishment through the next step in the epigenetic sequence of continuity or constancy in the content of self-recognition (self-constancy being analogous to the object constancy of Piaget's sensorimotor theory).

The importance of this phase for later adaptive flexibility in the personality is that self-schemata cannot be modified without, at least for a time, an access to perception or awareness.[EN4] Further, the achievement of a basic capacity for eventual self-recognition provides a basis for a sense of *continuity* in the human organism. This permits relatively greater independence from variation in outer or environmental regularities, on which organisms at a more primitive level depend for stability.

ISSUE 7: CONTINUITY OR "SELF" CONSTANCY

In the latter half of the second year the bifurcation in the progression of interactions with the mother widens with the appearance of a new quality in aggressive and destructive behavior.[8] This is a quality of directedness and intentionality in these behaviors, which up to this time have been seen usually as more immediately reactive to frustration or externally imposed conditions. Now they appear elective and initiated by the child in directed and provocative moves, often at some time removed from the defining of a rule or "don't"—most often first toward objects of the material environment and then toward the mother in the testing of an intended interpersonal encounter.

The restoration of a previously adapted equilibrium between toddler and caretaker environment, which has been perturbed by the child's new capacity to carry out intentionally destructive and directed acts of aggression, provides the condition necessary for a key experience of "reversal" in regard to self-constancy. The intentional disruption of previously reinforcing and facilitating exchanges with the caretaker disrupts the toddler's newly consolidating self and body representational framework. Reexperience of his own coherence, again at his own initiative or by outreach from the caretaker, provides a situation from which "self" constancy as an inner structure can be established. An interactional equilibrium in the infant–caretaker system is critical in terms both of providing the experience of the taking of a contrary position and of still providing the experience of specific recognition by the familiar caretaker when the intention resumes to restore facilitating reciprocation again. The necessity for reversibility in establishing self-constancy on the basis of "self-schemata" as "operations," in Piaget's sense, gives a rationale for some of the child's employment of directed destructive or aggressive behavior in the second 18 months of life. Should the caretaker be unable to differentiate or fail to aid in restoring the facilitating self as the toddler had previously experienced it, the toddler's own familiar "good self" as a constant frame of reference would be impaired.

In conceptualizing this issue as related to and immediately following issue 6, we envisioned the process as paralleling the notion of reversal in Piaget's sensorimotor theory, whereby operations become abstracted from action and thus freed for new combinations in thought.[9] The self-representation as a scheme has been discussed by Sandler and Rosenblatt (1962) and in this issue can be considered as gaining abstraction and thus mobility as an operation. Self as active initiator or as active organizer is thus "conserved."

The difference between mother–infant pairs in the way such directed intentional aggression was handled was striking in the range of tolerance to intolerance of any such testing. The ambivalent mother, who is in considerable doubt about setting her limits, permits more than another, but eventually she too comes to the point of standing her ground, usually by an angry display long overdue. After this, if the prior step has been negotiated, there follows an abating of the intensity and frequency of elective and provocative clashes with her.

An issue depending on experiences of "reversal" in establishing self-constancy, and introduced by the new capacity for directed aggression, may or may not be negotiated. The longitudinal data lead us to believe that optimally there may be an age-appropriate span to which this consolidation is limited. After 30 to 36 months the child becomes increasingly able to anticipate and consequently to *conceal* inner content that has been so ingenuously revealed in the expression of his intentions and wants between 15 and 30 months, associated at that time with an awareness shared between infant and caretaker via expectations held in common by both. After this age level, concealment (and "defense") renders inaccessible, even to the child himself, the awareness providing a relatedness between the elements necessary for this essential step.

This sequence of levels constructs an *ontogeny of interactive regulation* in the infant–caretaker system, at each level involving new elements that represent integrations of old accomplishments epigenetically. The sequence also suggests an ontogeny of awareness, the characteristics of which are becoming organized through the sequence of adaptations. As increasing numbers of elements enter the repertoire of coordinated behaviors and expectancies and constitute new contexts for action, even finer discriminations become targets of exploration and scheme formation and are drawn into the interactive regulatory process. Research contributions to an ontogeny of awareness have already begun in investigations based on the use of the novelty or surprise reaction in early infancy (Bower, 1972; Charlesworth, 1964) or the focusing of attention (a major means of regulating motility even in the neonate), especially the patterns of attentive focus developing in the exchanges between infant and caretaker (Stern, 1971). Piaget (1973) commented on the role of both conscious and unconscious aspects of early cognitive development, basing this theoretical position of the relationship of consciousness in scheme formation to the assumption, which he attributes to Claparede, that it is mismatch that provokes arousal and conscious experience. This is essentially the same notion as that proposed by others also (e.g., Hunt, 1961; Von Holst, 1950).

In tracing the extension of sensorimotor scheme-building of the infant in interaction with his caretaking environment, we have followed the emergence of his increasingly clear intentionality. Spitz (1957) suggested that this sets the stage for the emergence of the self at around 15 months of age in terms of the toddler's perception (awareness) of his own intention during the restriction of his volitional execution of his intended aims, an experience frequent at 15 months. Certainly the perception of, or inference of, direction of intentionality continues to play a major role in the regulations of interpersonal behavior. In the concept of the emergence of the self framework[10] as an essential self-regulatory mechanism in the second 18 months of life, much remains to be clarified regarding access to awareness, particularly the relationships between "inner" perception and feedback to expectations or goal-directed activity, that is, the child's synthesizing of readouts of his own state as *context* and goal-directed activities as *content*.

RECAPITULATION AND SUMMARY OF ISSUES

The first issue, in which coordination between activities of infant and caretaker takes place (months 1, 2, and 3), is the level of the basic regulation of infant states. Idiosyncracies in the organization of the self-regulatory characteristics of each partner demand a certain specificity in the modifications necessary for achieving harmonious reciprocal coordination, with wide variation to be found in different infant–caretaker pairs in the role accorded infant cues in determining the adaptation.

The second issue (months 4, 5, and 6) concerns the timed "fitting together" of the more active, voluntarily directed reciprocal behaviors characteristic of social (smiling) play and of the caretaking interactions of this period (e.g., diapering, bathing, and feeding of solids). The affect of joy or delight becomes established as a criterion for precision in the matching of interpersonal reciprocations.

The third issue of coordinations (months 7, 8, and 9) concerns the adjustments between infant and caretaker necessary to accommodate the more active initiation by the infant of the now more evidently intentional, goal-directed activities and the rapid acquisition of a widening repertoire of motor skills. Patterns of facilitation and interference (i.e., regulation) of infant initiative and intentionality become defined.

The fourth issue in which interaction must be coordinated between infant and caretaker (months 10–13) concerns the extension of the manipulatory activities of the infant from the area concerned with material objects to one concerned with active, intentionally directed manipulation of the responses of persons, especially the caretaker. The extent of availability of the caretaker's response to an intentional bid of the infant is being determined and is thus, in the usual mothering situation, determining the extent to which and the conditions under which the chief regulatory element of the infant's environment, namely, the caretaker, can come within his repertoire of active self-regulatory schemata.

The fifth issue (months 14–20), at the time of new gains in locomotor freedom, requires adjustment between infant and caretaker in terms of those new self-assertive behaviors of the infant deliberately (intentionally) initiated against the wishes and limitations of the caretaker. The restriction to volition at this time appears to be associated with an especially keen awareness of the intention, or inner motivational state, that is being frustrated.

The sixth issue (extending over the second 18 months of life) concerns coordinations achieved on the level of newly appearing "secondary-process" functions in the toddler, of representation and expression, stemming from his "inner" perception of his own intentions and his own state, his own fantasies or wishes, and so on, and depending heavily on the development of language for communicability. In the "fitting together" at this level, the toddler can experience that another is aware of what he is aware of within himself, providing an experience of personal recognition in a shared awareness and possibly facilitating a consequent capacity for self-recognition. Relatively stable infant–mother coordination at this level provides a context in which basic strategies can become established, allowing the child to use this awareness of "inner" events to guide his own behavior.

The seventh issue, paralleling the previous issue in time (the second 18 months of life), concerns the adjustment being made in regard to directly provocative, aggressive, and destructive behavior. The dimensions of the affect of anger in the caretaker environment come in for active exploration, exposing the toddler's self framework, which is being consolidated in issue 6, to disruption. Restoration can be initiated by either the toddler or the caretaker, but it is proposed that achieving (reciprocal) coordination at this level provides essential experiences of continuity of the self-framework especially when the toddler's interaction is in the context of his being in, or having taken, a contrary position vis-à-vis the caretaker.

CONCEPTUALIZATIONS OF ADAPTIVE BEHAVIOR

The rationale for proposing an epigenetic sequence of interactional adaptations as an approach to the understanding of emerging character organization is suggested by a number of widely different sources. These sources can be only briefly touched on here. They are intended as a stimulus for the reader's reflection on the sequence of interactional issues and on the relevance of an adaptive model. Such a model can order behavioral details of interpersonal interaction, and hypotheses suggested that relate idiosyncracies of adaptation with idiosyncracies of character organization. This is not intended as a comprehensive review of relevant literature but includes only a most limited selection from those sources that have contributed to this viewpoint.

From the psychoanalytic point of view, Erikson's (1950, 1959) proposal of an epigenetic sequence of adaptations through mutual and reciprocal adjustments between infant and caretaking environment was the basis of his concept of a sequence of stages in personality development. This contribution opened a whole new vista for the conceptualization of mechanisms responsible for "ego" development. Basically the sequence of adaptations proposed in our work can be seen as merely filling in the smaller details of Erikson's first two issues of basic trust and autonomy, and as implementing his basic plan[11] of adaptive behavior in a biologic system, in which we discern four basic assumptions.

1. A lawful relationship connects the actual characteristics of behavior of the interactors in the infant–caretaking situation and the organizing of certain features of the child's personality during that time.
2. There is a balance between the polarities constraining the interaction, with a crucial alternative or "issue" for each stage determining the direction of the outcome and settled by decisive encounter.
3. In the history-dependence of the organic system a generalization of early, more specific adaptive strategies later on broadly underlies the biases of ensuing adaptations (e.g., organ mode to social modality).
4. With increasing complexity consequent to growth and differentiation, there are necessary corresponding capabilities maintaining a coherence or unity of the individual—that is, "ego identity" and, later on, "integrity." Just what mechanisms underlie these capabilities has been of central interest.

The interactional, adaptive framework is only a leaf taken from the biologist's notebook. The biological literature is the major source of data and the conceptualizations of adaptive mechanisms in systems consisting of components in exchange. Adaptation most basically can be envisioned as being determined by mechanisms related to maintenance of the regulation of functions of each partner. The *bonding* between the interacting components, which keeps them exchanging as an enduring system, stems from the requirement that regulation of the intrinsic processes of each be provided by the properties and activities of the other. In other words, on the simplest level exchange (interaction) is determined by a requirement for regulation. One of the perspectives that the biological approach provides is that the concept of the "unity of the organism" relates to an organism functioning in its proper environment, that is, its situation of evolutionary adaptation. A major difficulty in conceptualizing at the psychological level arises from a tendency to view the organization of behavior as the property of the individual rather than as the property of the more inclusive system of which the individual is a part.

The notion of an epigenesis in adaptive behaviors within a biological system has been elaborated from the viewpoint of embryologists, for example, in the work of Bertalanffy (1952) and Weiss (1949).[EN5] The former, a principle architect of "systems" theory, pointed out that from the most primitive level upward, two features characterize all matter that can be said to be living, namely, "primary activity" and "organization." Adaptation cannot be conceived of adequately as a simple matter of cause and effect, stimulus and response, or the passive enduring of proximity. The living machine must be considered as already running, the complexly governed interactions with its support system already being specified as the conditions for the living state.

At the cellular level Weiss (1949) explored the neuroembryological mechanisms of adaptation governing the relations between the central and peripheral components of the nervous system and formulated the viewpoint of adaptation that has been the most useful. His definition (Weiss, 1969) of a *system* in the sense in which it is being used here clarifies a number of points:

> Pragmatically defined, a system is a rather circumscribed complex of relatively bounded phenomena, which within these bounds, retains a *relatively* stationary pattern of structure in space or of sequential configurations in time in spite of a high degree of variability in details of distribution and interrelations among its constituent units of lower order. Not only does the system maintain its configuration and integral operation in an essentially constant environment, but it responds to alterations of the environment by an adaptive redirection of its componental processes in such a manner as to counter the external change in the direction of optimum preservation of its systemic integrity. ... The complex is a system if the variance of the features of the whole collective is significantly less than the sum of variances of its constituents. ... In short, the basic characteristic of a system is its essential invariance beyond the much more variant flux and fluctuations of its elements of constituents. By implication this signifies that the elements, although by no means single-tracked as in a mechanical device, are subject to restraints of their degrees of freedom so as to yield a resultant in the direction of maintaining the optimum stability of the collective. The terms "coordination," "control" and the like, are merely synonymous labels for this principle. (pp. 11–12)

In relation to the central thread of this chapter, one might add the term *integration.*

From the vast contribution of investigations in the areas of ethology and animal behavior have come a number of widely inclusive perspectives of interactive regulatory mechanisms constituting adaptive behavior in the organism–environment system and relevant to both phylogeny and ontogeny (e.g., Hinde, 1966; Uexküll, 1934). The most relevant work of T. C. Schneirla (1959) and his colleagues has seemed to be their study of the mechanisms by which "ontogeny progressively frees processes of individual motivation from the basic formula of prepotent stimulative intensity relationships" (see also Rosenblatt et al., 1961).

Cybernetics and its offshoot, information-processing theory, have provided a body of more formalized conceptualization by which the adaptive and self-organizing behavior of biological systems can be represented. This formalized conceptualization has been of enormous influence in bringing a wide range of phenomena under simplifying propositions that model much of the apparent complexity of the living process:

> One of the basic notions is that the system possesses inner criteria to which new inputs are matched. A certain "error signal" results if there is a mismatch. This activates effector apparatus which can then carry out activities to reduce the error signal. If these activities repeatedly require certain modifications necessary to achieve a match (e.g., on encountering consistent features of the environment) the modifications become part of the inner criteria. The criterion (or schema) then comes to represent the organism–environment relationship more precisely. Miller et al. (1960) have expressed these points in their concept of the TOTE unit as the basic unit of behavior. The cogency of the information processing model for the developmental process has been suggested by D. MacKay (1956). He proposes that an inner criterion on which an error signal is based must itself have an ontogeny, differentiating more specifically from earlier more global routines. The information-processing model provides a means of visualizing the organization of self-modifying system, which can take a changing relation to environment into account in terms of changes within itself as it maintains goal direction. In his application of the model to an understanding of neurophysiology and especially the regulatory function of the brain stem, Pribram (1963) emphasizes the optimal response of the system when such changes take place relatively slowly and by small increments. This provides an optimal "error signal" to which the system is best suited to respond. The concept of an error signal optimal for acquisition of new behavioral schemata sheds further light on the picture we have drawn of regulation and its relation to the sequence of interactional issues.
>
> The governing in biologic systems is in large part carried out through cybernetic or feedback control in which part of the output is fed back as input to the system, and, in terms of its match or mismatch with a criterion governs ensuing output. Such systems tend to oscillate and are usually in a continuing cycle of variation requiring constant input to maintain the limits congenial to any enduring existence of the system. This input can be provided by a second cybernetic system so a given state in one system provides the criterion for the control of the other, each system then setting a bias on the other, locked, so to speak, in a reciprocating or phase-synchronized relationship. (Sander, 1969)

Contributions of cybernetic theory and the information-processing model to the problem of adaptive and integrative mechanisms have been suggested by a wide variety of investigators (e.g., Bowlby, 1969; Von Holst & Mittelstaedt, 1950). Hunt (1961) provided a most comprehensive perspective of the relevance of the information-processing model in organizing data that relate early experience to cognitive development and especially to the conceptualizations of Piaget. In 1965 Hunt broadened this perspective in stating his theory of intrinsic motivation and proposing its role in psychological development. In this theory he suggested a three-stage epigenetic development of intrinsic motivation in the infant.

Piaget (1936) anticipated far in advance, and yet in detail, the essentials that have already been described for the information-processing model. His sensorimotor theory first combined the essential elements of the model in implementing his preoccupation with the mechanisms of adaptation.

Piaget's "schema" obviously proposes a basic mechanism of integration. For the schema all prior experiences of a particular kind are drawn on in determining the necessary modifications to achieve a consistent match in a new accommodation. In other words, by means of schemata the history of the system is integrated with the present context in organizing the final common path of action.

Polarity and the processes of the equilibration of polarities (e.g., decentering) form a central theme by which integration is carried further. Piaget (1969) summarized the three lessons that he drew from biology and that never ceased to illuminate his thinking:

> The *first* is that all adaptations of the organism ... imply the closest interaction between organism and environment: ... No subject without action on objects and no objects without a structuration contributed by the subject ... [The *second* is that] any biological adaptation implies two poles by virtue of these interactions; on the one hand, it is an accommodation, i.e., a temporary or lasting modification of the organism's structures under the influence of external factors; [and on the other] ... A complementary pole, the assimilation pole, which has the task of integrating external factors into the organism's structures. ... A third analogy is obviously necessary: if biological or cognitive adaptation requires two poles, they both tend toward total harmony by means of successive equilibrations. From the embryological regulations, whose fundamental stage Paul Weiss called "re-integration," or from the numerous cybernetic circuits described by Waddington at the heart of his "epigenetic landscape," up to the self regulations which the study of mental development is continually bringing to light, we find a quite remarkable continuity. ... We are struck by the generality of these vital fundamental processes, whose knowledge is just as indispensable to the psychologist as to the biologist. (page 157–158)

There is currently much interest in applying sensorimotor theory to the process by which the child gains lawful relationship with aspects of his interpersonal environment (see Escalona, 1963; Gouin-Decarie, 1965; Hunt, 1961). The polarity referred to by Piaget (Piaget & Inhelder, 1969) in the development of "object relations" is the polarity of *self* and *other*. The decentering of affectivity onto the other as an alternative to the self is part of a single integrated process correlated with cognitive decentering.[12]

The chronology of interactions described earlier and the correlated epigenetic sequence of adaptive issues can also be viewed as an effort to apply Piagetian concepts. The concept of *equilibrium*, for example, can be represented empirically here in the achievement of stable interactional coordinations. These levels of adaptation provide a sequence of contexts permitting widening options (increasing selectivity) from which a next level of differentiated volition can take off in building interpersonal coordinations and schemata of interpersonal relations.

An application of Piagetian concepts to the empirical material of our longitudinal study, as assembled under issues 6 and 7, can be suggested. These contrasting interactions represent a polarity, that is, interactional coordination versus divergence. (In psychoanalytic terms this could be expressed as the polarity of libidinal and aggressive drives or, in Mahler's formulation for this age period, as the polarity existing in the rapprochement subphase of the separation–individuation process.) In terms of our emphasis on an ontogeny of awareness in focusing the infant's initiation and intentionality, the harmony achieved in the negotiation of the sixth and seventh issues should be considered also in its relation to emerging self-awareness (see Spitz, 1957) and the establishment of an initial conservation or constancy in the structuring of self. Here there is opportunity for an inner decentering between polarities of self-awareness: the self as facilitated and coordinated (issue 6) and the self as negated and not coordinated (issue 7). If the interactive regulation existing between the toddler and his caretaking environment allows an *option* for *exercise* of *choice*, or behavior initiated by the toddler, a conservation of self-as-initiator or of self-as-active-organizer should harmonize the polarity. The failure of a self-constancy here would leave the child vulnerable to polar oscillations in terms of the interaction that happened to be current, a vulnerability in regulation that would powerfully determine that child's subsequent adaptive strategies.

Finally, Ross Ashby's (1952) conceptualization and mathematical derivation of the "origins of adaptive behavior" provides a remarkable model for adaptive behavior in an increasingly complex system. Drawing on the same Bourbaki school of mathematics as did Piaget, Ashby provided a mathematical derivation for usable definitions of many of the usually imprecise terms thrown about when we speak of adaptation, systems, regulation, and so on. In addition he derived principles of adaptive mechanics that account for some of the usually more difficult areas to be explained in adaptive behavior—for example, system, regulation, essential variables, the law of requisite variety, channel independence, adaptation time, use of the recurrent situation, temporary and partial independence, and the mechanism of disjoin of a subsystem made possible by constancy or stability (richness of equilibria) within a complex system. This mechanism of disjoin makes possible differentiated adaptations with the environment at the level of subsystems, so that perturbation of or in the "disjoined" subsystem does not spread to the rest of the organism.

If we approach the early organization of infant behavior in terms of principles of adaptive behavior in an infant–caretaker system, the problem of coherence or integration takes on a somewhat different color than when it is considered as one of the many functions of the individual to be attributed to his "ego." A whole array of mechanisms becomes evident that contributes to the "coherence" of the organism functioning within the caretaking system to which it is adapted. In fact, different contributions can be identified for each of the seven issues.

The adaptations appropriate to each level may contribute basic interpersonal strategies or interactional parameters in the sense that they become characteristic constituents of the interactive regulations involved in later, more differentiated interpersonal adaptations. The adaptations related to each issue do not represent something established once and for all, but they are successive contributions to the maintenance of a continuous regulative process in interpersonal interactions.

Mechanisms of synthesis and integration must advance *pari passu* with increasing differentiation if "adaptation time" (Ashby, 1952) is not to become unduly prolonged. Ashby suggested that under conditions providing a richness of "regions of stability" or equilibrium in interactive regulation, the self-organizing core could itself gain relative "disjoin" as a subsystem and thereby possibly a "temporary and partial independence." Under these conditions such a subsystem would be capable, within limits, of participating in ensuing perturbations of adaptive encounters with the surround without the perturbation's spreading over the whole complement of subsystems that constitute the more basic biological functions of the individual. Ashby's argument thus provides the rationale that a "self" or a self-organizing subsystem is essential to the regulation of adaptive behavior in a system at the critical level of complexity.[13]

NOTES

Supported by NIMH Research Development Program K5-MH-20, 505. The data reported were obtained during project support NIMH 898C1, NIMH 3325, and NICHD 01766. Work carried out during current support by The Grant Foundation, New York, has contributed in a major way to the viewpoint presented herein.

From Anthony, E. J. (Ed.) (1975). *Explorations in child psychiatry* (pp. 129–152). New York: Plenum.

1. In his discussion of research in relation to the biological problems of synthesis and organization, W. A. Mason provided a comprehensive perspective, an inspiration, and an example of the way sufficient empirical data can be accumulated to bear directly on problems of biological organization and to suggest relevant models.

2. Von Holst (1950), an investigator of insect behavior, raised some of the same questions that the psychiatrist has. Given the same exact configuration of movement of a limb or muscle, which is at one time passively moved and at another time actively moved by the organism, how are these movements centrally distinguished? In other words, how does the organism distinguish what happens to him from what he makes happen? Von Holst's conceptualization includes many clues relating to intention, perception, consciousness, and so on.

3. See Erikson et al. (1950), Hartman et al. (1946), Mahler (1968), and Spitz (1959).

4. This research was supported by the Supreme Council of the Scottish Rite.

5. It should be kept in mind that this is an account of interaction and is not intended as a summary of developmental steps. Furthermore, any interactional sequence will be seen to parallel the developmental sequences proposed by others (e.g., Mahler, 1968). These will be touched on briefly later and referred to in part; it should be evident, however, that within the scope of this chapter a comprehensive cross-referencing cannot be undertaken. The interaction is between a growing infant who has arrived with a particular endowment in regard to the regulation of its functions and a maternal character whose various facets will reveal themselves at different points as the infant differentiates new capabilities for determining his actions. The sequence illustrates a progressive differentiation, on the part of both the mother and the infant, of behaviors constituting their exchanges—a progressive differentiation of increasing complexity. The fact that a sequence of adaptive issues between mother and infant was proposed primarily as a way of organizing observational material for analysis, does not mean an unawareness of or disinterest in the contribution of other figures (e.g., fathers) or other influences in the child's interpersonal environment.

6. For each issue several categories of items were individually rated as evidence for or against the adaptation and the degree of harmonious adjustment that had been reached. All evidence that could be discovered in the record both for and against was extracted and drawn on in the evaluation of the items. Agreement between independent analysts on the evaluation of such major trends, when taken in these large time blocks and based on extensive and repeated documentation, is not impossibly difficult (Sander, 1969).

7. The relevance of issues 6 and 7 to Mahler's (1968) rapprochement subphase and the establishment of "libidinal object constancy" is that the two issues are constructed here as a concurrent polarity necessary for a "decentering formulation" in the structuring of constancy of self as a framework for subsequent self-regulation. These points will be taken up to some extent later.

8. Again it must be recalled that this framework has been derived from data collected from a particular White urban population at a particular point in social change affecting this particular population. It was our impression that every step in the impact of the multiple potentials inherent in the maternal character eventually is acted out in clear and decisive behavior in interaction with her toddler. Thus the transmission of maternal "dynamics" in actual behavior is not a mystery if one has access to a sufficiently detailed longitudinal picture, suggesting an approach to the adaptive specificity that Wallerstein (1973) called for in understanding developmental organization of ego.

9. This was suggested by Spitz (1957): "The achievement of the faculty of judgment on the level of the capacity to signify 'no,' either by gesturing or by word will be found to correspond to the achievement of reversibility in terms of Piaget's Theory (1936)" (p. 144).
10. See Spiegel (1959) for his review of the self in relation to psychoanalytic metapsychological considerations.
11. Also see Spitz (1959).
12. In an application of Piagetian concepts to the developmental analysis of interpersonal behavior, Feffer (1970) discussed decentering in terms of reciprocating *role* schemata (e.g., giving–taking and punishing–being punished). The polarity of concern in our viewpoint, on the other hand, is that between self-as-coherent (confirmed or reinforced) and self-as-dispersed (negated or extinguished), the polarity being then resolved in recognition of self-as-having-option-to-initiate. This formulation is particularly relevant in conceptualizing the genesis of narcissistic personality disorder.
13. Complexity in behavioral adaptation should increase with the richness of the behavioral repertoire available (the law of requisite variety; see Ashby, 1958), thereby increasing the number of possible selections of appropriately differentiated behaviors when conditions permit options (i.e., in Ashby's terms conditions that do not displace "essential variables" from their regions of stability; such displacements would limit selectivity by preempting behavior to restore basic regulation). Such necessary complexity appears to accompany complexity in social interaction and communication. For example, a provoking question, motivating the detailed investigations by Dr. D. Ploog (in a personal communication to the author) and his colleagues regarding communication in the squirrel monkey, is why such a relatively small creature with such a relatively simple habitat has evolved such highly complex communicational behavior. If Ashby's model is right, the advantage gained in predator avoidance or food gathering for the squirrel monkey may be less important than the gain in complexity of repertoire, regions of stability, and, consequently, selectivity made available for the self-organizing function. The critical step in human evolution may have been at the point of both complexity and stability at which the organism's own "state" itself became conscious, i.e., both coherent enough and recurrent enough to become a criterion for match.

    The information-processing model, in the general sense being used here that it is mismatch that leads to perception and consciousness, indicates that an ontogeny of interpersonal regulation must indeed be also an ontogeny of awareness. For both, the conceptualization of the infant and the caretaking environment as a system is central, with an ontogeny of awareness depending heavily on characteristics of "state" as context and on goal-oriented activities as content.

EDITORS' NOTES

EN1 This article illustrates how original and unconventional Sander's proposals and directions of research were for the epoch of his writing from 1960 to 1970 (actually, even for us). Written more than 30 years ago, it was requested not only as a scientific communication on his research, but also to explain the extraordinary richness of his theoretical background, unique in those years and outside of the ordinary even today: We refer to his capacity to integrate, for example, psychoanalytic and biological knowledge, instead of considering them as coming from opposite domains. This was one of Sander's many pioneering characteristics that succeeded in gaining the reader's curiosity with this article, and that, we believe, continues to provoke, even today, the profound interest of the reader thirty years later.

EN2   According to Sander, clinical and empirical research are areas clearly separated and, at the same time, interdependent—a view that, in the actual psychoanalytic culture, still seems very rarely shared.

EN3   For the specifics of such programs, see Chapter 3.

EN4   The clinical work aims at gaining access to perception and awareness as well.

EN5   The conceptualizations of these two authors are further tackled, particularly in chapters 9, 12, and 13 of this volume.

REFERENCES

Ashby, R. (1958). *An Introduction to Cybernetics.* London: Chapman and Hall.
Ashby, R. (1970). *Design for a Brain.* London: Chapman and Hall.
Bertalanffy, L. Von (1952). *The Problem of Life.* New York: Harper.
Bower, T. G. R. (1972). Object perceptions in infants. *Perception,* 1, 15–30.
Bowlby, J. (1969). *Attachment and Loss, V. 1.* New York: Basic Books.
Charlesworth, W. R. (1964). Instigation and maintenance of curiosity behavior as a function of surprise versus novel and familiar stimuli. *Child Development,* 35, 1169–1186.
Erikson, E. H. (1950). *Childhood and Society.* New York: W. W. Norton.
Erikson, E. H. (1959). Identity and the life cycle. *Psychological Issues,* 1, 50–101.
Escalona, S. (1963). Patterns of infantile experience and the developmental process. *The Psychoanalytic Study of the Child,* 18, 198–201.
Feffer, M. (1970). A developmental analysis of interpersonal behavior. *Psychological Review,* 77, 197–215.
Gouin-Decareit (1965). *Intelligence and Affectivity in Early Childhood.* New York: International University Press.
Hartman, H., Dris, E., and Loewenstein, R. M. (1946). Comments on the formation of psychic structure. *Psychoanalytic Study of the Child,* 2, 11–38.
Hinde, R. A. (1966). *Animal Behavior: A Synthesis of Ethology and Comparative Psychology.* New York: McGraw-Hill.
Hunt, J. McV. (1961). *Intelligence and Experience.* New York: Ronald Press.
Hunt, J. McV. (1965). Intrinsic motivation and its role in psychological development. In D. Levine (Ed.), *Nebraska Symposium on Motivation.* Lincoln: University of Nebraska Press.
MacKay, D. M. (1956). Towards an information flow model of cerebral organization. *Symposium on Cerebral Activity, Advancement of Science,* 42, 392.
Mailer, M. (1968). *On Human Symbiosis and the Vicissitudes of Individuation, Vol 1: Infantile Psychosis.* New York: International University Press.

Mailer, M. and McDevit, J. B. (1968). Observations on adaptation and defense in statu nascendi: Developmental precursors in the first two years of life. *Psychoanalytic Quarterly*, 37, 1–21.

Mason, J. W. (1968). Over-all hormonal balance as a key to endocrine organization. *Psychosomatic Medicine*, 30, 791–808.

Miller, G. A., Galanter, E., and Pribram, K. (1960). *Plans and the Structure of Behavior*. New York: Henry Holt.

Piaget, J. (1936). *The Origins of Intelligence in Children*. English translation. New York: International University Press.

Piaget, J., and Inhelder, B. (1969). The gaps in empiricism. In Koestler, A., and Smythies, J. R. (Eds.), *Beyond Reductionism: New Perspectives in the Life Sciences*. Boston: Beacon Press, 118–160.

Piaget, J. (1973). The affective unconscious and the cognitive unconscious. *Journal of the American Psychoanalytic Association*, 21, 246–61.

Piaget, J., and Inhelder, B. (1969). *The Psychology of the Child*. New York: Basic Books.

Polany, M. (1959). *The Study of Man*. Chicago: University of Chicago Press.

Pribram, K. (1963). Reinforcement revisited: A structural view. In M. R. Jones (Ed.), *Nebraska Symposium on Motivation*. Lincoln: University of Nebraska Press.

Rosenblatt, J. S., Turkewitz, G., and Scheirla, T. C. (1961). Early socialization in the domestic cat as based on feeding and other relationships between female and young. In B. M. Foss (Ed.), *Determinants of Infant Behavior*. New York: Wiley.

Sander, L. W. (1962). Issues in early mother-child interaction. *Journal of the American Academy of Child Psychiatry*, 1, 141–67.

Sander, L. W. (1964). Adaptive relationships in early mother-child interaction. *Journal of the American Academy of Child Psychiatry*, 3, 231–64.

Sander, L. W. (1969). The longitudinal course of early mother-child interaction: Cross case comparison in a sample of mother-child pairs. In B. M. Foss (Ed.), *Determinants of Infant Behavior*. New York: Wiley.

Sander, L.W., Julia, H. L., Stechler, G., and Burns, P. (1969). Regulation and organization in the early infant-caretaker system. In J. R. Robinson (Ed.), *Brain and Early Development*. New York: Academic Press.

Sandler, J., and Rosenblatt, B. (1962). The concept of the representational world. *Psychoanalytic Study of the Child*. New York: International University Press.

Schneirla, T. C. (1959). An evolutionary and developmental theory of biphasic processes underlying approach and withdrawal. In M. R. Jones (Ed.), *Nebraska Symposium on Maturation*. Lincoln: University of Nebraska Press.

Speigel, L. A. (1959). *No and Yes: On the Genesis of Human Communication*. New York: International University Press.

Spitz, R. A. (1959). *A Genetic Field Theory of Ego Formation*. New York: International University Press.

Stern, D. N. (1971). A micro-analysis of mother-infant interaction. *Journal of the American Academy of Child Psychiatry*, 10, 501–18.

Uexkuell, J. Von (1934). A stroll through the worlds of animals and men. In C. H. Schiller (Ed.), *Instinctive Behavior: The Development of a Modern Concept*. New York: International University Press.

Von Holst, E., and Mittelstaedt, H. (1950). Das Reafferenz Prinzip. *Naturwiss*, 37, 464–89.

Wallerstein, R. S. (1973). Psychoanalytic perspectives on the problem of reality. *Journal of the American Psychoanalytic Association, 21*, 5–34.

Weiss, P. (1949). The biological basis of adaptation. In J. Romano (Ed.), *Adaptation.* Ithaca: Cornell University Press.

Weiss, P. (1969). The living system: Determinism stratified. In A. Koestler and J. R. Smythies (Eds.), *The Alpbach Symposium 1968, Beyond Reductionism: New Perspectives in the Life Sciences.* Boston: Beacon Press.

Part 2

Part 2 brings in our subsequent search for the way principles of life processes might operate in the infant–caretaker system at an initial level of the first 2 months of life. At this point we were interested in principles that bridge more directly from the biological level to the infant–caretaker level. The data for this section have been developed from a continuous infant bassinet monitor that provided a record of states of sleep, wakefulness, feeding, crying, and approach of caretaker to the bassinet, and presence of infant within or removal from the bassinet.

It illustrates the system's sensitivity at the level of biorhythms, sensory perception, state regulation, and bodily functions—to the specificity of an initial "fitting together" in time, space, and movement between infant and caretaker.

In particular, Chapter 7 proposes that awareness of inner experience, such as the infant's awareness of his or her own state in this regularly recurring sequence, and its connection with the infant's emerging and recurring expectancies and desires, must provide an essential matrix of self-awareness for the infant's initial developmental organization of consciousness.

Moreover, Chapter 8 elaborates the way resolution of a basic paradox in living systems—how the paradox of mother and infant being "together with" each other can allow each to be "distinct from" each other—begins the negotiation that endures over increasing levels of complexity over the ensuing life span of each.

Chapter 9 introduces the beginnings of the concept of a recognition process.

5

Investigation of the Infant and Its Caregiving Environment as a Biological System

The purpose of this chapter is to illustrate a research program designed and carried out as a way to study the infant and its caregiving environment together as a living biological system. There are at least three reasons that this account has relevance to this volume. The first is that psychoanalysis, in its current concern with the argument that a "self-psychology within psychoanalysis" (Kohut, 1977) is needed, is turning once again, as it has from its very outset, to both biology and early development for light on the matter of the ontogeny of behavioral and psychological organization (e.g., Basch, 1977). Psychoanalysis needs the conceptual and empirical perspective that recent advances in biological systems research are opening up.

The second is that research in the area of early development is currently experiencing a transition in emphasis from the classical experimental approach, which aims at isolating variables, reducing sources of variability, and pursuing a linear concept of causality, toward the study of concurrent and interactive effects of multiple variables, mechanisms of integration, and the formulation of nonlinear concepts of causality. Developmental research itself, then, is looking toward biological models and methods of investigating living processes from the holistic, evolutionary, and systems perspectives of biology.

115

The third is that intense pressure is being exerted on clinical facilities to intervene actively now at the earliest pre- and postnatal levels to accomplish aims of "primary prevention" of developmental deviations when either the infant or the caregiving environment is considered at risk for them. The pressure is for the predictable manipulation of the developmental process. We have but a meager empirical base of prospective data from which the conceptualization of process can be constructed, or the lawfulness of change, plasticity, or the integration of complex determinants in producing a predictable outcome can be well enough understood to guide "prevention."

It is not clear to many what the differences are between traditional research designs and the study of a living system; this includes the kind of questions that can and cannot be addressed by each, or the relationships between variables that are relevant to either. In what follows, then, certain perspectives drawn from the domain of biology will be introduced, an example of mechanisms of regulation in biological systems given, and an account presented of the design, methodology, and findings of a project aimed at operationalizing some of the implications of a biological systems viewpoint (Sander, 1977).

The first of these perspectives drawn from the biologist's observation of the living system is that time and the temporal organization of events constitute a domain of order that cannot be in any way neglected, avoided, minimized, or bypassed. It remains a central reality around which the significance of other phenomena become assembled. Its importance does not come into view unless one is considering the system, the living organism within its environment of life support.

To begin with, then, and at the most general level, the ecological niche of the newborn is one that must provide at least the essential conditions for the proper negotiation of a profound revision after birth in the temporal organization of the infant's various functions (Sander, Chappell, Gould, & Snyder, 1975). Those who have had the joy of caring for a new baby know what can happen in the wee small hours of the morning. Often, at first, more happens then than during the rest of the 24 hours of the day, until, that is, the baby's rhythms of activity and quiescence tune in to, or synchronize with, the day and night differences within his new environment. At first, in addition to being awake when the rest of the world is asleep, the newborn may be falling asleep himself when he is in the midst of eating or crying and hungry when he should be sleeping. He may swallow when he is in the midst of breathing or bite down on a nipple, closing it off, when sucking would allow delivery of milk.

On the basis of present investigations of newborn physiology, it is conceivable now to regard the new baby as a composite of semi-independent physiological subsystems, each with its own rhythm, such as those controlling heart rate, respiration, brain waves, and body movement (Luce, 1970). Infants arrive with varying degrees of coherence or phase synchrony between these component subsystems. Because they affect such activities as waking, sleeping, and feeding, and, under certain conditions, each has the ability to run on its own time track, they must become harmonized and coordinated within the new baby, and in turn, tuned up with the regular periodicities of the world and of the people who make up the baby's world.

There are many time levels involved. The rhythms involved may be circadian, that is, arranged in relation to an approximately 24-hour cycle of variation; or ultradian, higher frequency rhythms in relation to time spans less than 24 hours; or infradian, lower frequency rhythms over 24 hours (Sollberger, 1965). Periodic behaviors involved in the interaction between infant and caretaker can be explored at the level of seconds and even microseconds (Brazelton, Tronick, Adamson, Als, & Weise, 1975; Condon & Sander, 1974; Stern, 1971). The orchestration of such a complexity is one of the major accomplishments of the postnatal caretaking task. Its aim is to bring the infant to function as a unified organism in coordinated harmony with an ecology based on a 24-hour cycle, arranged in day–night organization, with the day arranged in subunits such as morning, afternoon, and evening. On the background of harmony at this more macroscopic level, caretaker and infant are engaging in exchanges, cycling at a much higher frequency, in seconds or microseconds, and so on. But how does one approach the problem of investigating such complex organization and the mechanisms depending on location of events in time?

We started out trying to conceptualize the lawfulness governing longitudinal changes in the transactions between infant and surround postnatally, in terms of the biological concepts of adaptation and the adaptive process (Sander, 1962). The biologist, however, begins at an even more basic level, namely, with the problem of regulation—the regulation of exchange between the organism and its environment of life support. It is at this most basic point that time plays the fundamental role. I am referring here, again, to the matter of biorhythmicity, a subject that represents one whole discipline of biology, which for more than 50 years has been investigating the adaptive process in terms of mechanisms of temporal organization regulating exchanges in different ecological systems.

THE BIOLOGICAL SYSTEM

An illustration can be given by the way time in the biological system provides the basic organizational structure for a life-support framework by providing for the phase synchronization, or for the cooccurrence of essential periodic encounters between the organism and its niche, such encounters being sparsely distributed, but at precisely the right time (see Figure 5.1).

In this figure, Enright (1960) illustrates the activity of three batches of synchelidium (amphipods or "sand fleas") collected from three dif-

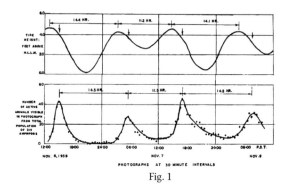

Fig. 1

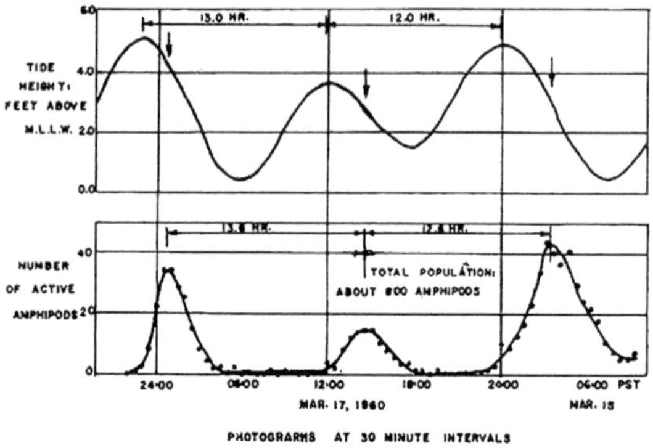

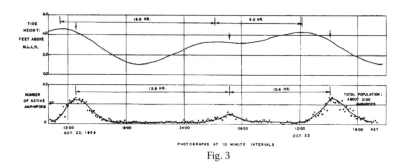

Fig. 2

Fig. 3

FIGURE 5.1. Activity rhythms in *Synchelidium* n.sp. isolated in laboratory, compared with tidal movements (U.S.G.S predictions) on beach from which they were collected. Vertical arrows on tide graph indicate position of estimated maximal activity of amphipods. Note that the time scales differ. Courtesy of Cold Spring Harbor Laboratory Press.

ferent beaches in Southern California, some 319 in one, 2,100 in another, and 600 in a third. Because of coastal configurations, the time and character of tidal ebb and flood on different beaches vary from one beach to another. The time and configuration of tidal peaks and troughs characteristic for the three beaches from which the samples of amphipods were collected are illustrated in the top line of each of the three sections of Figure 5.1. It is to be noted that the time between tidal peaks is 14.4 and 11.2 hours for one beach, 16.0 and 9.0 for another, and so on. The ecology of the amphipod is such that the time for its greatest activity on the beach occurs at the onset of the ebbing tide, estimated for the three populations by the arrow. The meaning of "fitting together," or adaptation, in respect to the organization of the ecological system is dramatically portrayed by the lower line of the graph for each of the three sections. This represents a count of the numbers of actively swimming amphipods in each sample at a sequence of time points; this line shows peaks of swimming activity in the creatures that correspond to the estimated time of expected peak activity on their respective beaches. However, when being counted, the amphipods now are *not* at the beach at all, but in the laboratory, each group isolated under the same controlled and constant conditions. Regulation of the timing of the recurrent activities essential for its survival from *endogenous* sources within the amphipod adjust it to, or synchronize it with, resources provided by essential recurrent events in its environment being regulated by a separate independent and *exogenous* source of periodicity. The meaning of phase synchrony for the organism as a whole is that of establishing a general *state of readiness* for the encounter. If properly timed, evidently the key exchanges between the interacting components of the system need only be episodic, not continuous.

Much has been learned of the various mechanisms governing phase-control of biorhythms (Aschoff, 1969). Investigators of the role of biological rhythms in different ecological systems suggest that both the processes of adaptation without and of integration within the organism can be resolved as matters of phase-synchronization of interacting components (Aschoff, 1969; Halberg, 1960; Pittendrigh, 1961).

Each infant arrives with a unique set of regulatory characteristics, and each meets a caretaking environment with its own unique regulatory features, two disparately organized entities at the outset, to say the least. The way they finally adjust themselves to exist together around the clock in some reasonable harmony consequently involves exchanges that must also be uniquely configured. However, unique configurations become manageable as with the three different beach configurations of Figure 5.1, at least conceptually, when one focuses on the timing of recurrence of certain specific variables relevant to each of the interacting partners and on the temporal pattern that the timing of such recurrence establishes.

THE INFANT AND CAREGIVING ENVIRONMENT AS A SYSTEM

The initial strategy of our investigation, then, was to make the unit of observation not the infant alone, or the caretaker as a separate entity, but the two in concurrent action together around the clock. Systems constituted differently in terms of the particular characteristics of infant or of caretaker provide experiments in nature. The strategy of comparing the 24-hour course of events over time in different systems provides clues to mechanisms of regulation. The second step, then, was to devise methods by which we could chart day by day, the values of multiple variables related to the different functions or subsystems mediating between the participants. Variables would be selected that could be given quantitative values and could be continuously recorded or frequently sampled. The third step, finally, was to compare across the infant–caregiving systems at some outcome point the progress in the development of the functions and the sensorimotor subsystems on which the measurements of variables had been recorded. The effect that having a role in the regulation of essential exchanges has on the developmental process of infant functions provides further clues as to *mechanism* and *process*, especially if such infant functions can be assessed in terms of the specific way they contribute to regulation of the system. This can be carried out, for example, by perturbing the system and charting the course of recovery of variables related to particular subsystems (Cassel & Sander, 1975).

A combination of methods therefore is necessary to study the organization of events in the infant–caretaker system and the changes in this organization over the first days and weeks of postnatal life. The scope of the chapter does not permit more than the briefest description of the methods we have used and the three major categories of variables that have been combined to describe the temporal organization of events in the postnatal infant–caregiver system over the first weeks of life.

METHODS

It was while working with a stabilimeter to measure the motor activity of the newborn, which we first had constructed in 1958, that the idea emerged of using the infant's bassinet itself to monitor, continuously, automatically, and around the clock, the timing of events in the infant and the way they matched the clock time of occurrence of activities and interventions of the caretaker. It was important that this bassinet be exactly like any infant's ordinary bassinet, both for the mother and for the infant, so that their developing interaction would not be disturbed—no wires on the baby, no special maneuvers by the mother.[1] The present model, almost indistinguishable from an ordinary nursery bassinet, provides unattended a continuous record on a real-time basis, around the clock and day after day, of seven different states[2] of sleep or wakefulness in the infant, its crying, its respirations, its activity, the time when it is removed from and when it is returned to its bassinet, and the presence of its caretaker at the side of the bassinet.

This first set of variables provided by the monitor record was combined for analysis with sets of infant, caretaker, and interactional behavioral variables that had been obtained by event-recorded observations[3] during a feeding or over the entire course of an awake period from transition to awake until the onset of the first subsequent non-REM substage of sleep. These measures were chiefly those of frequency, duration, and sequence, with a rough intensity scale for certain of the variables. In one project, event-recorded observations of feeding interaction were carried out daily for the first month of life and twice weekly over the second month.

A third category of variables was measured by a third set of methods to obtain repeated assessments of specific sensorimotor functions of the infant. These involved infant behaviors on presentation of visual stimuli, especially that of the human face (Stechler, Sander, Burns, & Julia, 1973); the use of specific perturbations to the ecological system by altering important visual configurations, such as by masking the mother's face[EN1] during a feeding (Cassel & Sander, 1975); sucking behavior (Burns, Sander, Stechler, & Julia, 1972); crying behavior (Van Melle, Sander, Stechler, Julia, & Burns, 1973). In more recent independent research by Boston University investigators, substitution of a strange feeder (Chappell & Sander, 1978) and acoustic stimulation, especially that of the human voice (Condon & Sander, 1974), have been used to further examine avenues of adaptive exchange. It should be self-evident that continuous monitoring entails the generation of huge amounts of data. On the heels of the problem of developing relatively nonintrusive methods to obtain such data came the problem of developing procedures and programs to reduce and analyze them, and hard on the heels of that problem came the problem of display and communication of the data.

Thus far in the chapter certain points have been made: (a) about regarding infant and caretaking environment, taken together, as an interactive regulative ecological system; (b) about the charting of changes over time in the organization of events within the system; (c) about individual uniqueness of the interacting partners who constitute different infant–environment systems (the unique organization of the individual requires unique exchange patterns by which the partners can achieve adapted coordination and maintain mutual regulation); (d) about the specificity of events and exchanges that bond the partners so regulated; and (e) about a connection between the role of specific infant functions in the early regulation of exchanges with the caregiver, their course of development, and their adaptive employment at later points in development.

The following examples illustrate the way these points have been operationalized in study of the infant–caregiver system and are not intended as a comprehensive review of the project findings.

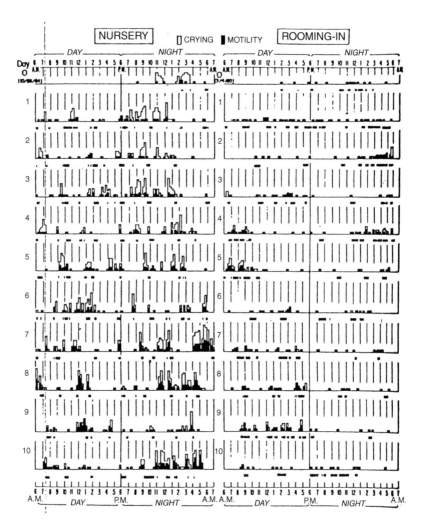

FIGURE 5.2. Relative frequency, duration, and distribution of motility, crying, and care-taking blips as measured by bassinet monitor for a nursery and a rooming-in baby over the first 10 days of life. Caretaker interventions for each baby and for each day of life are represented by black marks directly below solid lines indicating days of life. Reprinted from Sander and Julia (1966). Copyright 1966, American Psychosomatic Society.

RESEARCH FINDINGS

Figure 5.2 provides an illustration of the relationships that come to light as simple variables from infant and caregiver are recorded continuously, around the clock in real time, and are charted for visual display (Sander, 1969). The infant variables were occurrence of crying and of movement; the caregiver variable was removal and return of infant to bassinet. Such simple variables, continuously and automatically recorded, provide an observational window on a two-partner system, illustrating the way change over days can be displayed and indicating those features of the adaptive process that distinguish differently constituted systems.

The data were obtained over the first 10 days of life from two ecological systems: an infant boarded in a general hospital newborn nursery, on 4-hourly scheduled feedings given by many different nurse caretakers on frequently changing duty hours; and an infant roomed on the maternity floor with its own experienced (multiparous) mother providing complete care and breast feeding on an infant-demand regimen. The legend identifies the data displayed. The display shows (a) the gross asynchrony in the nursery in timing between the recurrent caretaking interventions and the recurrent episodes of activity in the infant; (b) the persistence in the nursery of a high degree of activity and crying over the entire 10 days, with the greatest portion of activity and crying produced per 24 hours remaining in the 12 night hours; and (c) in contrast, the baby rooming-in with a single caretaker showing far less total activity and crying. There is an evenly distributed amount of activity all through Day 2, with a great many frequently repeated responses by the mother. By Day 3, for the rooming-in pair, there is already synchrony emerging between episodes of activity in the infant and episodes of caretaking events, between which there are long periods of no exchange. Not only is there coordination of caretaker with infant at the onset of an infant activity span, but a correspondence of activity of the mother over the total duration of the infant's activity span. Then, between Days 4 and 6, for this pair the 24-hour distribution shifts so that the greatest amount of the activity and crying of the infant begins to settle in the 12 daytime hours, with long sleep periods and only rare exchanges at night.

The essential points presented in Figure 5.2 have been confirmed in larger samples of normal infants reared in the neonatal nursery and in samples of normal infants roomed-in with a single caretaker, receiving a demand feeding regimen (Sander & Julia, 1966; Sander, Julia, Stechler, & Burns, 1972). In the latter group, those receiving infant-demand feeding, predictable organization of the 24-hour day begins during the first 10 days of life. The shift of the major occurrence of motility and crying from night to day hours occurs for the sample between the fourth and sixth day. By 10 days of life the major part of the longest sleep period each day has settled within the 12 night hours.

By contrast, for samples of normal infants boarded in the newborn nursery for 10 days, circadian rhythmicity does not begin at all during the first 10-day period. Activity and crying remain greatest during the 12 night hours, as in Figure 5.2. On Day 11 we have transferred the infants of such a sample, one by one, to the individual care of a single foster caretaker who roomed-in with them around the clock as sole caretaker. The caregiving response shifts at this point from a clock-scheduled timetable to interventions contingent to the infant's change of state; that is, the individual caregiver provides a demand feeding regimen.

Within 24 hours the motility and crying output of the infants dramatically reverse the day–night distribution and assume the normal pattern. Persistent effects of these very stressful first 10 days in the 4-hourly scheduled nursery on circadian rhythmicity are seen when such infants are kept with the single rooming-in foster surrogate mother over the next 2 weeks while being monitored. During this subsequent 2-week period, a precocious advance in day–night differentiation takes place, which during the same days of life significantly exceeds that of the infant rooming in with a single caretaker from birth. Furthermore, there are clear differences between male and female infants in this effect, with the female infants responding to the stress with a significantly more advanced degree of day–night difference. Infant effects, caretaking effects, and age-in-days-of-life effects thus interact in producing the different courses that differently constituted systems reveal when we can chart them day by day.

Figure 5.3 illustrates the day-by-day distribution over the first month of life of the total duration per 24 hours of awake-active states, plotted here in terms of 3-day means for 30 infants. What we see is a daily duration of awake-active states over the first 3 days of life that is not reached again until the end of the first month. This effect is independent of caretaking regimen. The same curve is obtained whether the infants are boarded in the nursery or cared for by a single caretaker in the rooming-in situa-

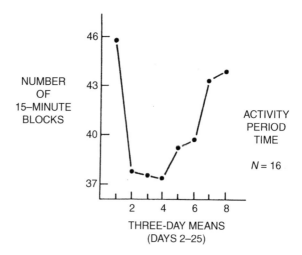

FIGURE 5.3. Awake-active states per 24 hours. Each point represents a mean for 3 days of the number of 15-minute segments of the 24-hour record, which are characterized by activity increase above sleep level or crying or removal from bassinet by caretaker. $N = 16$ babies, 8 cared for in nursery, and 8 in rooming-in condition. Quadratic $F = 27.85$; $df = 1/84$; Cubic $F = 7.37$; $df = 1/84$; Linear $F = 1.464$; $df = 1/84$. Reprinted from Sander et al. (1972).

tion. This phenomenon of increased duration of awake states in the first 3 days of life we have interpreted to be a result of disruption of the temporal organization of infant physiology that, up until the time of birth, had depended on the 24-hour fluctuations of maternal factors responsible for maintaining the fetal temporal framework. The longer duration of states of relative arousal over the first 3 days serves nevertheless to provide necessary conditions for increased frequency and duration of exchange with the caregiver and an increased frequency of trials through which the two can achieve adapted coordinations. Through these exchanges, new entraining cues that *recur* in the interaction at specific points in the caregiving sequence can reestablish a new postnatal temporal organization of the 24-hour day (as we saw for Day 2 in the rooming-in baby illustrated in Figure 5.2). When one couples the finding of greater 24-hour arousal over the first 3 days of life with the evidence that in the rooming-in, demand-fed infant appropriate day–night distributions of sleep and awake states begin between Days 4 and 6, one is faced with the possibility that something essential is jelling during those first 3 days regarding the organization of circadian rhythmicity. Further evidence that these first 3 days of heightened arousal may have a different significance than the ensuing days is provided by the crying record of the nursery-reared group. Although in the nursery there is no change in caregiving regimen, the high level of total 24-hour crying of the first 3 days falls strikingly in this group after the third day. By the end of the first week of life, the clock-scheduled, nursery-reared infant appears to conserve energy. Instead of crying until something happens—an effort early in the week that may go on uninterrupted for 1 to 2 hours if there is no caregiving response—by the end of the week there is a burst of crying, then a pause during which a drowsy appearance may be present, then another arousal and outburst of vigorous crying and a subsequent pause. We have seen this go on over and over, then, for as long as 2 hours or until the nurse intervenes. Such behavior often can be observed in the night hours, when the nursing staff is reduced and long delays in response to crying are unavoidable, as was pointed out by Aldrich, Sung, and Knop (1945).

Wide differences between nursery and rooming-in groups in motility and crying output were shown by infants under these different postnatal caretaking circumstances, as demonstrated by the 24-hour monitoring method (Figure 5.4).

On the other hand, wide individual infant differences were demonstrated between infants under the same caregiving regimen. Figure 5.5 shows the length of each sleep period over the first month of life plotted in sequence as it occurred for two infants receiving the same caregiving regimen over the first month of life, namely individual fostering in the rooming-in (demand-fed) situation.

The gradual postnatal appearance of circadian rhythmicity is illustrated for one infant in Figure 5.6. Here the data were cast in terms of minutes of sleep per hour. One-hour, lagged, autocorrelations were performed for a

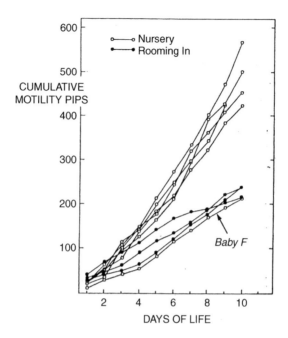

FIGURE 5.4. Cumulative graph of motility blips (24-hour totals) recorded by monitoring bassinet for six nursery and three rooming-in infants over the first 10 days of life. By Day 4, the two populations have diverged in activity generated, except for Baby F, who belonged to the sample boarded in the neonatal nursery. Reprinted from Sander and Julia (1966). Copyright 1966, American Psychosomatic Society.

210-hour span (Days 2–10) and a consecutive 240-hour span (Days 11–20). The ultradian rhythm that appears clearly in the first 210-hour analysis is replaced by a major 24-hour rhythm in the subsequent 240-hour analysis. It has not been generally recognized that 24-hour sleep–awake organization begins to occur between Days 4 and 6 under optimal circumstances, nor that circadian rhythmicity can be established in the second week of life.

Continuous sleep state data also reveal individual differences related to the rate of achieving circadian rhythmicity. Figure 5.7 shows the autocorrelations obtained over Days 11 to 20 of life for two infants, both having had the nursery experience of care over the first 10 days, and both having had the same caretaking regimen of individual surrogate mother rooming-in over the second 10 days. The first subject is a male and the second a female. The individual differences seen here are consistent with the differences between males and females that we found in comparing males and females for extent of day–night difference in sleep occurrence during the second 2 weeks of life. The effect of the stressful initial 10-day nursery experience seems to *advance* precociously the rate of organization of the 24 hours for females so they sleep significantly more at night and less in the day. The same 10-day nursery experience appears to *retard* the rate of

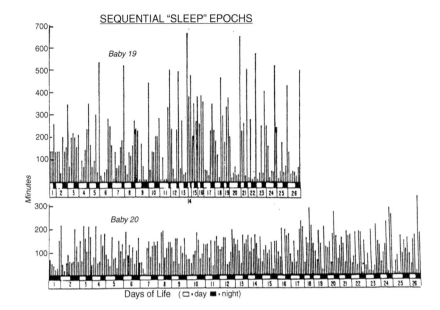

FIGURE 5.5. Real-time durations of all sleep periods plotted in actual sequence over the first 29 days of life for two infants. Black sections represent hours between 6 p.m. and 6 a.m. each day. Sander (1975). Reprinted with kind permission of Springer Science and Business Media.

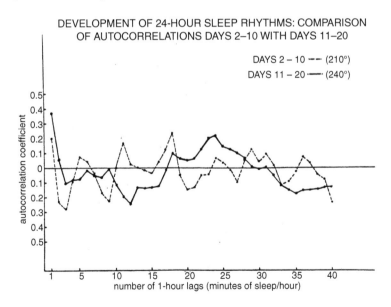

FIGURE 5.6. One-hour, lagged autocorrelations of minutes of sleep per hour for sleep, Days 2–10 (210 hours) and Days 10–20 (240 hours) for infant rooming-in with single surrogate foster mother.

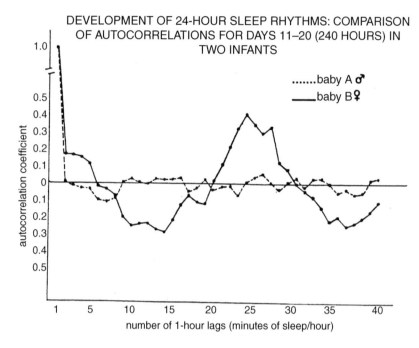

DEVELOPMENT OF 24-HOUR SLEEP RHYTHMS: COMPARISON OF AUTOCORRELATIONS FOR DAYS 11–20 (240 HOURS) IN TWO INFANTS

......baby A ♂

___baby B ♀

number of 1-hour lags (minutes of sleep/hour)

FIGURE 5.7. One-hour, lagged autocorrelations of minutes of sleep per hour, over Days 10–20 (240 hours) on two babies, (a) male and (b) female, each having had nursery caretaking during the first 10 days and single surrogate foster mother rooming in over

day–night organization during the second 2 weeks of life for the males, who are also receiving the same caregiving regimen as the females during the second 2 weeks, that is, an individual surrogate mother rooming-in (Sander et al., 1972).

Comparison by Julia (Sander, Stechler, Julia, & Burns, 1970) of auto-correlations calculated over 240 hours during the second 10 days of life, obtained from infants individually fostered in the first 10 days ($n = 8$) with those boarded in the newborn nursery in the first 10 days ($n = 8$) indicates that whereas the former show their circadian peak of sleep occurrence at precisely 24 hours, the latter group shows a wider range of deviations from a 24-hour peak in a significant number of the sample, that is, peaks at 23 to 25 or 26 hours.

In the differentiation of a longest sleep period per 24 hours, individual differences in 24-hour organization between infants receiving the *same* caregiving regimen can be demonstrated, as well as the group differences in 24-hour organization between *groups* of infants receiving *different* care-giving regimens. In Figure 5.5, the first baby, Baby 19, shows the presence of an excellent differentiation almost from the outset. There is a clear long-est sleep period per day with a number of clearly shorter periods. After

Day 3 the occurrence of the longest sleep period per 24 hours becomes consistently located in the night segment. This was a responsive, well-organized baby, and easy to care for. The second infant, Baby 20, by contrast, although also meeting our rather stringent criteria for normality, and cared for under the same individual demand feeding caregiving, produced a record that showed many more sleep periods of briefer duration, and little differentiation of sleep-period length. It was difficult to identify one clear longest sleep period per 24 hours. Period-length differentiation appeared only toward the end of the first month, and the stable occurrence of the longest sleep period per 24 hours within the 12 night hours was only getting under way on the tenth day of life. This infant was reported by both the foster mothers to be the most difficult to care for of all the infants of the sample.

We found, for the babies ($n = 27$) of this project (three samples differently constituted as to caretaking system, of 9 infants each), that there was a significant positive correlation between length of longest sleep period per 24 hours and length of longest awake period per 24 hours, a period-length factor, if you will (as Figure 5.5 suggests).

There was also an interaction of length of longest sleep and longest awake period per 24 hours with the effect of the individual caretaker. Over Days 11 to 25 of this study, with each nurse fostering 8 babies, we found evidence that one of the two foster nurses produced infants with significantly longer longest-sleep and longest-awake periods per 24 hours than did the other. For any given infant-caretaker ecological system, interactions between infant determinants and caretaking determinants set the stage for individual uniqueness of their exchange patterns.

As one looks more closely at infant differences in sleep and awake behavior, it is evident that the way babies wake up and go to sleep is quite different. For some, crying begins during the last REM period and increases steadily to imperative levels; the last thing to occur in the awakening sequence for such infants may be the opening of the eyes. In other instances, the infant, with but very little increase of movement over that of his last REM period, may open his eyes and lie relatively quiet for 10 to 15 minutes, until finally the first whimper will be produced.

In addition to the many obvious, as well as subtle, differences between our two principal foster nurses, with which we became familiar in detail, there were striking differences in style of caretaking by our natural mothers also (Group C). Each of these had had experience with at least one previous baby of her own and had developed a measure of confidence in her own way of doing things. For example, one such mother's dictum, apparently handed down from her mother, was that she would not pick up her baby until the infant had cried for 5 minutes. Our records showed a crying curve for this pair that was just an order of magnitude above that of the other natural mother pairs. However, everything otherwise went well. Another mother, who tended to keep the bassinet with her in the room in which she was working, would respond at the very first sign of arousal, scarcely ever allowing her infant more than a whimper before she responded. We were hard put to locate the few scattered single crying blips that were accumulated on that record.

Time does not permit a review of the data from which we have studied the matter of specificity of the synchronization or bonding between the individual infant and the individual caretaker. We have done this by rearing infants with one experienced foster mother rooming with the infant 24 hours a day from birth and then on the 11th day changing to another experienced foster mother. The change is marked by significant increases in the occurrence of distress events during feeding and in 24-hour crying over hours and days subsequent to the change (Van Melle et al., 1973). Another way of studying specificity by event-recorded interactional observations is to change caretakers for a single feed on Day 7, when only one individual has done all the feeding up to that point; still another is to mask the familiar caretaker during a feeding on Day 7, comparing infant behaviors and state distributions during the awake period, including latency to first non-REM sleep period, with values obtained on Day 6 and before (Cassel & Sander, 1975).

Finally, the repeated assessment of the developmental course of key sensorimotor functions that are involved in transacting the regulatory exchanges between the partners in differently constituted infant caregiving systems indicates important relationships to be understood. We have carried out repeated assessments twice weekly over the first 2 months of life of a variety of infant behaviors related to the visual system, when the infant is presented with the human or drawn face under systematically different stimulus conditions of presentation. These have included "looking" and "looking away" time, peripheral gaze, motility, crying, and so on (Stechler et al., 1973). The course is quite strikingly different in the three different caregiving systems over the first 2 months of life, significant differences appearing, for example, in total looking time and crying during stimulus presentation (Sander, Stechler, Burns, & Lee, 1979; Stechler et al., 1973). It is our conviction that in spite of the more careful individual fostering after the 10th day of life, the effects of those first 10 stressful days of being boarded in the newborn nursery persist over the rest of the first 2 months of life and influence the integration of sensorimotor functions in state and interactional regulation.

SUMMARY

In summary, then, the study of infant and caregiver as an interactive regulative system by continuous monitoring and methods of repeated measurement on infant and caregiver variables centers our attention on the temporal organization of events. We have indicated the following.

1. Birth is a point of profound rupture in mechanisms of temporal organization in the fetal-maternal system.
2. The ecological niche of the newborn must provide for a reestablishment of this temporal organization postnatally in terms of a framework of new exchanges between neonate and environment that constitute the initial processes of regulation and adaptation and represent interactions of infant, caretaker, and age-in-days-of-life determinants.
3. The first 3 days may be a crucial span of time in which the interaction of events responsible for optimal 24-hour temporal organization is established. Events such as the recurrence of maternal entraining cues in consistent relation to state changes in the infant provide the necessary conditions for the array of biorhythms that characterize both the infant and its caregiving environment to gain the organization that will ensure their role in the regulation of the system.
4. Individual infant differences in periodicities and rates of change over the first days of life, interacting with individual differences in caretaking configurations, eventuate in specific patterns of 24-hour exchange between the two. Mechanisms of bonding are based on the way specificity of regulation is established and maintained in the system. Much of this specificity depends on time and the timing relationships between events in critical recurring caregiving situations.
5. This specificity of regulatory fittedness between a particular infant and a particular caregiver can reach an appreciable degree by the 10th day of life.
6. The later adaptive employment of sensorimotor functions on which the establishment of regulatory coordination in the system has depended is influenced by this earlier role that they have played in establishing that regulation.

DISCUSSION

The material that has been presented of an investigation of the infant and its caregiving environment together as a biological system illustrates the perspective that such an approach provides, directing attention to mechanisms and processes of change in the organization of events in the system, as one goes from fetal to postnatal life. Fundamental to this perspective are the role of time and the central place of temporal organization as a first level in the construction of the behavioral framework of interaction between the participants making up the system. The central role of biorhythmicity in the achievement and maintenance of coherence in the living system cannot be underestimated. Biorhythmicity requires a consideration of 24-hour, around-the-clock time as well as the time structure of events in briefer durations. Events between infant and caregiver assume importance in terms of the exactness of their synchrony, of the temporal characteristics of their phase relationships, and of their characteristics of asynchrony. There is a *background* in the low-frequency rhythms (e.g., states of sleep and awake or activity and quiescence) that is necessary for the analysis of characteristics of interaction between the higher frequency rhythms that make up the *foreground* of the interaction (e.g., sucking, linguistic-kinesic, gaze and gaze-aversion rhythms, etc.). Time requires a holistic perspective of different levels in the system as well as providing the framework for studying the precise individual specificity of the process of fitting together by which adapted interaction in a given *moment* of time is achieved. The process of fitting together affects connection or bonding between the unique dispositions and behavioral configurations of partners that have behavioral organizations that are highly disparate, that is, the newborn infant and its caregiver.

The methodological and analytic requirements for the investigation of change in the organization of living systems during the life span differ from the more traditional experimental paradigm, the questions one asks are different, and the route of discovery is different. For example, from the visual display of continuous and repeated measures, points of change come into focus or the relationships between interacting variables change, differences in rates of change appear, or the "history dependence" of the system becomes evident.

In other publications (Sander et al., 1979) based on the same biological systems perspective, data have been presented as illustration of the way particular sensorimotor systems of the infant (e.g., the visual system) become integrated over the first 2 months of life in relation to their role in the achievement and maintenance of initial regulation. Visual behavior plays an important role in the regulation of the initial feeding interaction, and the feeding interaction is in turn directly related to the regulation of states in the sleep–wake continuum. In other words, the infant's employment of specific sensorimotor systems becomes shaped by the contribution such systems make to more basic state regulation as an around-the-clock adaptive requirement for infant and caregiver. This viewpoint suggests that the "ordering function" proposed by Basch (1975), as being a function central to the ontogeny of self, is itself determined by an interactional ontogeny integrating basic biological processes in a specific adaptive context. The infant's active organization of his world involves the inseparable nature of the endogenously active biological processes that underlie our conceptual domains of regulation, adaptation, integration, and organization.

In still other publications (Sander, 1962, 1964, 1969, 1975; Sander et al., 1975), the changing organization of events and interactions over the first 3 years of life in the infant–caregiver system has been described as a sequence of levels of fitting together between infant and caregiver. These extend from a beginning level of coordination concerned with biological issues, such as those related to regulation of states of sleep and waking and the basic functions of feeding, motility, and so on, to the levels of adaptation concerned with fitting together between toddler and caregiver on the basis of correct inferences of intentions, goals, feelings, words, and expressions. Each new task of "fitting together" is ushered in by new activities or capabilities that the infant can begin to introduce into the interaction with its caregiver. The preservation of an active role for the infant in the adaptive sequence is the basis for the establishing and maintenance of the infant's or toddler's "sense of agency" (Lewis, 1977) in actively organizing his adaptive repertoire. Such an active role is essential in the widening achievement of effectance in self-regulation. Self-regulatory capability becomes crucial as the complexity of adaptation increases over the second and third years of life. Such increasing complexity calls into play additional newly emerging mechanisms of integration as a means of maintaining the coherence of the individual in his unique adaptive situation. These integrative mechanisms must involve the development of a language and of symbolic representations that have gained common usefulness both to the individual and his caregivers; they must involve also a certain awareness of one's own state, dispositions, intentions, and thought content.

This epigenetic sequence of issues of adaptive coordination constructs an ontogeny of self-regulation, each issue for the infant relating specific caregiving contexts to his own individual adaptive content, and depends on additional increasingly differentiated and, for the infant, newly employed mechanisms of integration. The negotiation of the sequence of issues provides the basis for proposing that the ontogeny of self-regulation is paralleled by an ontogeny of awareness and self-awareness. The latter are functions that increasingly enter the construction of the repertoire of adaptive strategies by which infant and caregiver become coordinated, especially in the second and third years of the child's life. From the adaptive perspective, consciousness (or awareness) is not a generally uniform or unitary state, the same for everyone, but involves an individual organization of state and content of awareness in terms of the moment-by-moment configuration of the ongoing process of that individual's adaptive encounter. Here, the static imagery of structures is not adequate to capture the conceptualization of temporally organized process. The necessary conditions for the ontogenetic progression of self-awareness as a mechanism of self-regulation depend, then, on the capacity for changing organization of events and processes in the system and not only on the potential of the individual infant.

Obviously, the later steps in the establishing of this sequence of adaptive coordinations, which now involve "secondary process" functions such as representations and their recognition, require a partner also capable of specificity of fittedness in these more subtle levels. Prior to this level of adaptation during the second 18 months of life in the infant–mother system there has been the foundation of a long history of regulatory achievements that have been gained by the partners over the first 18 months. These coordinations now provide a mutually experienced context in which the "meaning" of each other's behavior is already clear for the most part. This context of mutual familiarity provides the necessary condition to set the stage for precision of fitting together on these next, more subtle levels of thought and inner perception that involve the "reading" of intentionality, feeling states, emotional expression, and so on. It is the correct reading of intentionality that is critical for the preservation of initial trust during negotiation of the later issues. Correct and specific recognition by the "significant other" during the second 18 months may be a necessary requirement for a consolidation of the experience of self-recognition and for the establishment of the function of self-recognition in further adaptation. Validation of the toddler's perception of his own state and inner content by the partner's act of recognition is essential for the toddler to learn to depend on his own inner perception to guide his continuing active organizing of his widening repertory of adaptive strategies. Conversely, at this chronological point in development, the invalidation of his own inner percepts in the adaptive encounter requires him to turn to alternative "defenses"—inhibition, compliance, and so on. A new level of recognition in the second 18 months of life involving the coordination of mutual awareness, then, is a system achievement, an "emergent property" of the whole, setting the stage for an integration greater than the part properties of either of the partners alone. It is a matching or meeting by which the system comes to be regulated at the level of the spirit, so to speak, a regulation that provides "states" in the system necessary for the successful inclusion of subsequent, even more subtle mechanisms such as those of long-term goals, identifications, values, and so on.

There are other conditions as well that are provided by the state of organization in the system. These constitute necessary contextual elements for the progression of changes in organization that mark the ontogeny of self-regulation. Here I am referring not only to the maintenance in the system, as a system's characteristic, of the infant's role as "agent" in organizing his world, but the construction of the "intermediate area" as formulated by Winnicott (1951). From the systems perspective, the context for "the intermediate area" is that of the mother "holding the situation in time"—a condition that allows the infant to experience inner and outer percepts at the same moment in time without his option for the initiation of activity in the service of integrating the inner and outer domains being threatened or preempted by demands for regulation. The "intermediate area" can be viewed as an "emergent property" of the system, an "open space" in regulatory exchanges when these are considered in terms of their temporal organization. The formulation of the "open space" in the postnatal infant–caregiver system has been discussed in more detail elsewhere (Sander, 1977).[EN2] It is mentioned here only to illustrate the alternative conceptualizations, offered by the systems perspective, from which to consider conditions necessary for change in organization during development.

There is a fundamental polarity of events and directions in the biological system (i.e., attachment and detachment, bonding and isolation, synchrony and asynchrony, combination and differentiation, togetherness and separation, complexity and unity, etc.) that provides the context for organizing processes that allow for unique adaptive and integrative solutions to be arrived at in each system. In formulating a "self-psychology" from the perspective of the biological system, the necessary conditions for the emergence of a coherent self as a step in the ontogeny of self-regulation will fall into the domain of emergent properties of the system.

There are new vistas currently in biology that elaborate the properties of open systems, especially those that are far from equilibrium. These formulations are concerned with new concepts such as the difference between information and instruction, that between resilience and stability, the "amplification of adaptation," "order through fluctuation," mechanisms related to "boundary properties," and the role of "attractor surfaces" (Holling, 1976; Prigogine, 1976; Waddington, 1976).

As psychoanalysis now turns again both to biology and to early development to implement the formulation of a self-psychology, it is to newer data and newer conceptualizations in both disciplines that we must look for more adequate tools to grapple with the task. Obviously, there is a great distance to go, but what must be done now is to orient our research directions and designs so that the exploration of development in terms of the infant and its environment together as a biological system can begin. Data are needed to provide the empirical base from which to formulate and document the rapid and lawful process of changing organization of the system, as exchanges between its component parts increase in scope and complexity over the first years of life, both within the developing individual and in relation to his larger environment of life support.

NOTES

The projects reported in this chapter were carried out while the author was Professor of Psychiatry in the Division of Psychiatry at Boston University Medical Center. Project support was provided by funds from U.S.P.H.S. Project No. NICHD 01766 (1965–1969). L. Sander, Principal Investigator, G. Stechler, Co-Principal Investigator, in collaboration with P. Burns and H. Julia. Funds from the Grant Foundation, New York, supported work from 1972 to 1974 that was carried out in collaboration with W. Condon (Co-Principal Investigator), P. Chappell, P. Snyder, and J. Gould. Supplemental funds were provided by the University Hospital General Research Support Funds, and Dr. Sander was recipient of NIMH Research Scientists Awards, No. K5-MH20-505, between the years 1968–1973, and 1973–1978. In addition, Dr. Stechler was recipient of NIHM Career Development Award Level II, No. 5-K2-MH-18. Reports of the data included in the chapter were presented at the International Society for the Study of Behavioral Development Biennial Conference, July 1975, Surrey, England, and at the annual meeting of the American Academy of Child Psychiatry, October

1975, St. Louis, Missouri. G. Van Melle was responsible for analyzing a major portion of the infant crying data for this report.

Published in Pollock, G. H., & Greenspan, S. I. (Eds.). (1980). *Infancy & Early Childhood* (Vol. 1, pp. 177–201). Bethesda, MD: National Institute of Mental Health.

1. Over the years the ideas and efforts of a number of engineers and research-ers have contributed to the present monitoring bassinet model, especially those of Dr. Don Jackson, Dr. Gerald Stechler, Mr. Richard Burwen, Dr. Her-bert Teager, Dr. Jeffrey Gould, and Mr. Paul Miller.
2. The research team has accomplished the computer interfacing of the monitor output, giving high agreement between sleep-state distributions obtained by the analysis of monitoring data using computer-state recognition programs and the scoring of concurrent five-parameter sleep polygraphy (Sander et al., 1976).
3. Event recording methods were begun by the Boston University group in 1965 by Padraic Burns, M.D., using a Rustrak 4-key event recorder (Burns et al., 1972). The present method has been developed by Dr. Patricia Chappell from her original infant–mother interactional variables and her recording method using a 15-second epoch (Boismier, Chappell, & Meier, 1970). Dr. Chappell's present method utilizes a 60-key computer interfaced keyboard recorder based on the White Recording and Transcription System (White, 1970) as modified by Mr. Paul Miller (Chappell & Sander, 1978).

EDITORS' NOTES

EN1   See Chapter 9 for the mask experiment.
EN2   In Chapters 7 and 8 of this book.

REFERENCES

Aldrich, C., Sung, C., & Knop, C. (1945). The crying of newly born babies: II. The individual phase. *Journal of Pediatrics, 27,* 89–96.

Aschoff, J. (1969). Desynchronization and resynchronization of human circadian rhythms. *Aerospace Medicine, 40,* 844–849.

Basch, M. F. (1975). Toward a theory that encompasses depression: A revision of existing causal hypotheses in psychoanalysis. In E. J. Anthony & T. Benedek (Eds.), *Depression and human existence.* Boston: Little, Brown.

Basch, M. F. (1977). Developmental psychology and explanatory theory in psycho-analysis. *Annual of Psychoanalysis, 5,* 229–263.

Boismier, J., Chappell, P., & Meier, G. (1970). *A behavior inventory for assessing states of arousal in the human newborn.* Paper presented at the meeting of the South-eastern Psychological Association, Louisville, KY.

Brazelton, T. B., Tronick, E., Adamson, L., Als, H., & Wise, S. (1975). Early mother–infant reciprocity. In *Parent-infant interaction* (CIBA Foundation Symposium 33, pp. 137–154). Amsterdam: Elsevier.

Burns, P., Sander, L., Stechler, G., & Julia, H. (1972). Distress in feeding: Short-term effects of caretaker environment on the first 10 days. *Journal of the American Academy of Child Psychiatry, 11*, 427–439.

Cassel, T. Z., & Sander, L. W. (1975). *Neonatal recognition processes and attachment: The masking experiment.* Paper presented at biennial meeting of the Society for Research in Child Development, Denver, CO.

Chappell, P., & Sander, L. (1978). Mutual regulation of infant–mother interactive process: The context for the origin of communication. In M. Bullowa (Ed.), *Before speech: The beginnings of human communication* (pp. 89–109). Cambridge, UK: Cambridge University Press.

Condon, W. S., & Sander, L. W. (1974). Neonate movement is synchronized with adult speech: Interactional participation and language acquisition. *Science, 183*, 99–101.

Enright, J. T. (1960). Discussion (tidal rhythmicity). *Cold Spring Harbor Symposia on Quantitative Biology, 25*, 487–498.

Halberg, F. (1960). Temporal coordination of physiologic function. *Cold Spring Harbor Symposia on Quantitative Biology, 25*, 289–310.

Holling, C. S. (1976). Resilience and stability of ecosystems. In E. Jantsch & C. Waddington (Eds.), *Evolution and consciousness* (pp. 73–92). Reading, MA: Addison-Wesley.

Kohut, H. (1977). *The restoration of the self.* New York: International Universities Press.

Lewis, M. (1977, February). *The search for the origins of self: Implications for social behavior and intervention.* Paper presented at the Symposium on the Ecology of Care and Education of Children Under Three, Berlin.

Luce, G. G. (1970). *Public Health Service Publication No. 2088.* Washington, DC: U.S. Government Printing Office.

Pittendrigh, C. S. (1961). *Harvey Lecture Series 1960–61.* New York: Academic.

Prigogine, I. (1976). Order through fluctuation: Self-organization and social system. In E. Jantsch & C. Waddington (Eds.), *Evolution and consciousness.* (pp. 93–126). Reading, MA: Addison-Wesley.

Sander, L. W. (1962). Issues of early mother–child interaction. *Journal of the American Academy of Child Psychiatry, 1*, 141–166.

Sander, L. W. (1964). Adaptive relationships in early mother child interaction. *Journal of the American Academy of Child Psychiatry, 3*, 231–264.

Sander, L. W. (1969). Regulation and organization in the early infant caretaker system. In R. J. Robinson (Ed.), *Brain and early behavior* (pp. 311–315). New York: Academic.

Sander, L. W. (1975). Infant and caretaking environment: Investigation and conceptualization of adaptive behavior in a system of increasing complexity. In E. J. Anthony (Ed.), *Explorations in child psychiatry* (pp. 129–166). New York: Plenum.

Sander, L. W. (1977). The regulation of exchange in the infant-caretaker system and some aspects of the context-content relationship. In M. Lewis & L. Rosenblum (Eds.), *The origins of behavior: Vol. 5. Interaction, conversation, and the development of language* (pp. 133–156). New York: Wiley.

Sander, L. W., Chappell, P., Gould, J., & Snyder, P. (1975). *An investigation of change in variables of infant state and infant–caretaker interaction over the first seven days of life.* Paper presented at the biennial meeting of the Society for Research in Child Development, Denver, CO.

Sander, L. W., Gould, J. B., Snyder, P., Lee, A., Teager, H., & Burwen, R. (1976). Continuous non-intrusive bassinet monitoring of neonatal states on the sleep-awake continuum. *Sleep Research, 5,* 208.

Sander, L. W., & Julia, H. L. (1966). Continuous interactional monitoring in the neonate. *Psychosomatic Medicine, 28,* 822–835.

Sander, L. W., Julia, H. L., Stechler, G., & Burns, P. (1972). Continuous 24-hour interactional monitoring in infants reared in two caretaking environments. *Psychosomatic Medicine, 34,* 270–282.

Sander, L. W., Stechler, G., Burns, P., & Lee, A. (1979). Change in infant and caregiver variables over the first two months of life: Integration of action in early development. In E. Thomas (Ed.), *Origins of the infant's social responsiveness* (pp. 349–407). Hillsdale, NJ: Lawrence Erlbaum Associates, Inc.

Sander, L. W., Stechler, G., Julia, H., & Burns, P. (1970). *National Institute of Child Health and Human Development Project No. 01766: Terminal report.* Washington, DC: U.S. Government Public Health Service.

Sollberger, A. (1965). *Biological rhythm research.* Amsterdam: Elsevier.

Stechler, G., Sander, L., Burns, P., & Julia, H. (1973). *Infant looking and fussing in response to visual stimulation over the first two months of life in different infant-caretaking systems.* Paper presented at the biennial meeting of the Society for Research in Child Development, Philadelphia.

Stern, D. N. (1971). A micro-analysis of mother–infant interaction behavior regulating social contact between a mother and her 3½-month-old twins. *Journal of the American Academy of Child Psychiatry, 10,* 501–518.

Van Melle, G., Sander, L., Stechler, G., Julia, H., & Burns, P. (1973). *In-crib crying over the first month of life in different caretaking systems.* Paper presented at the biennial meeting of the Society for Research in Child Development, Philadelphia.

Waddington, C. H. (1976), Evolution in the subhuman world. In E. Jantsch & C. Waddington (Eds.), *Evolution and consciousness* (pp. 11–15). Reading, MA: Addison-Wesley.

White, R. L. (1970). *WRATS (White Recording and Automatic Transcribing System): A computer system for automatic recording and transcribing data.* Unpublished paper prepared at Rutgers University, Institute of Animal Behavior, Newark, NJ.

Winnicott, D. W. (1951). Transitional objects and transitional phenomena. In *Collected Papers: Through Paediatrics to Psycho-Analysis.* (pp. 229–242). New York: Basic Books.

6

Investigation of Interactive Regulation in Three Infant Caretaking Systems

The Boston University longitudinal study led to a viewpoint about how to apply conceptualizations of the adaptive process to early human development. It is a particular viewpoint of adaptive behavior by which data from the first 18 months of life can be related to the second 18 months of life and the biological level can be related to the psychological level. Therefore in 1963, when the opportunity arose through the National Institute of Mental Health research development program to begin a new program of investigation, we decided to study the infant and caretaker as a system with a more detailed examination of the mechanisms of regulation, their relation to interactions and to events within the system, and their changes over time. One of our findings when we rated and assessed the sequence of infant–mother interactional issues was that the characteristics of negotiation of the first issue tended to predict the negotiation of subsequent issues, at least through issue 6. In other words, if we assessed the characteristics of adaptation between the partners right at the outset, when the system was first getting underway, we might gain basic insight into the idiosyncracies of adaptation that that particular system might show at subsequent levels of coordination, and something like an adaptive potential or adaptive capacity for any given infant–mother pair might be indicated.

To investigate differences in adaptive progress in different systems, one should have access to some striking but uniform contrast in infant–caretaker "fitting together," which should not be confounded with differences in endowment of the infants. The contrast in harmony of fitting together ideally should be studied only over a limited time span, so that the extent

139

of recovery from perturbation to the system can be examined. For such an investigation we wanted measurement that would be reasonably precise without upsetting naturalistic observation. The subject samples to be observed also had to provide a contrasting analysis without experimental manipulation. Three samples of normal infant–caretaker pairs were chosen for study, nine pairs to be in each sample. The first two samples had specific contrast in caretaking condition; the third sample consisted of neonates reared by their own experienced, multiparous mothers. We used five principal methods of data collection over the first 2 months of postnatal life to get parallel observation of several infant variables and several caretaker variables that would be quantitative and would occur frequently enough and over a long enough time span to permit the identification of significant changes in values or the appearance of a regular recurrence or a relative stability of values.

DESIGN

The study[1] sample consisted of three groups of nine normal[2] infants each (Table 6.1). Two groups were composed of infants given up by their mothers for adoptive placement and cared for by surrogate mothers. Of these, the infants in Group A spent the first 10 days in the newborn nursery being cared for by the usual nursery staff (multiple caretaking) on a fixed 4-hour nursery feeding schedule. These infants were then shifted to an individual rooming-in arrangement in a regular hospital room, where each infant was cared for by a single caretaker on a demand schedule 24 hours a day for the next 18 days. At the end of the first 4 weeks the infant was placed in a regular agency foster home and was there followed for a second 4-week period.

The infants in Group B (also going to adoptive placement) went directly into rooming in (usually 24 hours after delivery), where they had a first

TABLE 6.1
Design for Investigation of Interactive Regulation in Three Infant–Caretaking Systems

Group	N	Caretaking Period 1 (0–10 Days)	Caretaking Period 2 (11–28 Days)	Caretaking Period 3 (29–56 Days)
A	9	Nursery	Single caretaker (X or Y) rooming in	Foster home
B	9	Single caretaker (X or Y) rooming in	Single caretaker (Y or X) rooming in	Foster home
C	9	0–5 days: 6–10 days: Natural mother at home	Natural mother at home	Natural mother home rooming in

single surrogate-mother caretaker from Day 2 through Day 10 and were shifted to a second such caretaker from Day 11 through Day 28. These infants were always on a demand schedule while cared for in the hospital. After the first 4 weeks they also went to foster homes, where we continued to observe them for a second 4 weeks.

Group C was composed of infants of experienced, multiparous mothers. These infants were cared for by their own mothers, in rooming in for 5 days, and then were followed at home for the remainder of the 8-week study period.

Groups A and B were designed to elicit differences in infants cared for over the first 10 days by multiple caretakers on a rigid feeding schedule, that is, one not allowing modification of timing of caretaker intervention, in contrast to caretaking by single caretakers on infant-demand feeding schedule. The subsequent caretaking conditions (from Day 11 onward) were the same for Groups A and B: single surrogate mother rooming in 24 hours per day and infant-demand feeding. The assignment of infants to the two groups and to the two nurses who did most of the rooming-in surrogate mothering was unbiased. Group C provided a basis for comparison rather than a strict control group. Obviously home rearing by a mother differs in many ways from hospital and foster rearing. Group C was designed to provide normative data for the parameters measured, with which to compare the more closely monitored Group A and B infant–caretaker pairs.

METHODS OF DATA COLLECTION

The four methods employed are briefly described.

1. *Around-the-clock observation.* Experience with the infants and the mothers in the longitudinal study impressed us with the obvious fact that adaptation between a mother and her infant is not carried out only in the time units customarily sampled in mother and infant observations but in all 24 hours of the day. "Relationship" must first involve living together.

   Observation around the clock can be carried out if one considers that the continuous observation of even one variable of a complex system provides an observational window on the state of that system over time. For example, if one could measure automatically, around the clock and day after day, only the infant's presence in or absence from the bassinet, one could derive a great deal of information about the pattern and the change in pattern of caretaking events. Couple this variable with one monitored from the infant while in the bassinet—for example, time of the occurrence of crying—and one has a means of observing interactions between infant and caretaker.

Essentially, the monitor was a recording bassinet, operating without instrumentation of the baby; it utilized an Esterline-Angus event recorder moving at 12 inches per hour to record continuously, by separate pens in parallel, several channels of digital inputs. These represented (a) small summations of infant activity obtained via an air mattress, a strain gauge, an amplifier, and an integrator system; (b) infant crying (occurring while the infant was in the bassinet); (c) the caretaker's removal of the infant from the bassinet, the duration of the removal, and the return of the infant to the bassinet; and (d) the proximity of the caretaker to the bassinet.

2. *Observation of time of onset of awake state and sleep state for Group A and B infants during the first month of life.* These observations of clock time of major change of state were made by the registered nurses acting as surrogate mothers with high reliability in terms of a simple dichotomous definition based on eyes remaining open or closed over a span of at least 5 minutes. These observations by nurses fully accustomed to 24-hour duty and to accurate charting permitted an around-the-clock correlation of the monitor with the observed state and gave information about the periodicity of state changes in the infant—their day–night distribution and the striking individual differences between infants who had been reared by the same surrogate mother.

3. *Observation of feeding interaction.* Daily during the first month of life and twice weekly during the second month, a feeding was observed and recorded in real time on a Rustrak 4 key event recorder. The feeding was divided into three phases: prefeed, feed proper, and postfeed. Coded entries recorded various infant states; mutual regard between infant and feeder; infant regard of feeder's face; postural change for feeding, burping, visual regard, or "other"; insertion and removal of nipple; onset and end of sucking; signs of infant distress; intensity of stimulation; and so on. These measures were mostly durations and frequencies. The amount of formula taken was recorded for each period of "nipple-in time" by having the feeder put the bottle down on a scale instead of the table.

4. *Systematic observations of infant behavior on experiencing visual stimuli.* Approximately twice weekly in the first month and weekly in the second month of life the infant was presented a series of stimuli, each for a 1-minute duration, at a 10- to 12-inch distance, with a 15-second interstimulus interval. The stimuli consisted of the following sequences: (a) a line drawing of a face; (b) the experimenter's face still, (c) nodding, (d) in full social approach using smile, voice, and movement to elicit infant attention, (e) a line drawing again, (f) the mother's face still, (g) nodding, (h) social, (i) a line drawing again, (j) the experimenter's face still, (k) nodding, (l) social, and (m) a line drawing again. Using the same Rustrak 4 key event recorder, occurrence and durations of the following behavioral categories were

made in real time: look, look-excite, look-excite-vocalize, look-excite-smile, look away, eyes closed, fuss. Looking included any orientation of infant gaze to the whole stimulus or any part of it, including its periphery and including gaze with one eye only. The testing of the infant was carried out only in optimal states of quiet alertness.

The analysis of data generated by these many variables, which were measured repeatedly on the three groups of neonates over their first 2 months of life, cannot be covered within the scope of this chapter. A number of findings have been reported (Burns, Sander, Stechler, & Julia, 1972; Sander, 1969; Sander & Julia, 1966; Sander, Julia, Stechler, & Burns, 1969, 1972; Sander, Stechler, Burns, & Julia, 1970), and others will be reported in the near future. Many of the findings are relevant to the adaptive process in an interactive regulative system, contributing toward answers to basic questions although not fully answering them. For example, one asks: How early does an interactional bonding between infant and caretaker become established? Which infant variables appear to play a primary role in this process? What are some of the effects on the adaptive process of a limited perturbation of the system at this early point?

In regard to the first question, our evidence confirms the impression that a "bonding"—that is, a specific adaptation between the infant and the individual providing sole care—is established within the first 10 days[3] of postnatal life. In this adaptation it is assumed that the infant's idiosyncracies of regulation have become coordinated to some extent with the caretaker's idiosyncracies. This adaptation was shown by the immediate and significant rise in 24-hour crying output on Day 11 for Group B infants, who had experienced a change in surrogate mother on that day, an increase in crying that persisted for a number of days. (The same two surrogate mother nurses cared for all but one of the Group B infants. Each new infant subject admitted to the study was assigned to one or the other alternately in an unbiased way, so that on Day 11 infants went as often from Nurse A to Nurse B as from Nurse B to Nurse A.)

The feeding data demonstrated the same effect of change of caretaker on Day 11 for Group B as did the crying variables. "Distress events" during feeding, which over the first 10 days of life had settled down for Group B infants to a low level relative to the number occurring for infants in Group A, also showed a sudden, significant, and persistent rise at Day 11 for the Group B infants. (Distress events consisted of the number of episodes during the feeding of spitting up, crying, gagging, vomiting, turning away, etc.) In current research[EN1] we are pursuing the question of which variables will be the most sensitive indicators of perturbation of the initial coordination with a single caretaker.

In regard to the second question, certain infant variables do appear to play a primary role in the interactions through which regulation is carried out. The important variables are those related to the various "states" of the infant. These evidence oscillation or periodicity, both in the active and quiet cycles of REM and N-REM sleep and in the longer epochs of wakefulness and sleep. It seems evident that the sequence infant-state-change-caretaking-intervention is a first and most basic contingency and that caretaker-intervention-infant-state-change is an equally basic contingency, which bonds or links the pair in reciprocal regulation from the very outset. We have encountered marked individual differences in the length of the gross sleep and awake epochs characteristic of each infant. The relative length of these two epochs is significantly intercorrelated, suggesting the existence of individual differences in an epoch "duration factor." The modification of the overall lengths of sleep and awake epochs and of their day–night distributions is one of the important sites of adaptive pressure as the caretaker seeks to bring her infant's 24-hour temporal organization into some coordination with the 24-hour pattern of events in the household. The data suggested that the shifting of epoch length toward shorter or longer periods may be related to the style of caretaking of the particular nurse who is doing the surrogate mothering.

Research on biological rhythm has made a key contribution to the conceptualization of the adaptive process and the temporal organization of interaction in the system. This contribution is an insight into the control of the phase relations of oscillating systems, which makes synchrony between them possible. Phase control involves quite a different array of mechanisms from those included in the traditional stimulus–response or learning perspective (see Aschoff, 1965). Franz Halberg (1960) concluded that "Temporal organization of physiologic function usually involves a circadian time structure, with great although not unlimited plasticity. … By synchronization with environmental routines integrative circadian systems gain adaptive value. Temporal coordination in physiology has both integrative and adaptive facets. Periodicity analysis provides for resolution of adaptation as a function of integration and vice versa."

Figure 6.1 shows the progress of infant and caretaker variables over the first 10 days of life in the nursery (Group A) and in the single-caretaker rooming-in situation (Group B). Not only do crying and motility continue to increase under the nursery (Group A) condition, but they remain greatest in the 12 night hours. In the rooming-in (Group B) condition, not only are motility and crying at a much lower level and not only does a shift occur between Days 4 and 6 to their predominance in the 12 *day* hours, but also a synchrony appears between the larger epochs of activity and crying in the infant and both the time of occurrence of and the duration of caretaking interventions.

The "temporal coordination in physiology has both integrative and adaptive facets" and has been documented beautifully, for both the normal and the neurologically at-risk neonate, by the work of Prechtl (1968) and his colleagues. These investigators obtained simultaneous recordings from a number of physiological subsystems during extended 6- to 8-hour polygraphic studies of neonate's cycling through subphases of sleep. The

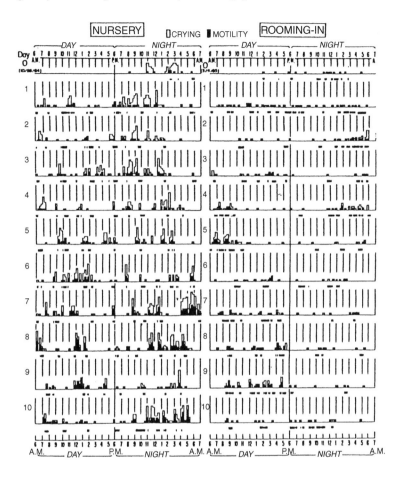

FIGURE 6.1. Relative frequency, duration, and distribution of motility, crying, and caretaking pips as measured by the activity and interactional monitor for a nursery and a rooming-in baby for the first 10 days of life. Caretaker intervention for each baby and for each day of life are represented by the black marks directly below the solid lines indicating day of life.

group of infants designated as hyperexcitable (and those who have been found later to pose greater behavioral difficulty in rearing) is found to show poorer "coherence" or synchrony between physiological subsystems at the points of change as they pass through REM to N-REM cycles. The distinctness of states in these infants is less clear than in the normal infant, making it difficult for the caretaker to read the cues indicating which state the infant is in. These are cues that usually guide the mother in selecting which intervention is in order or, indeed, whether an intervention is in order. The "state" itself, then, represents a summation or an integration of multiple subsystems comprising the infants' physiology. Phase synchrony between the cycling infant states and episodes of caretaker activity constitutes a next order of integration in the system. Variables that indicate the state of the infant[4] may be among the most critical for assessment of both mechanisms of regulation in the infant and progress of adaptation between infant and caretaker.

The design described earlier has allowed us to chart the course of sleeping and waking over the first month of life, both in Group A infants (who did not experience caretaking response as contingent on their changes of state) and in Group B infants (whose caretaking was contingent on their changes of state). Day–night organization of sleeping and waking (i.e., sleeping more between 6 p.m. and 6 a.m. and waking more between 6 a.m. and 6 p.m.) became statistically significant within the first 10 days of life for Group B infants but not for Group A infants. However, within a few days after Group A infants had been transferred from the nursery to the contingent caretaking environment of the surrogate mother who was rooming-in (on Day 11), they abruptly showed a precocious advance in 24-hour periodicity, with a significantly greater day–night difference in the organization of sleep and wakefulness between Days 11 and 25 than was shown by Group B infants during this time. Interestingly enough, this reaction of advance or precocity was shown mostly by the female infant, the male infant tending to show his most rapid progress in day–night differentiation when he had had the contingent caretaking of the Group B condition during the first 10 days of life (Sander et al., 1972).

Although Group A infants had exposure to a noncontingent environment only during the first 10 days of life, they continued to show marked differences from the Group B and C infants over the remainder of the investigation (to the end of the second month of life). One of the most noteworthy differences was the variability between babies when they were examined week by week. Significant stability of rank order from week to week was never obtained for Group A infants in terms of a number of variables, for example, crying, sleeping, and "looking" time on perceptual testing. In other words, stable individual differences were less evident in Group A. On the other hand, stable individual differences were most striking in the Group C infants, in whom the interactional idiosyncracies between infant and caretaker for a number of variables (e.g., crying before intervention) were already most strikingly evident by the end of the first 10 days. An illustration of the stability of rank ordering of subjects within groups over Weeks 2 through 8 is given by Kendall's coefficient of concordance. Although Group B and C infants showed different degrees of stability depending on the stimulus presented, Group A infants never achieved a significant rank order correlation over these weeks for any of the stimuli used in the perceptual test, nor for rank ordering in terms of time spent crying during the presentation of visual stimuli. Both Groups B and C had coefficients of concordance greater than the $p < .025$ level of significance for these stimuli.

The history dependence of the infant–caretaker system is illustrated also by other effects of first 10-day experience shown during the ensuing weeks. For example, Group A infants evidenced significantly greater crying over the 2 months of the study in reaction to the presentation of visual stimuli on the perceptual test, indicating lower tolerance than the others in this situation for this particular kind of visual stimulation (i.e., the human face; see Figure 6.2). In relation to the notion of a connection between the consistency or stability of the system and the progress of visual discrimination or differentiation of the infant's reaction to visual stimuli, only the Group C infants, reared from birth by their own mothers, showed a significant difference over the 2 months in the amount of time spent looking at the mother's face during the perceptual test in comparison with the amount of time spent looking at the stranger's face. In approaching interaction in the system from the viewpoint of an ontogeny of regulation, these data support the suggestion already made, that one is dealing also with an ontogeny of awareness. Furthermore, from this piece of evidence one might say that greater specificity and stability in initial adaptation may be associated with the earlier development of a more differentiated discrimination. From the adaptive viewpoint, however, an early and highly precise fitting together may create certain vulnerabilities for the infant should the system become unstable or be disrupted later. To place a value judgment on behavior from the perspective of adaptation, one must know the environment and the adaptive tasks that the infant will be encountering later.

The research approach that we have been reviewing has provided a rich source of hypotheses and possibilities for new research aimed at a better understanding of the early organization of behavior and perhaps eventually personality. Although work is still going on in the study of data obtained in the prior projects, survival in the research world demands new projects and new data. The same general direction has been continued, that of investigating mechanisms of the adaptive process in an infant–caretaker system, but employing advances in technology and new methods.

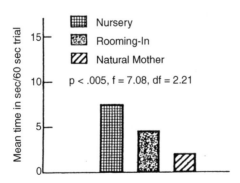

FIGURE 6.2. Infant fussing during perceptual test for all stimulus presentations over Weeks 2 through 8 of life, showing caretaker group differences (Stechler, 1973).

In a current project being supported by the Grant Foundation entitled "An Investigation of Change in Infant–Caretaker Interaction Over the First Two Weeks of Life," the monitoring bassinet has been further advanced in design so that from the prone but otherwise free-lying infant in the bassinet, the occurrence and duration of five states of the infant can be recorded around the clock, along with time of occurrence and duration of caretaking intervention. The five states are awake and active, awake and crying, transitional sleep, REM sleep, and N-REM sleep. The continuous 24-hour record obtained is interfaced with computer tape storage through an optical scan system that makes possible analyses of the complex sequence and the time series as well as the usual statistical analysis of variables. The monitor discriminates a range of differences in state regulation between infants within the normal range and allows study around the clock of changes over the first week of life in sleep cycling and in longer sleep–wake epoch characteristics. The monitor now promises to be an instrument that will make possible a quantitative study of the ontogeny of regulation in at-risk infants of various types and a way of evaluating a variety of caretaking regimens that will optimize their early course of development.

As part of the same project, receiving Grant Foundation support, new methods of precise analysis of interaction between the infant and his interpersonal world have been developed by Dr. William Condon. Dr. Condon has developed a method of independent frame-by-frame analysis of soundtrack and film track of neonates who have been filmed in the awake and active state while being spoken to by an adult or for whom speech is being played on a tape recorder. The frame numbers of the two tracks match, so that an analysis can be made of the points at which change in movement configuration and in speech occur, for example, at word or phoneme boundaries. As early as 12 hours after birth there is evidence of synchrony at microsecond levels between the movements of the awake and active neonate and these linguistic components of human speech (Condon & Sander, 1974). Dr. Condon's work constitutes evidence for a wholly unexpected microscopic level at which bonding in the infant–caretaker system is taking place, and it opens a whole new systems approach to the acquisition of language and to the paralinguistic aspects of communicational behavior. Stern's (1971) film analysis at the microsecond level of the regulation of head turning and facing behavior between mother and infant indicates that at 3½ months initiation of facing behavior by one or the other can be reciprocally regulated at interactional levels of less than a half-second.

RECAPITULATION

These current findings provide evidence of the embeddedness of the human infant in a microscopic interactive regulative system as well as a macroscopic one. The first question that comes to mind might be this: How does the individual ever extricate himself from the obligatory demands on behavior that this necessity for continuous regulation imposes? However, the question is misleading, as one is never extricated from the life support system or the exchanges that it provides as long as life prevails. One asks, rather, how regulatory interactions are incorporated into behavioral organization in a way that provides a measure of relatively stable continuity in the presence of both a varying environment and a changing organism, so that new modifications and adaptations can continue to differentiate within a reasonably brief adaptation time. Ashby's (1952) model of adaptive behavior in complex polystable systems, along with other, already-existing ideas, has been drawn on in the construction of an interactive regulative perspective that encompasses the behavioral coordinations necessary for regulation both on the more biological level of the first 18 months and on the more psychological level of the developments of the second 18 months that are related to functions such as language, representation, and inner awareness.

At each level we have tried to pay attention to the mechanisms of integration and synthesis that are represented by the interactive coordinations relevant to regulation at that level. In an epigenetic sense the relative harmony of reciprocal equilibrium between partners in the system sets the stage for active differentiation of a next level, and finally for the partial and often temporary independence or "disjoin" of a self-regulatory subsystem. These subsystems are accessible in some degree to more conscious levels of function and synthesize feedback elements related both to the ongoing "state" and to active goal direction. Intrinsic, matching criteria provided as a consequence of the disjoin constitute a new basis now for continuity and self-constancy. Perturbations of the system requiring adaptive modifications can begin to be limited to modification in the "self" framework instead of requiring modifications at all levels of linkage, including the biological level. Disjoin requires a certain complexity ("requisite variety") of stable equilibria and in this sense provides a solution for the initial, seemingly paradoxical, features of complexity and coherence mentioned at the outset.

The synthesis of a number of views of the adaptive process appears to offer a way to order empirical interactional data of considerable diversity and complexity and to provide a hypothetical framework that can be applied to the ordering. The focus becomes centralized on the problem of regulation and its connection with the exchange between component parts of a system and with the necessity to define and determine the regularity or the relative stability of variables, as well as to determine the introduction of new behaviors. Obviously, in working from the empirical approach, one tends to carry observation and analysis to ever-finer levels but hopefully remains equally sensitive to concurrent determinants of synthesis and coherence.

NOTES

This chapter is the second half of a chapter, "Infant and caretaking environment" (pp. 153–166), in the book edited by E. T. Anthony (1975), *Explorations in Child Psychiatry*. New York: Plenum.

1. "Adaptation and Perception in Early Infancy," USPHS HD01766, carried out in collaboration with G. Stechler, Ph.D., H. Julia, Ph.D, and P. Burns, M.D.
2. Normality was precisely defined and controlled by prenatal history, observation of delivery, and postnatal examination.
3. Regulatory exchange between infant and mother has existed from conception onward. Anderson (1973) stressed the critical role of the initial hours postpartum with possibly enduring consequence to the way the transition to postnatal regulation is accomplished.
4. Escalona (1962) was one of the first to call attention to the central significance of the infant's state for both investigator and mother. A current report by Anders and Hoffman (1973) assesses the neonate in terms of sleep–wake states.

EDITORS' NOTE

[EN1] A research study that the author was conducting at the time when this paper was written.

REFERENCES

Anderson, G. C. (1973). Paper presented at annual meeting of the International Society for the Study of Behavioral Development, Madison, WI.
Aschoff, J. (1965). Response curves in circadian periodicity. In J. Aschoff (Ed.), *Circadian clocks: Proceedings of the Feldafing Summer School*. Amsterdam: North-Holland.
Ashby, R. (1952). *Design for a brain*. London: Chapman & Hall.
Ashby, R. (1958). *An introduction to cybernetics*. London: Chapman & Hall.
Bertalanffy, L. Von. (1949). *The problem of life*. New York:.
Bower, T. G. R. (1972). Object perception in infants. *Perception, 1*, 15–30.
Bowlby, J. (1969). *Attachment and loss* (Vol. 1). New York: Basic Books.
Burns, P., Sander, L., Stechler, G., & Julia, H. (1972). Distress in feeding: Short-term effects of caretaker environment of the first 10 days. *Journal of the American Academy of Child Psychiatry, 11*, 427–439.
Charlesworth, W. R. (1964). Instigation and maintenance of curiosity behavior as a function of surprise versus novel and familiar stimuli. *Child Development, 35*, 1169–1186.
Condon, W., & Sander, L. (1974). Synchronization of neonate movement with adult speech: Interactional participation and language acquisition. *Science, 183*, 99–101.
Erikson, E. H. (1950). *Childhood and society*. New York: Norton.
Erikson, E. H. (1959). Identity and the life cycle. *Psychological Issues, 1*, 50–101.

Escalona, S. K. (1962). The study of individual differences and the problem of state. *Journal of the American Academy of Child Psychiatry, 1*, 11–38.

Escalona, S. (1963). Patterns of infantile experience and the developmental process. *The Psychoanalytic Study of the Child, 18*, 198–201.

Feffer, M. (1970). A developmental analysis of interpersonal behavior. *Psychological Review, 77*, 197–215.

Glassman, R. B. (1973). Persistence and loose coupling in living systems. *Behavioral Science, 18*, 83–98.

Gouin-Decarie, T. (1965). *Intelligence and affectivity in early childhood.* New York: International University Press.

Halberg, F. (1960). Temporal coordination of physiological functions. *Symposia on Quantitative Biology, 25*, 289–310.

Hartman, H., Dris, E., & Loewenstein, R. M. (1946). Comments on the formation of psychic structure. *Psychoanalytic Study of the Child, 2*, 11–38.

Hinde, R. A. (1966). *Animal behavior: A synthesis of ethology and comparative psychology.* New York: McGraw-Hill.

Hunt, J. M. (1961). *Intelligence and experience.* New York: Ronald Press.

Hunt, J. M. (1965). Intrinsic motivation and its role in psychological development. In D. Levine (Ed.), *Nebraska symposium on motivation.* Lincoln: University of Nebraska Press.

MacKay, D. M. (1956). Towards an information flow model of cerebral organization. *Symposium on Cerebral Activity, Advancement of Science, 42*, 392.

Mahler, M. (1968). *On human symbiosis and the vicissitudes of individuation: Vol. 1. Infantile psychosis.* New York: International University Press.

Mahler, M., & McDevit, J. B. (1968). Observations on adaptation and defense in statu nascendi: Developmental precursors in the first two years of life. *Psychoanalytic Quarterly, 37*, 1–21.

Mason, J. W. (1968). Over-all hormonal balance as a key to endocrine organization. *Psychosomatic Medicine, 30*, 791–808.

Miller, G. A., Galanter, E., & Pribram, K. (1960). *Plans and the structure of behavior.* New York: Henry Holt.

Piaget, J. (1936). *The origins of intelligence in children.* New York: International University Press.

Piaget, J. (1973). The affective unconscious and the cognitive unconscious. *Journal of the American Psychoanalytic Association, 21*, 249–261.

Piaget, J., & Inhelder, B. (1969a). The gaps in empiricism. In A. Koestler & J. R. Smythies (Eds.), *Beyond reductionism—New perspectives in the life sciences* (pp. 118–160). Boston: Beacon Press.

Piaget, J., & Inhelder, B. (1969b). *The psychology of the child.* New York: Basic Books.

Polanyi, M. (1959). *The study of man.* Chicago: University of Chicago Press.

Prechtl, H. F. R. (1968). Polygraphic studies of the full term newborn. In H. Bax & R. C. MacKeith (Eds.), *Studies in infancy clinic in developmental medicine.* London: Heinemann.

Pribram, K. (1963). Reinforcement revisited: A structural view. In M. R. Jones (Ed.), *Nebraska symposium on motivation.* Lincoln: University of Nebraska Press.

Rosenblatt, J. S., Turkewitz, G., & Scheirla, T. C. (1961). Early socialization in the domestic cat as based on feeding and other relationships between female and young. In B. M. Foss (Ed.), *Determinants of infant behavior.* London: Methuen.

Sander, L. W. (1962). Issues in early mother–child interaction. *Journal of the American Academy of Child Psychiatry, 1,* 141–167.

Sander, L. W. (1964). Adaptive relationships in early mother–child interaction. *Journal of the American Academy of Child Psychiatry, 3,* 231–264.

Sander, L. W. (1969). The longitudinal course of early mother–child interaction: Cross case comparison in a sample of mother–child pairs. In B. M. Foss (Ed.), *Determinants of infant behavior* IV, pp. 189–227. London: Methuen.

Sander, L. W., & Julia, H. L. (1966). Continuous interactional monitoring in the neonate. *Psychosomatic Medicine, 28,* 822–835.

Sander, L. W., Julia, H. L., Stechler, G., & Burns, P. (1969). Regulation and organization in the early infant–caretaker system. In J. R. Robinson (Ed.), *Brain and early behavior,* pp. 311–333. New York: Academic.

Sander, L. W., Julia, H. L., Stechler, G., & Burns, P. (1972). Continuous 24-hour interactional monitoring in infants reared in two caretaking environments. *Psychosomatic Medicine, 34,* 270–282.

Sander, L. W., Stechler, G., Burns, P., & Julia, H. (1970). Early mother infant interaction and 24-hour patterns of activity and sleep. *Journal of the American Academy of Child Psychiatry, 9,* 103–123.

Sandler, J., & Rosenblatt, B. (1962). *The concept of the representational world: Psychoanalytic study of the child.* New York: International University Press.

Schneirla, T. C. (1959). An evolutionary and developmental theory of biphasic processes underlying approach and withdrawl. In M. R. Jones (Ed.), *Nebraska symposium on maturation.* Lincoln: University of Nebraska Press.

Spiegel, L. A. (1959). The self—The sense of self and perception. *The Psychoanalytic Study of the Child, 14,* 81–109.

Spitz, R. A. (1957). *No and yes—On the genesis of human communication.* New York: International University Press.

Spitz, R. A. (1959). *A genetic field theory of ego formation.* New York: International University Press.

Stechler, G. (1973). *Infant looking and fussing in response to visual stimuli over the first two months of life in different infant-caretaking systems.* Paper presented at annual meeting of the Society for Research and Child Development, Philadelphia.

Stern, D. N. (1971). A micro-analysis of mother–infant interaction. *Journal of the American Academy of Child Psychiatry, 10,* 501–518.

Uexkull, J. Von (1934). A stroll through the worlds of animals and men. In C. H. Schiller (Ed.), *Instinctive behavior—The development of a modern concept.* New York: International University Press.

Von Holst, E., & Mittelstaedt, H. (1950). Das Reafferenz Prinzip. *Naturwiss, 37,* 464–489.

Wallerstein, R. S. (1973). Psychoanalytic perspectives on the problem of reality. *Journal of the American Psychoanalytic Association, 21,* 5–34.

Weiss, P. (1949). The biological basis of adaptation. In J. Romano (Ed.), *Adaptation.* Ithaca, NY: Cornell University Press.

Weiss, P. (1969). The living system: Determinism stratified. In A. Koestler & J. R. Smythies (Eds.), *The Alpbach Symposium 1968—Beyond reductionism—New perspectives in the life sciences.* Boston: Beacon Press.

7

The Event-Structure of Regulation in the Neonate– Caregiver System as a Biological Background for Early Organization of Psychic Structure

To have the chance to reflect on the papers of Drs. Beebe and Demos is an enriching experience.[EN1] Each of their papers has been developed from sets of data that are as close to the empirical beginnings from which the self is organized in postnatal life as can possibly be studied. Each grapples with the four fundamental questions that grip all of us: (a) On what basis do we describe precursors of a phenomenon as elusive and complex as the self? (b) In terms of observable behaviors, can we correctly infer inner experience? (c) How is inner experience welded into the psychic structure we call the self? (d) What are the changes in organization and representation that both inner experience and the self as a psychic structure undergo over the longer term spans of development?

Both presenters couched their work and their thinking within the systems perspective, each particularizing dimensions of inner experience that belong in different time domains and involve different functional and regulatory subsystems of the human organism. At this point, most of us who are dealing with the complexities of early development anchor our thinking in the systems perspective. It must be realized that one of the drawbacks of taking a systems viewpoint of organization is that the living system ultimately includes everything—particularly the entire range of *time dimensions* within which interactive structures of mutual influence can be organized.

I propose here that this longer temporal dimension is occupied by the basic requirement for biological regulation of infant states along the arousal–quiescent continuum, that is, initially the sleep–awake continuum. It is essential in gaining a wider perspective on infant and caregiver, as an example of a living "system," to recognize that we are dealing with the fundamental property of self-regulation that characterizes all living organisms from single cells upward. The function of self-regulation characterizes the infant and it characterizes the caregivers. What we are seeing in this earliest example of regulation in the living infant–caregiver system is the interaction of two uniquely self-regulatory subsystems, that of the newborn and that of the caregivers. Solutions to their interaction that allow infant and caregiver to reach the harmonious and enduring coordination required for "regulation" of each will be individually unique in its temporal organization, and its perceptual, motor, and sensory configurations. (Note: The course of special features of character organization and of pathogenesis can be seen to begin immediately in early derailments of coordination and regulation. We consider in this chapter only the usual course in which reasonably stable regulation is achieved over the first 3 months of life.)

The neonate's distribution of states on the sleep–awake continuum that the caregiver can observe from birth onward is endogenously determined. The daily, around-the-clock distribution of a newborn's states on this continuum varies from individual to individual as do the characteristics of the events that can modify this temporal organization of states as infant and caregiver move toward their achievement of an initial regulatory equilibrium in the system.

My comments on this earliest context within which we observe affect and interactional structure are based on data of continuous, around-the-clock, noninvasive bassinet monitoring of infant and infant–caregiver interaction. From these data has emerged a background picture we have termed the "event-structure" of the infant–caregiver system. This event-structure becomes a characteristic background configuration of events that emerges from the recurrent patterning of interactions that are needed to establish and maintain the infant's self-regulation of state. Within this framework, microsecond interactions are occurring and affects are experienced, both of which are coming via mutual modifications to gain their meaning for the regulation of the system.

The event-structure of an infant–caregiver system stems from the *recurrent* interactions between a mother with her agenda, a father with his agenda, and a generational family system with its agenda within a social system with its agenda. Into the midst of this comes a new infant with its agenda. The individually unique features of each infant's state organization, with its own particular requirements for regulation, are basic to the agenda that the neonate introduces now into this already complex system. These features of state organization and state regulation influence the interactions that take place between the neonate and the caregiver as they move via mutual modifications toward a stable, harmonious, and enduring adapted coordination. When the configurations of state regulatory interaction settle down to a predictably recurrent pattern, a daily event-structure, uniquely configured for each system, can be said to have become organized, becoming thereby part of the regularly recurring *configurations* of *expectancy* for both infant and caregiver. This forms the background of at least a 24-hour time frame, against which shorter term events in the foreground must be described. The actual *time* organization of this uniquely configured background event-structure becomes shared by both infant and caregiver in the harmoniously regulated system. This time background begins to serve as a reference structure for ascribing meaning to foreground events or events that perturb the unique background structure.

To illustrate just how soon after birth the individually unique features of a particular caregiver become part of the event-structure of the regulatory interaction, we have included Figure 7.1.

Figure 7.1 illustrates the situation in the early infant–caregiver system when one highly experienced surrogate mother caregiver is replaced on the 11th day of life by another, equally experienced and able surrogate mother. In this study, the surrogate mothers provided the only caregiving around the clock for only one infant at a time, beginning at birth. In the sample of nine infants, only two surrogate mothers were used; the initial assignment of the infants to caregiver alternated between these two without bias. The crying and distress measures after Day 10 indicate the disruption of the adapted coordination that had already been established over the first 10 days of life between the neonate and the initial caregiver.

It is helpful to review a bit further some of the biological features that govern neonatal state organization and underlie the recurring structure of events the infant requires of the caregiving system. These features, as mentioned earlier, begin with the 24-hour time organization of the infant's states on the sleep–awake continuum. This organization is governed by the phenomena of biorhythmicity and their related rhythms: circadian, ultradian, and others. This represents a different biology than Freud began with. The facts are that a fundamental property of organization is given to living systems as a whole and to each of their living components by the cyclic oscillations that characterize them. The mechanisms by which a multiplicity of endogenously arising physiological rhythms can become harmoniously phase-synchronized within the individual generate an organism that has coherence as a whole. The empirical demonstration of "coherence" among the various oscillating physiological subsystems of the infant and the relation of this coherence to infant sleep organization and to later problems of caregiving was reported by Prechtl (1968, 1969) and Kalverboer, Touwen, and Prechtl (1973).

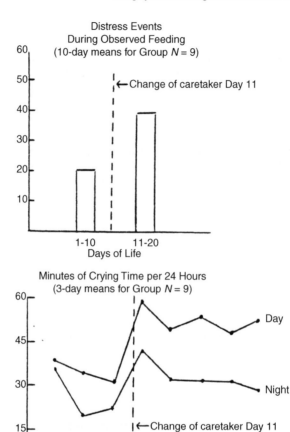

FIGURE 7.1 The effects of caretaker replacement on child-caregiver interaction after 10 days of life.

Our group has demonstrated the powerful influence played by individual differences in this 24-hour temporal organization and its relation to the regulation of both infant and of caregiving systems. We have demonstrated the way adaptation between the two then establishes a framework of recurrent events in which specific functions, behaviors, and strategies are carried out (Sander, 1969).

It is helpful to think of this event-structure of a system, and the affects that may or may not be associated, as each related to separate domains. Affects may, but do not necessarily, determine the event-structure of the system. Recurrent goal organization of both infant and caregiver and the motivations that promote the recurrent goal realization, which establishes the adapted coordinations on which enduring state regulation rests, may be amplified and shaped by affects but do not necessarily arise from affects.

Within the organization and regulation of the event-structure of the larger system, we can identify at least a half-dozen features or constraints that this fundamental property of biorhythmicity imposes on the framework of recurrent events that characterize the infant–caregiver system. Among some of the properties that the elemental biorhythmic nature of living systems impose are: (a) the preeminent role given to timing, that is, to the temporal organization of events in the regulation of the system; (b) the assurance that situations will be recurrent; when recurrence becomes dependable, it provides a condition essential for habituation and adaptation; (c) that within this recurrence, there will be a capacity for the reorganization needed to reach harmonious coordination; phase-shifting and phase-synchrony of rhythms between functions of infant and caregiver that have different periodicities take place, and this is a mutual modification that makes coordination achievable; (d) that there will be a patterned specificity of cues specifically timed and recurrent that provide the *entrainment* necessary for this coordination of rhythms. Entrainment by specific and regularly recurrent patterning of perceptual and sensorimotor cues within a specific temporal framework of events is the mechanism by which rhythms of one period length in one oscillating system can be phase linked to periodicities in another such system. Much attention is being given to this critical phenomenon now in premature nurseries and intensive care units to facilitate phase-synchrony and coherence in infants who are seriously impaired in the temporal organization of their sleep states and of their related physiological subsystems. At the same time, they are being exposed to an environment that provides few if any of the rhythmically recurrent events that are necessary for entrainment; and (e) that coherence and equilibrium in regulation of the system over longer time spans provides a temporal organization of events in the system that allows for what has been called loose-coupling (Glassman, 1973) or disjoin (Ashby, 1952). This is a temporary and partial *disengagement* of infant and caregiver when they are in a state of coordination and harmony of regulation.[EM2] Such disengagement in a state of equilibrium in the system is a condition that favors the achievement of a sense of agency in the infant and the sense that its motivations and goals are its own.

I am suggesting, furthermore, that, in addition to underlying the event-structure of the system in adapted equilibrium, the property of biorhythmicity also sets the background for the regularities of the interactive situations in the system that are necessary for the infant's regularly recurrent *experience of its own inner states*. Successful regulation in the system on a 24-hour basis is an important condition for recurrence of this inner experience. We find that individual characteristics of sleep organization provide one of the most sensitive indicators of risk in the neonate. And, of course, this risk is a risk for the infant–caregiver system in its task of achieving a harmonious and enduring regulation. Consequently the qualities of infant's inner experience related to the recurrent states and the interactional context in which they are regularly reexperienced quickly become part of the infant's recurrent expectations and organization of his or her own self-regulatory behaviors.

The well-organized normal infant wakes up four to six times a day. Each awakening exhibits a sequence of clearly identifiable states until the infant falls back to sleep. These states are recognizable with a high level of interobserver reliability, and provide the first specific observational cues as to the infant's inner experience that the caregiver intuitively infers and reads from moment to moment. It is from these inferences that the caregiver regularly makes her decisions. This is a first link in the neonate between the observable and the inner experience. Around these decisions, a regularly repeated interactive context becomes established so that state, and thus inner experience, is experienced by the infant within a specific behavioral context. The time frame of each awakening has direction to it—a sequence that progresses in terms of both state and interaction. Within this directional context, affects acquire their meaning, and motivations their specific goals. As was pointed out earlier, in the competent system the recurrent sequence of states on the sleep–awake continuum can be seen as the first level of initiative that the infant introduces into the system.

I am in full agreement with Demos that there is evidence that affect systems are identifiable from the beginning—especially in the awake end of the continuum—and that they become engaged from the outset in the interactive patterns with the caregiver. Almost at once affects of surprise and interest can be described in the awake infant. In a description of self-regulation of earliest infant states coupled with the infant's inner experience of them, affects can be referred to as recognizable states that begin in the context of, or combined with, state position on the sleep–awake continuum. In this earliest time of state regulation, affects can be seen to be embedded within a recurrent sequence of sleep–awake state organization, a subsystem of its own, distinct from but interacting with affect systems that are brought into play as initial caregiving coordination is being achieved in the process of establishing harmonious and enduring state regulation. From the start, qualities of, sensitivity to, and regard for the endogenous determination of the timing and duration of sleep–awake states of the baby can be observed and assessed in the caregiver's decisions. Similarly, one caregiver's sense that the states of the baby should be contingent on her control, and their occurrence and timing should be her responsibility, contrasts with that of another, who perceives the timing and direction of state change in the baby as an endogenously arising primary property of the baby, with *her* proper response then being contingent to that state change.

What has become strikingly clear is the mutual influence at this initial level and how very early in the normal infant–caregiver pattern the system gains 24-hour temporal organization through this mutual influence of infant and caregiver. Day–night differentiation in the location of sleep and awake states (sleep predominating in the nighttime 12 hours, and awake states in the daytime 12 hours) becomes evident between the fourth and sixth day of life in such a system. This differentiation does not appear when such recurrent mutuality is lacking. This is illustrated in Figure 7.2, which illustrates the 24-hour distribution of sleep states in an infant experiencing the noncontingent caregiving of the neonatal nursery with multiple caregivers.

In the instance of the experienced natural mother or caregiver, there is regularly recurrent caregiving contingent to the endogenous rhythms of neonatal states. This sets the stage necessary in state regulation for both entrainment and the necessary adaptive modifications involving habituation, learning, and goal organization. Given these features, the entire 24 hours can become organized in a pattern of napping and waking periods by the seventh day of life. After some days of regularity, there are days of changing organization followed by the appearance of a new stability of nap organization. In Figure 7.3, the infant begins three daytime naps and a night nap on Day 7. This continues through Day 11. There is a reorganization between Days 12 and 14, and we see two daytime naps and a still longer night sleep period on Days 15 through 19. There is a second reorganization, Days 20 and 21, and we find a shorter morning nap, a longer afternoon nap, and the long night sleep. Although not shown in the figure, this latter pattern for the infant endures stably over the rest of the first 2 months of life.

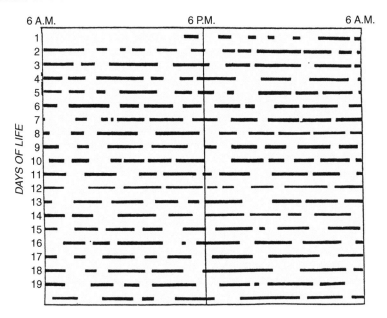

FIGURE 7.2 Distribution of sleep states in an infant experiencing noncontingent caregiving of neonatal nursery with multiple caregivers.

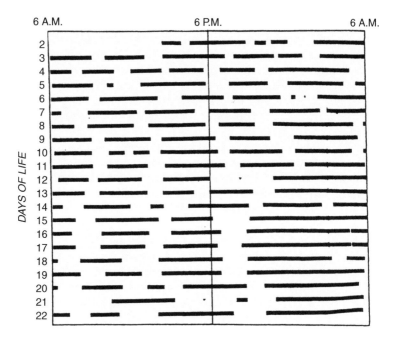

FIGURE 7.3 Distribution of sleep states in an infant experiencing regularly reccurrent caregiving of experienced mother or caregiver.

We have demonstrated also the mutual interactive influence between caregiver behavior and the longer sleep–awake periodicities. In two samples of nine infants each, each infant was cared for around the clock, one at a time, over the first month of life by a single surrogate mother. There were two such mothers, each caring for a sample of nine infants. The infants of one mother emerged with significantly longer longest awake and significantly longer longest sleep periods over 24 hours than did the infants cared for by the other surrogate caregiver (see Figure 7.4).

The interactive sequence over an awake period itself becomes part of episodic memory. In our experiment in which the natural mother's face is masked just before the first awakening on the seventh day of life, we showed infant reactions of notable surprise to this violation of expectancy. This reaction began at one specific moment in the feeding interaction, which had become by 7 days a familiar sequence of caregiving events. The context for experience is being learned with the content. As Ashby (1952) first delineated in the early 1950s, state is a configuration of variables that recurs and can be recognized when it recurs again. This can be a highly complex configuration of variables, but a pattern, however, that can be recognized, often, as a single recurrent cue for the observer. This is, of course, the same model Demos has pointed out in thinking about the emotions, highly complex configurations of behavior and physiology that can be recognized when they recur by a single configuration of cues. The

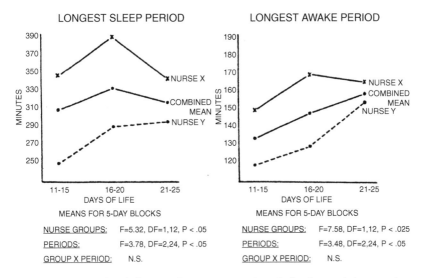

FIGURE 7.4 Interactive influence between caregiver behavior and longer sleep-awake periodicities.

question has also been raised whether or not the neonate comes equipped to recognize recurrent states of the caregiver (Meltzoff, 1985; Stern, 1985).

In the caregiver system, where the states of the infant become the infant's first initiative in modifying the system to achieve regulation, the infant gains actual agency in self-regulation within that system. We can call a harmoniously regulated infant caregiving system that makes it possible for the infant to exercise agency in its own state regulation a competent system.[EN3] The extent to which an infant can be an agent in his or her own self-regulation differentiates one infant–caregiver system from another from the outset. Differences between systems and their relative competence can be traced from the earliest interactions. As time goes on, the harmony of regulation can persist, improve, or deteriorate. Systems differ in their resilience or rigidity to maintain or alter such organization.

In regard to regulation in the competent infant–caregiver system at this early point, we make three simple proposals: (1) That the inner experience of the infant first consolidates around this recurrent sequence of states on the sleep–awake continuum, particularly those at the awake end; that is, transitional, drowsy, awake active, awake quiet or alert, fussing or crying. As just noted, state comes quickly to include affects (e.g., surprise or interest). (2) That because of this regular daily recurrence in the competent system, these particular experiential states, as well as the state of sleep, become goals for the infant and begin to determine goal-organized behavior within the familiar recurrent event-structure of the infant–caregiver system. The self-regulatory capabilities of the infant become activated and organize infant behavior to reconstruct situations associated with reexperiencing desired states and avoiding states not desired; and (3) That in the competent system that ensures infants as agents in their own self-regulation, such recurrent inner states as goals become the inner criteria, or set points, for generating increasingly varied and complex goal-organized behavioral schema. These bring about the situations in the competent system associated with the experience of the desired states. This is a sequence in which infants change the situations that then directly change their own states via their own initiative.[EN4] Arrived at as part of the mutual influence of regulatory coordinations, such schemes become part of the organization of the system as well as of the infant. One's own states are indeed one's own when such competence is achieved.

In terms of this organization of coordinated behavior, which becomes characteristic for a system, the infant's sense of continuity over time can be considered to be carried by this recurrent conservative configuration of inner experiences associated with the regulatory strategies that have now become characteristics of the system. The importance of thinking in terms of the systems perspective is that the mutual adaptation, which is achieved between infant and caregiver in the "competent" system, establishes for the infant that one's own actions can directly affect one's own states in desired directions. In such a system, self-regulation becomes an active interpersonal skill. Hence, the role of the infant's inner experience in the organization of his or her adaptive behavior becomes central to the effectiveness of the interactive strategies he or she develops. At the same time, the organization of awareness of inner experience (which can be thought of here as an awareness of one's own state) is given a central role in self-regulation. In the stable and competent system (which is characterized by recurrent situations related to state regulation), these strategies become organized as structures of psychic organization; that is, proceeding by goal organization of behavior from the regularly recurring experience of an awareness of one's own inner experience—awareness of own state—to alter it in a familiar, goal-ordered fashion to a more desired state. This contrasts with the situation in the incompetent system, in which the infant reexperiences its own state as being a result of or secondary to a more primary structure of outer events.

At this point in the discussion of the earliest development of psychic structures related to the sense of self, discussed here as awareness of own inner experience, we realize we must begin to address the question of ontogeny in the organization of awareness (i.e., consciousness). In the model presented here, such ontogeny would revolve around the conditions that influence the unique way in the caregiving system that awareness of inner experience in the individual is allowed or is not allowed to organize the generation of that individual's adaptive behavior. It is here that derailment in the development of the sense of self can be seen to begin. This, however, is the subject for another paper, addressing the role within an infant's own particular system that infant awareness of own inner experience is allowed to play in that infant's organizing of his or her own self-regulatory goals.

There is another point: How can the origins of the self as a psychic structure emerge from the mutuality of influence required to achieve enduring state regulation? With such a powerful mutual shaping of behavior and of biological responsivity going on, it is easy to envision the shaping effects of projective identification and the unconscious response to another's attribution. These conditions make it difficult, even impossible, for the individual to make any distinction between which experience is his or her own endogenously arising one, and which is part of this mutual interactive influence elicited by or in response to the other.

Elsewhere, based on the concepts of regulation, adaptation, and integration in living systems, we (Sander, 1983) have proposed the idea of a disengagement between infant and caregiver in terms of "open space," a first edition of Winnicott's (1958b) intermediate area. The idea in this is that in the competent system, in which regulation can be maintained at a well-balanced equilibrium, there is during an awake period often a time span of long enough disengagement between infants and caregivers to allow the infants to proceed from clearly endogenously arising motivations and interests. These are quite clear, because the disengagement is quite clear at that point of regulatory equilibrium so that there is no preemption of action by regulatory needs that are imposed either from within or from without. This is only a span of time in the longer time frame of the awake sequence that I have been talking about, in which such disengagement is possible; but it is, I think, similar to what Winnicott has been describing in his suggestions about the origins of the capacity to be alone. This longer time frame of regulatory stability he spoke of in terms of "the mother holding the situation in time" (Winnicott, 1958a). He described the disengagement in the following way:

> The infant is able to become unintegrated, to flounder, to be in a state in which there is no orientation, to be alone to exist for a time without being either a reactor to an external impingement or an active person with a direction of interest or movement. The stage is set for an id experience. In the course of time there arrives a sensation or an impulse. In this setting the sensation or impulse will feel real and be truly a personal experience. (p. 34)[EN5]

I suggest, then, that it is in the system in regulatory equilibrium related to a longer time domain of regulation, namely, the 24-hour day, that such endogenously arising directions of infant initiative can be pursued repeatedly by the infant. Under these conditions the infant will experience inner experience, with its endogenously arising motivations and goals, as his or her own. This is associated with option as agent to act on this inner experience, in both reconstruction and new construction. This begins the possibility for the infant to experience an alternative to the indistinctness of agency in the experiences associated with mutuality. How one comes to regard one's own inner experience as a of sense of self emerges over the first 2 years in the context of the outcome to these initiatives that emerge within the "open space." Their success or failure biases the long-term trajectory, as do the regulatory conditions that permit or deny option to pursue them. We can see a model for formative influences on the quality of this regard as a systems property from the outset. What we have tried to do is to draw attention to the lawfulness that governs this very earliest edition of inner experience in the success or failure of self-regulation of one's own recurrent states. For example, one can see here the powerful role that the intrusive, controlling caregiver or the nonresponsive mother would play in compromising such a dyadic opportunity for allowing the infant a working role in the active organization of inner experience.

The capacity for psychic structuralization is indeed a systems characteristic, but all levels of temporal and goal organization need to be considered if we are to start from the beginning to understand the complexity and role of an inner frame of reference in the ontogeny of a sense of self.

NOTE

In regard to this more inclusive system we can ask, What are the *larger regularities,* and the more extensive time spans within which Beebe's interactive structures of microsecond mutual influence fit, and within which Demos's affect systems are organized?

EDITORS' NOTES

EN1   Such writings are included in: Goldberg, A. (1987). *Frontiers in Self Psychology: Progress in Self Psychology,* Vol. 3

EN2   These arguments will be revisited and elaborated in the next chapters.

EN3   Therefore, not a competent child, but a competent system favors a harmonious adjustment that leads to the *sense of agency.*

EN4   Sander's thinking seems clear in this particular point: systems theory doesn't diminish the individual responsibility on the changes of one's states.

EN5   This same quote from Winnicott is reported by Sander in another work (see chapter 8). Its richness and intensity make it worth being read more than once.

REFERENCES

Ashby, W. R. (1952). *Design for a brain.* London: Chapman & Hall.

Glassman, R. B. (1973). Persistence and loose coupling in living systems. *Behavioral Science, 18,* 83–98.

Goldberg, A. (Ed.). (1988). *Frontiers of Self Psychology* (Vol. 3, pp. 64–77). The Analytic Press, Hillsdale, New Jersey.

Kalverboer, A. F., Touwen, B. C. L., & Prechtl, H. F. R. (1973). Follow up of infants at risk of minor brain dysfunction. *Annals of the New York Academy of Sciences, 205,* 172.

Meltzoff, A. (1985). The roots of social and cognitive development: Models of man's original nature. In T. Field & N. Fox (Eds.), *Social perception in infants.* Norwood, NJ: Ablex.

Prechtl, H. F. R. (1968). Polygraphic studies of the fullterm newborn infant II: Computer analysis of recorded data. In M. Bax & R. Mackeith (Eds.), *Studies in infancy.* London: Heinemann.

Prechtl, H. F. R., Weinman, H., & Akiyama, Y. (1969). Organization of physiological parameters in normal and neurologically abnormal infants: Comprehensive computer analysis of polygraphic data. *Neuropaediatric, 1,* 101–129.

Sander, L. W. (1969). Regulation and organization in the early infant-caretaker system. In R. J. Robinson (Ed.), *Brain and early behavior.* London: Academic.

Sander, L. W. (1983). Polarity, paradox and the organizing process in development. In J. Call, E. Galenson, & R. Tyson (Eds.), *Frontiers of infant psychiatry*, pp. 333–347. New York: Basic Books.

Sander, L. W. (1985). Toward a logic of organization in psychobiological development. In H. Klar & L. Siever (Eds.), *Biologic response styles: Clinical implications* Washington, DC: APA.

Stern, D. (1985). *The interpersonal world of the infant.* New York: Basic Books.

Winnicott, D. W. (1958a). *The capacity to be alone: The maturational processes and the facilitating environment.* New York: International Universities Press.

Winnicott, D. W. (1958b). Transitional objects and transitional phenomena. In *Collected papers.* New York: Basic Books.

8

Paradox and Resolution
From the Beginning

Among the dynamic forces that shape organization in the developing infant and in the infant–caregiver system, a number of apparent paradoxes can be discerned. This brief chapter on early human development addresses only one of these paradoxes. The viewpoint is one that has emerged from nearly 40 years of experience with the subjects of the Boston University Longitudinal Study in Personality Development (Sander, 1984). As with a wide range of research on both the animal and human levels, this study has revealed the singularity, the uniqueness of each newborn, each family system, and each individual's own particular pathway of development. The other side of the apparent paradox emerges from the extensive research on the minutiae of events within the flow of interaction between infant and caregiver: These studies have been carried out at the level of microsecond film and video analysis (Condon & Sander, 1974; Stern, 1974; Trevarthen, 1979). From this viewpoint, the now well-established concepts of intersubjectivity and attunement have been defined—that is, how infant and caregiver can function rhythmically and synchronously with each other.

The paradox is that we begin with two biological "givens": the requirement for self-regulation (the agency to initiate action to self-regulate within the context of one's unique life support system must be the individual's own agency to initiate; the "being distinct from" pole) and the capacity for microsecond synchrony and attunement with an "other" (not cognitively managed by the individual; the "being together with" pole). Both givens are there from the beginning of life and provide the essential conditions for the experience of "connection with" another and for the positive affects that are the basis of motivational systems underlying healthy relationships, including the experiences of loving and being loved as we come to encounter, and then "know" them in later life.

It is the sharing of a focus of attention in these "moments of meeting" that sets the stage for the microsecond tuning, the capability with which we are born. The experiencing of such "attunement" organizes positive affects, their motivational role, and the organization of consciousness.

It seems evident from the diversity of possible developmental pathways that integration of these two poles is a relative matter, ranging from the derailments of gross pathology at the one extreme to what we consider "health," or the optimization of potential that lies within both the new individual and the system, at the other. Indeed, many of the difficulties in childrearing relate to the confusion and indefiniteness that obscure the presence of each pole of the paradox, the very essential role that each pole plays, and the awareness that it is their integration that lies at the heart of the early developmental process.

Infant research is intended to explore, identify, and comprehend the essential principles that govern the early developmental process. It is hoped that such findings can and will be assimilated into the way caregivers both think and feel as they begin to construct an environment for their newborn. "Essential" principles of the developmental process exist from conception and persist throughout life. This chapter offers two brief clinical vignettes and notes their relation to the highly complex, but centrally vital, task of integration that confronts caregiver and infant from the moment of conception. The real problem is the *translation* from the discovery of principles governing the developmental process to their incorporation within the exchanges and interactions that will be the shaping forces in new infant–caregiver systems.

Every field, infant research included, has its own language. If space allowed, it would be appropriate to consider here how that language applies to how caregivers think about early development. What would it mean for caregivers to think in terms of systems instead of individuals; in terms of process instead of structure; in terms of a flow of sequence, recurrence, and expectancy within the recurring exchanges between themselves and their charges instead of thinking in terms of isolated events? How does one think in terms of temporal organization (e.g., the 24-hour day and its regular recurrences, whether reflecting change or stability), or in terms of the distribution of "moments of meeting" between components of the system and the specificity such meetings convey? Space limitations preclude a discussion of the necessary background biology brings to our thinking.

In psychology, we sometimes fail to address that underlying yet unavoidable mystery of biology, *organization* that is essential for life itself. Biology constantly confronts this mystery driven on the one hand to analyze the unending process of engagement between organism and environment on a scale or hierarchy of levels—subsystems within larger systems—yet always constrained, on the other, by the vital necessity of maintaining the coherence, or unity, required for the enduring existence of both the living organism and the living system.

From such an effort at translation could emerge a way of thinking about the early developmental process—about the role of time, place, and movement in the organization of the infant–caregiver system and its processes of regulation, adaptation, and integration: about the central issue of where the impetus for initiation of action lies in the exchanges between infant and caregiver, or why the essential features of self-regulation and self-organization that are required of every living organism cannot be bypassed when dealing with the developing human infant. In exactly the same way, translation from the language of the neurosciences would enrich our thinking about longer term consequences of infants' experiences. Relevant here are current concepts of the way anatomical and functional organization of the brain itself is being shaped, while regulatory and adaptive modifications of behavior are taking place between infant and caregiver. In the presence of this broader perspective, our thinking could be extended to include the role of conscious experience in shaping the early developmental pathway. This is especially relevant in the place being given now to experiences of awareness and self-awareness; as a result, brain organization constantly is being revised and updated through processes of categorization, mapping, and, especially, reentry (Edelman, 1992). Translation at this point from neuroscience to psychology would open the door to discussing the experience of "recognition" (Sander, 1991) as being one of specificity in a "moment of meeting" between the complexities of two unique subsystems—the infant and the caregiver. Recognition can be thought of as a way of representing how one individual comes to savor the wholeness of another—that is, the experiencing by one of some configuration of the whole, some gestalt of the state of coherence of the other (Sander, 1995a, 1995b). I propose that the experience of recognition represents a specificity in the meeting of such gestalts, one that provides the critical condition for the reorganization of both interacting partners as they progress toward new integration. Recognition, as a process moving toward increasingly precise specificity, serves as an essential operational metaphor for both developmental process and therapeutic process. It also provides a broader base on which coherence in the larger infant–caregiver system can be built (Sander, 1995a).

Obviously, this chapter cannot provide the necessary theoretical framework required to integrate philosophies from among the complexity of disciplines involved. But it is important to recognize that such an integration can open us up to new ways of thinking. Next I illustrate and enlarge on the two poles of the paradox and the diversity of possible developmental pathways that are available to provide resolution.

ILLUSTRATIVE EXAMPLE OF "BEING TOGETHER WITH"

This example illustrates the "being together with" pole, and opens consideration of the powerful place of intersubjectivity in comprehending the glue that binds together infant and caregiver as a living system. The following description is an example of the way that "primary intersubjectivity" (Trevarthen, 1979) can enter the caregiving situation, shape it, and yet remain quite outside the awareness of either participant. The scene, drawn from some 3 minutes of movie film,[1] can be described as follows.

Case Example

The research team was filming one of our new neonatal subjects on the eighth postdelivery day out on the lawn in front of the parents' house. In those days (1958), that was 3 days after mother and baby had returned from the hospital. One of the team was standing on the lawn talking with the father. The mother was sitting nearby with the new baby talking with another member of the team. The baby became increasingly fussy, with mother trying unsuccessfully to quiet her. The mother became a bit embarrassed and decided it was time to bring out refreshments, so she gave the baby to the father, who was standing nearby talking, and went into the house. The next 2 or 3 minutes of film shows the father standing on the lawn, holding the baby in his left arm, continuing to talk to the researcher, during which time the baby simply falls asleep and the two go on talking. Run at normal film speed of 30 frames per second, this is all that can be seen.

When, however, the film is rerun frame by frame over the same few minutes, it can be seen that the father glances down momentarily at the baby's face. Strangely enough, in the same frames, the infant looked up at the father's face. Then the infant's left arm, which had been hanging down over the father's left arm, began to move upward. Miraculously, in the same frame, the father's right arm, which had been hanging down at his side, began moving upward. Frame by frame the baby's hand and the father's hand moved upward simultaneously. Finally they met over the baby's tummy. The baby's left hand grasped the little finger of the father's right hand. At that moment the infant's eyes closed and she fell asleep, while the father continued talking, apparently totally unaware of the little miracle of specificity in time, place, and movement that had taken place in his arms.

This example makes clear immediately the first pole of our dynamic: The principle of intersubjectivity. *Webster's Dictionary* defines "relation" as "connection." We begin life "connected," as part of each other. We begin in relationship. Intersubjectivity as a principle of first relationships has been demonstrated richly, both empirically and conceptually, by both Stern (1974) in "attunement" and Trevarthen's (1979) "primary and secondary intersubjectivity." Opportunities for the engagements of intersubjectivity hinge largely on the way the caregiver's attention is organized and available. As Murray (1988) pointed out, it is here, in the organization of attention, that postpartum depression in the mother plays such a critical role. In Trevarthen's "secondary intersubjectivity"—in the extension of the role of intersubjective organization to the enacting of play, games, and all forms of cooperative engagement between individuals—we realize that we have a further elaboration of the way each participant assimilates aspects of the complex organization of the other to achieve new integration at the systems level. A game represents the integration of a system; in this it is akin to the achievement of a relative stability in regulation of infant states of sleeping and waking as the case example illustrated.

ILLUSTRATIVE EXAMPLE OF "BEING DISTINCT FROM"

At the same time, Tronick, Als, Adamson, Wise, and Brazelton (1978) demonstrated vividly just how vulnerable the infant in the first months of life is to derailment of this elementary experience of connection by showing the infant's collapse in both mood and engagement when confronted with a caregiver's unresponsive, still face. This brings us to the second pole of our paradox.

Almost from the very outset, an infant begins to organize his or her own unique set of expectancies, which emerge from the diversity among recurring engagements with the caregivers; this organization is apparent in the system of the infant as "being distinct from" the caregiver. Throughout the 24-hour day, as expectancy probabilities are becoming established for both, a dynamic field of forces begins and surrounds the recurrent moments of meeting between the infant and the caregiver. Exchanges of intersubjectivity, along with their positive emotional amplification, are being balanced by negative emotions as the infant meets a mismatch of expectancy, as when he or she encounters the still face or some equivalent interdiction. A dynamic balance emerges between initiatives for approach or for avoidance; this, in turn, begins to constrain the flow of behavior in the infant–caregiver system. The essential requirement that each living organism be self-regulating means that the initiative to choose a direction must arise from within the organism itself, not from an extrinsic source. We are all too familiar with avoidance and negative affects, but we also are beginning to track and appreciate the irreplaceable inward-motivating role played by positive affects in the initial adaptive encounters that make up "the first relationship."[2] Inasmuch as positive affects also energize, amplify, and motivate the infant as the "agent-to-initiate" in organizing his or her own goals, we can begin to describe both poles of the paradox as contained within the framework of positive affects. In the language of chaos theory (Gleick, 1987), rather than represent opposition and conflict, this would constitute a "strange attractor." We understand adaptation as a fitting together over time between infant and caregiver that constructs a new and enduring system: This builds on the idea that positive affects must embrace both the pole of being together with (intersubjectivity) and that of being distinct from (singularity). The singularity of an infant as he or she initiates action in his or her own self-organization is experienced by both the baby and the caregiver. It has been demonstrated (Papousek, 1967) that the early infant's realization of an expectancy, or the achievement of a goal is accompanied by positive affects. At such moments, the caregiver can express positive affects that match and amplify those of the infant; whether she does so depends in large measure on the extent to which she has, in her own psychological organization, already granted the infant this essential role as agent to initiate the action required for his or her own self-regulation and self-organization.

To glimpse how this all "works" in the earliest relationships brings us to our second case example: A state of relative stability in the regulation of the infant–caregiver system is established by means of mutual adaptations. The example illustrates an initial adaptation of this kind between the two. Biology has long pointed out that systems maintained in states of relative stability of regulation begin to show new, or "emergent" properties. The conditions under which sleep states gain 24-hour organization in the infant–caregiver system is one such emergent property that will be described. It illustrates the way we can think of the infant as a self-regulating subsystem, and demonstrates how the infant becomes loosely coupled or disembedded within the broader stability of regulation achieved within the larger system—that is, a new, emergent property of the infant–caregiver system appears. Such loose coupling or disembedding of infant as self-organizing agent would represent the "being distinct from" pole of our paradox.

I should clarify here just what is meant by loosely coupled or disembedded ("disjoined," as Ashby [1952] described it). Ashby introduced this concept in describing the significance of reaching the adapted state in a richly complex system. When there is a stable equilibrium in regulatory balance among a requisite variety of component functions, a selected function can itself (within its own phase-space) interact with the context—the organism's network of engagement—without a perturbation in the selected function spreading to or upsetting the stability of the rest of the system. On the other hand, a system may not be in such a state of regulatory equilibrium, or it may be trying desperately to maintain its coherence. Under such circumstances, component functions remain tightly coupled with the system as a whole, so that a slight perturbation of one part spreads at once to the rest of the system. To illustrate this Ashby used the metaphor of someone learning to drive a stick-shift automobile:

Adaptation may demand independence as well as interaction. The learner-driver of a motor car, for instance, who can only just keep the car in the center of the road, may find that any attempt at changing gears results in the car apparently trying to leave the road. Later, when he is more skilled, the act of changing gears will have no effect on the car's travel. Adaptation thus demands not only the integration of related activities, but the independence of unrelated activities. (p. 157)

In systems language, within the coherence of a stably regulated infant–caregiver system, conditions should allow the infant to function as a "self-as-agent," self-organizing subsystem that becomes loosely coupled, or disjoined. Yet another framework would describe the systems condition under which Winnicott's (1965b) "true self" development could begin. The empirical evidence of all this was presented in Chapter 6 of this volume by illustrating initial 24 hour sleep-awake state organization in the neonate in 3 different caretaking environments.

RESOLUTION OF PARADOX

The bassinet-monitoring study illustrated another emergent property of a system maintained in a state of relatively stable regulation—the appearance over the course of an infant's awake period of an "open space" (Sander, 1977) in time, one that allows the endogenously activated, self-organizing initiative of the infant to emerge and begin the process of constructing its own idiosyncratic goals—the pathway to be pursued in "being distinct from." Integration at this point, clearly, must be thought of in terms of process within a system.

Open space, as I have formulated it, begins to become recognizable during the course of an awake period toward the end of the first month of postnatal life. The mother feels she is coming to "know" her infant within what is now a relatively stable 24-hour framework of expectable states in her infant's cycling and sequencing. During an awake period, after the infant has been picked up, changed, fed, and socially interacted with, the baby still is in an awake-active or quiet-alert state, not yet ready to return to sleep. The mother puts the infant in a reclining chair where the baby can see and hear her and goes about her other work or interests. This is a moment of disengagement but one in a state of regulatory stability, a coherence in the infant–caregiver system as a whole. During this open space in time, the infant's "primary activity," his or her agency for generating self-organization, can take off and initiate and organize an idiosyncratic network of proximal engagement of his or her own. This may involve grasping his or her own fingers, or watching mother, or banging against a mobile hanging before the infant. The infant is free from the need to manage or restore the regulation of his or her own state as a whole, and self-regulation can be carried out within a specific component sensorimotor subsystem. The infant's agency can pursue its own interests in a variety of ways: The child can engage in active selective exploration either of self or the low-intensity stimuli or discrepancies in the surroundings. Feedback and self-correcting action become related specifically to the goals of the infant's own interests and action.

Here we have a systems model, then, of equilibrium constructed by an enduring coordination between infant and mother over time, a balance that provides containment without impingement. We can apply this model to our understanding of succeeding tasks for new adaptive coordination that will arise within the system as the infant matures over the ensuing months.

In the open space segment of the awake period there is documentation for Winnicott's paradox: "The basis of the capacity to be alone is a paradox: it is the experience of being alone while someone else is present" (Winnicott, 1965a, p. 30). And, further "it is only when alone (i.e., in the presence of someone) that the infant can discover his own personal life. The pathological alternative is a false life built on reactions to external stimuli" (p. 34). The open space segment can be thought of as a first level of Winnicott's "intermediate area" and "true self" engagement with it.

If we think of the first relationship from the perspective provided by basic biological principles that govern the interactive exchange process in all living systems, we begin to appreciate that the integration of dynamic polarities inherent within such systems is their essential direction. The idea of stages in development has provided important descriptive markers but tends to obscure such common, essential, underlying dynamics. For example, the process of separation and individuation has long been conceptualized and studied as part of the early developmental process, but it has been assumed to enter the picture at some later point, after initial "togetherness" has been established. As I have tried to illustrate, if we can translate from the biological level and think in terms of systems and process, it becomes evident that the same fundamental dynamic is there in the system from the first relationship. This suggests that we can view the progress of the developmental process as one of integration, one that brings together apparently contrasting poles on levels of new and increasing complexity. Ultimately it is this process that constructs the wide spectrum of pathways that, at the same time, preserve the uniqueness of the individual.

NOTES

Published in J. D. Noshpitz (Series Ed.) & S. Greenspan, S. Weider, & J. Osofsky (Vol. Eds.). (1998). *Handbook of Child and Adolescent Psychiatry* (Vol. 1 pp. 153–160). New York: Wiley.

1. The film sequence being described was first demonstrated to me by Daniel Stern some 25 years ago. The film itself was taken in 1958.

2. By adaptive encounter (Sander, 1962), I am referring to the epigenetic, selective process of mutual modification required to reach an essential specificity of coordination over time between the uniquely organized infant and the uniquely organized caregiver. This is a fitting together, long described in biology as that coherence in organization of exchange at the level of both the infant and the system that provides the conditions necessary for continuity of existence. The failure-to-thrive infant attests to this necessity.

REFERENCES

Ashby, W. R. (1952). *Design for a brain*. London: Chapman & Hall.

Condon, W. S., & Sander, L. W. (1974). Neonate movement is synchronized with adult speech: Interactional participation and language acquisition. *Science, 183*, 99–101.

Edelman, G. M. (1992). *Bright air and brilliant fire: On the matter of the mind*. New York: Basic Books.

Gleick, J. (1987). *Chaos: Making a new science*. New York: Viking-Penguin.

Murray, L. (1988). Effects of post-natal depression on infant development: Direct studies of early mother–infant interaction. In R. Kumar & I. Brockington (Eds.), *Motherhood and mental illness (Vol. 2)*. London: John Wright.

Papousek, H. (1967). Experimental studies of appetitional behavior in human newborns and infants. In H. W. Stevenson, E. H. Hess, & H. L. Rheingold (Eds.), *Early behavior: Comparative and developmental approaches*. New York: Wiley.

Sander, L. W. (1962). Issues in early mother–child interaction. *Journal of the American Academy of Child Psychiatry. 1*, 141–166.

Sander, L. W. (1977). The regulation of exchange in the infant caretaker system and some aspects of the context-content relationship. In M. Lewis, & L. A. Rosenblum (Eds.), *Interaction, conversation, and the development of language* (pp. 133–156). New York: Wiley.

Sander, L. W. (1984). The Boston University Longitudinal Study—Prospect and retrospect after twenty-five years. In J. Call, E. Galenson, & R. Lyson (Eds.), *Frontiers of infant psychiatry* (Vol. 2, pp. 137–145). New York: Basic Books.

Sander, L. W. (1991). *Recognition process—Organization and specificity in early human development*. Paper presented at the University of Massachusetts Amherst Conference, Amherst, MA.

Sander, L. W. (1995a). Identity and the experience of specificity in a process of recognition. *Psychoanalytic Dialogues, 5*, 579–595.

Sander, L. W. (1995b, April). *Wholeness, specificity and the organization of conscious experiencing*. Paper presented at the meeting of the American Psychological Association, Division 39, Santa Monica, CA.

Stern, D. N. (1974). Mother and infant at play: The dyadic interaction involving facial, vocal and gaze behaviors. In M. Lewis & L. A. Rosenblum (Eds.), *The effect of the infant on its caregiver* (pp. 187–213). New York: Wiley.

Trevarthen, C. (1979). Communication and cooperation in early infancy: A description of primary intersubjectivity. In M. M. Bllowa (Ed.), *Before speech: The beginning of interpersonal communication* (pp. 321–347). New York: Cambridge University Press.

Tronick, E., Als, H., Adamson, L., Wise, F., & Brazelton, T. B. (1978). The infant's response to entrapment between contradictory messages in face-to-face interaction. *Journal of Child Psychiatry, 17,* 1–13.

Winnicott, D. W. (1965a). The capacity to be alone. In *The maturational processes and the facilitating environment* (pp. 29–37). New York: International Universities Press.

Winnicott, D. W. (1965b). Ego distortion in terms of true and false self. In *The maturational processes and the facilitating environment* (pp. 140–153). New York: International Universities Press.

9

Recognition Process
Context and Experience of Being Known

Although I feel highly honored to have been invited to participate in this conference[EN1] titled "The Psychic Life of the Infant: Origins of Human Identity", Ed Corrigan can tell you I was very reluctant to accept the invitation. My reluctance began with the words to the title. I had to ask myself, just what is the "psychic life" of the infant? And, really, just what is "human identity"? I found I just didn't know exactly what either of those two terms really meant.

There were at least three major obstacles that seemed to be in the way of my accepting the invitation: the first, as I have said, being the meaning of the words in the title. The second obstacle appeared as I thought of the wide range of professions and disciplines that would be represented in the audience: highly disciplined researchers, a whole range of clinicians dealing with infants, parents, children, families, and communities—psychologists, psychiatrists, pediatricians, and world-renowned psychoanalysts. Each individual would bring a different point of view, a different database, a different theoretical framework, each couched in its own language—its own vocabulary. So this obstacle seemed to be that whatever one said, there would be an essential necessity to translate across these different languages. But each time you tried to explain what you meant by some term you wanted to use, you would have to explain the meaning of the words you were using to explain the meaning of the term.

For me this present is a time of convergence of interdisciplinary thinking; It is a time of excitement and movement toward new integrations; it is also a time of new ideas and new words used to express them. I thought here of Colwyn Trevarthen's (1979) notion of the "learning pump," and Christopher Bollas's (1987) term, "genera." New words enable us to think new thoughts and to become aware of new relationships, but it takes a whole paper to explain what each means.

Now, as if these two obstacles weren't enough, the third obstacle to my acceptance of the invitation was the challenge the title posed to confront what is probably one of the most central and ultimate issues in personality development. Probably no challenge could be greater for either the infant researcher or the clinician than to be asked to integrate what each might construct of the inner life of the infant with whatever experience they each might have had with that lifelong process that concerns the matter of human identity. For this, not only must we move between the realm of healthy-normal development and the realm covered by the whole spectrum of pathologies and derailments, but, at the same time, we must deal with one of the essential paradoxes in the developmental process. For me this paradox begins with one of the unavoidable actualities that our longitudinal study has drummed into us, namely, the singularity, the uniqueness, of each individual, each newborn, each family system, and each developmental pathway. On the other hand, however, what we will be hearing a great deal about tomorrow is intersubjectivity; that is, how we are each a part of the other. The challenge as I see it for our integrative talents in this conference is the ultimate one: How can we both be part of each other and singularly unique at the same time?

I was confronting myself with all three of these obstacles as I expressed my reluctance to accept to Ed Corrigan[EN2] in our telephone discussion. On hearing this, he brought his clinical wisdom to the situation: "You don't have to know the answers to all those questions," he said. "We just want to hear how you're thinking about them." Ah, well, that did it, which is why I'm here today.

Before launching into the real task at hand, I would like to say a few words about the broader background for our meeting. As I have said, this is a time of a great convergence of thought, a time of complex interdisciplinary communication, of integration of concepts, of vocabularies, and of efforts. This is exemplified in such books as *Cosmogenesis: A Growth of Order in the Universe*, by David Layzer (1990), professor of astrophysics at Harvard. In this one volume Layzer brings together realms of diverse scientific inquiry in an amazing breadth of information, integrating a present understanding of the creative process from the beginning of the universe to the evolution of human consciousness. Another such extraordinary convergence is that proposed by Gerald Edelman (1992): the process of synaptic selection of neural groupings in development that he calls neural Darwinism. Edelman's conceptualization provides a solution to the way a brain can have evolved that can be aware of its own functioning. It is just the observational and clinical basis now for how self-awareness in the developmental process gains its unique organizational configuration for each developing individual that will be the focus of this chapter.

With Edelman's theory, new significance of previously unrecognized details becomes apparent, such as the two great synaptic flowerings in early development, the one between 8 and 12 months postnatally, and the one between 18 and 24 months. These two spans of time underline the profound significance during those months of the nature of the infant's experience as agent in actively organizing his adaptive behavior and the impact of this agency in the selection of his more enduring neural groupings.

Such details bring to the fore the constructionist perspective on the developmental process.

But, not only is there a convergence of interdisciplinary thinking in the present day, but new theories with new paradigms are appearing, such as chaos theory, that have their own vocabulary of descriptors for the complex, dynamic, nonlinear systems in nature. One key notion in chaos theory is that a minute amount of change, or of new information, if introduced into the iterations of the differential equation representing the system process, becomes an initial condition eventuating in a major later change of direction or an amplification or a diminishment; the system taking some alternative pathway not predictable in any linear fashion from its preceding position. A metaphor might be, that for one approaching this conference with an open mind, receptive to new information, the stage is set for the possibility that a new detail incorporated into that individual's processes of categorization and thought might change the organization of his theoretical construction, and possibly even the direction of his work.

These current exciting happenings make up some of the background then for my approach to our conference title, but my actual approach to our subject is *not* from current sources. It does not begin from psychoanalytic theory and language. It stems from a past generation of biologists who introduced me to the dynamic open systems view of life process. In particularly, I am thinking of Ludwig von Bertalanffy (1949) and Paul Weiss (1968), whose perspectives have provided me with the viewpoint from which I begin. Parenthetically I should say at this point, by the use of the word *infant*, given in our title, I will be thinking of the prerepresentational period of early development.

Von Bertalanffy emphasized that there were two essential features of every living system. One of these was organization and the other was primary activity.

From the level of the cell to the level of the human being, living organization is an active ongoing process, a process of exchange with a context of life support. This is a process of integration that generates and maintains a vital coherence—a unity—of the organism as a whole in the presence of its awesome complexity.

This organizing process is one of active ongoing, endless exchange between the organism as a whole and its own components on the one hand, and, on the other hand, between the organism as a whole and its context of life support—its "network of engagement," so to speak. The organism as a whole has emergent properties beyond the sum of its parts Whatever "structures" may seem permanent to us, whether physical or psychological, are also in process, the impression of permanence being only a consequence of the relative time frame of the observer.

Second, von Bertalanffy emphasized that this active engagement of the organism in the process of exchange is a "primary activity" generated endogenously from within the organism, and not initiated from without. It is an inner impetus that determines each living thing to be self-regulating, self-correcting, and self-generating. In the language of our level of interest in the infant, this impetus is called "agency," which in turn becomes "initiative," and, in my thinking, must be basic to whatever other conditions undergird the "origins of human identity." This endogenous agency or primary activity governs and organizes the essential exchanges between the organism and its context of life support, in which the organism modifies itself or modifies the context to achieve that enduring coordination with its context that the biologist knows as the adapted state. Enduring is the critical word here. Coordination must be enduring to be consistent with the requirements for continuing existence of the organism. Thus, coordination means *over time* as well as *within time*, so to speak. Those organizing themes that govern this process of exchange over time can be even more difficult to define than the more proximal processes in the more immediate foreground of time. An example that is coming to light in the present day is that of "intergenerational transmission" of such themes in the organizing processes of individual behavioral and psychological development.

I would suspect that an association that some of you are having at this moment is to Winnicott's description (1958, 1965) of the infant–mother system, in which the mother is "holding the situation in time." We can ask what does it mean to hold the situation in time? The way I have understood it is that mother and infant engage around the clock in a framework of recurrent "moments of meeting." (*Moments of meeting* is a term I have derived from Martin Buber's observation that "all real living is meeting.") This recurrent framework of moments of meeting in turn sets up a framework of expectancy, a framework that both partners can share in the longer dimensions of time, as a contextual background of continuity of *needed events*, regardless of what *unexpected events* may occur in the foreground. Confirmation of expectancy for the recurrence of such needed events gives a sense of continuity over time. If there continues a recurrent confirmation of that needed expectancy, something like Erickson's sense of basic trust would emerge. Basic trust best defines the nature of a fundamental context for development, namely, that of the organization of the infant–caregiver system as a whole, that stems from this framework in time. Within this framework in time, the infant's "primary activity" becomes its "agency" for self-regulation—the self regulation of its own state, that now becomes a recurrent context, giving the infant's expectancy the quality of enduring continuity. Thus, the idea of enduring as being continuity in some larger contextual framework of reference suggests it as an essential building block at the very origins of the emergence of human identity.

The presence of such an enduring framework of continuity may not be noted in a healthy situation, but its role becomes more obvious when the opposite prevails, and discontinuity and mismatch of expectancy becomes the expectancy. We can ask how then can the situation be "held in time"? Such self-modifications in the elemental organization of the infant, which are necessary to maintain an enduring existence must follow, whenever it is that the infant now must hold the situation in time for itself.

At one extreme we may see the self-modification of "the failure to thrive" infant. At the other extreme may be an effective organization of lively aggressive behavior—or self-concealment behind constant vigilance. (Here we could take a side road and look at the fascinating implications of the genetics of individual differences in the capacity to hold an expectancy, over time, or, to endure over time. How long is it to "wait" for each of us? Here we are at the subject of what resilience is, or at the role of an inherent brevity in a necessary time dimension that contributes to a vulnerability to a later depression.)

Time has a spectrum of highly significant dimensions in the developmental picture. We will hear much of microsecond levels of exchange, and the briefer rhythms from 1 to 2 seconds to 10 to 15 seconds, as well as the longer rhythms of 4 to 6 hours, to those of 24 hours, and even the longer span between major organizational changes over the longer developmental course. Within the different levels in this complex time framework, the agency, that is, the primary activity of the infant, is governing its initiative for its own self-regulation, whether this may be in the direction of approach or of withdrawal. For an organism that has evolved a brain capable of being aware of its own functioning, as Edelman outlined, we can begin to think that some capacity—however dim—that would provide for the higher organism's experience of an awareness of its own agency in initiating and regulating its exchange with its context, would provide a powerful evolutionary advantage. This would be especially so if such capability for self-awareness exposed the organism at the same time to the necessary network configuration that contained the array of options or choices for selection that were available among the organism's alternative pathways of regulatory strategy.

The necessity for an elemental distinction between what any organism makes happen through its initiation of action and what happens to it that is unrelated to its initiation was proposed by von Holst and Mittelstadt (1950) some 50 years ago, as the basic requirement for the organism's construction of a goal-organized plan (what we call now the schema, or scheme).

This emerged from von Holst's study of the goal-organized strike action of the preying mantis, and was formulated in his "reafferrence principle" and his notion of an "efference copy," the central neural configuration organizing the behavior output in the insect to which the reafferrence is essentially compared.

Essentially this is the feedback loop, now elaborated in the concept of reentry and the brain's capacity to be aware of itself, described by Edelman (1992).

I mention this because it suggests a basic reason at the biological level for a process differentiating one's agency to initiate action as being central also to organization at the psychological level. Although psychological complexity is at a next level of magnitude, the problem is the same. The psychological system must, of necessity, also distinguish its own agency for generating action from the agency of the other. In a system comprised of two self-regulating organisms, the infant and the caregiver, the confusion in boundaries at the outset is quite familiar to all of us, especially if we realize the presence of phenomena such as Trevarthen's primary intersubjectivity or projective identification. If these boundaries within the system are confused, indeed, before the infant's capacity for self-awareness has emerged, it is easy to see the confusion, in the process of identity formation and maintenance that must gradually have to resolve later, as the emerging organization of awareness becomes consolidated. We look to the beginnings of the recurrent organization of events in the infant–caregiver system to help explain why the identity process can take an entire lifetime, or never be resolved, or again why it never need be a problem.

What I would like to come to in a few moments in a brief glance at our infancy data are the elements that operate to begin the definition of boundaries as a systems function almost from the outset, but before doing so I would like to draw a bit longer on additional principles from the biological world, basic to ongoing life processes, that may have further relevance both to the "psychic life of the infant" and to "the origins of human identity."

Just as von Bertalanffy saw the essence of living systems to rest on a process he called organization, so Paul Weiss, in a paper of some 30 years ago, pointed to organization in living systems as one of the two great unsolved problems in biology. *Organization* he defined as a "collective property of groups of elements, whose interrelations bind them dynamically into a unit of higher order."

Weiss's illustration of the challenge posed by the matter of organization was dramatic. I quote here from his 1970 paper:

> I have pointed to the "organized" character of brain function. What does that mean? It means the operation of a principal order that stabilizes and preserves the total pattern of the group activity of a huge mass of semiautonomous elements (in this case, brain cells), notwithstanding a tremendous range of individual variation and flux of and among the elements themselves. Our brain contains more than 10 billion nerve cells, each of which averages about 10,000 connections with others; each cell, in turn, contains at a minimum, 10,000 complex macromolecules, not only in constant agitation but being renewed about 10,000 times in a life span. Thus, looking at it from the worm's eye-view of the macromolecule, brain action must deal in a lifetime with at least 10 to the 22nd power (that's 10 with 22 zeros) macromolecular constellations in various degrees of instability and impermanence. A fact that the individual molecule, of course, cannot know, but which our integral brain cannot help but ponder, is that throughout all that *churning and changing* of a population of molecules, which is 10,000 billion times as

large as the human population on earth, we retain intact our sense of individual unity and identity, our habits and our memories.

So Weiss has brought us exactly to the mystery in the phenomenon of human identity, the mystery of coherence, of unity in complexity, that can be found in the entire hierarchy of living systems.

Weiss went on to say:

> Just what sort of principle will be revealed, or will have to be postulated in order to account for that relative stability of a pattern as a whole, despite the infinitely greater autonomous variability of its elements—order in the gross with freedom in the small—is as obscure for the case of brain action as it is for the coordinated activities of all life, or for the integrated wholeness of the development of an individual from an egg. It is one of the great unsolved questions that biology temporarily has bottled up under the label, "organization."

In addressing Weiss's great "unsolved problem" in our confrontation now with the "origins of human identity," which we are addressing at the psychological developmental level, it may be important to begin our thinking with this unity of the living organism as its given essence, rather than trying to construct unity from diverse functions by some subsequent process. Because each infant is already a complexity of unique organization, what we would be looking for in conceptualizing human identity in terms of process would be how maintenance of the coherence of this singularity of organization might be carried out, in spite of a wide range of developmental contexts. Weiss's second great unanswered question in biology may give us a clue to that process. This second question concerns what Weiss calls the chief biological device for establishing and maintaining just those bonds on which this mysterious unity of organization in the living system rests. He identified this as the device of *specificity*. Weiss began with the dictionary definition of *specific* as "having a special *determining* quality." He continued: "In the living world such (special determining) qualities are used universally as means of communication, recognition, affinity relations, selectivity—the basic principle being matched specificities—a sort of resonance between two systems attuned to each other by corresponding properties." Weiss, in effect, in 1970 was proposing a universal principle of matched specificities that determine and maintain the wholeness, the unity implied in the concept of organization.

So, here we are 30 years later addressing the matter of this essential unity, now at the psychological level, in addressing the origins of human identity, but now for our search for understanding we have at our disposal Trevarthen's (1979) primary intersubjectivity, Condon and Sander's (1974) linguistic kinesic synchrony, and Stern's (1985) attunement. If we are to proceed, then, to the level of consciousness in our pursuit of the device of specificity as being the essential key to the coherence in organic unity, we may need to propose a specificity at the level of awareness; that is, to the specificity in another's awareness of what we experience being aware of within ourselves. This specificity I have called recognition process.

Weiss went on to list a dozen examples of the diversity of ways living nature applies this principle of specificity, including the selective recognition of sound waves by the ear in tonal identification, the selectivity that enables nerves growing out from given nerve centers to make functional connections only with predestined types of peripheral tissue to be innervated, the complex array of specificities of recognition on the molecular level that characterize the function of the immune system, and are the substance of molecular biology and genetics.

In general, it is easier to think in terms of specificities related to the foreground of the interactions and exchanges between the component parts of the organism, than to perceive specificities that characterize the organism as a whole in exchange with its larger context. That we can think and perceive the individual in terms of the whole is illustrated by Prechtl, Weinman, and Akiyama's (1969) procedure for assessment of the neurological intactness of both neonate and fetus. This specific observation is that of the overall quality of the infant's spontaneous (i.e., not elicited) general movement. His variables concern the quality of movement of the whole body. He wrote, "It is not surprising that only terms such as complexity, fluency, and elegance capture the characteristics of normal general movement, or, that their absence or reduction indicates an abnormality."

In using his method of direct observation, and, in the fetus, ultrasound imaging for the recognition of quality, interobserver agreement is at the $R = .90$ level and the accuracy in assessing neurological intactness is far greater than can be obtained using elicited movement or any combination of quantitative measures.

Prechtl defined this powerful instrument for analysis of movement as a Gestalt perception, quoting from Conrad Lorenz's famous paper "Gestalt Perception as a Source of Scientific Knowledge":"Gestalt perception is able to take into account a greater number of individual details and more relationships between these than in any rational calculation."

But Lorenz warned:

> Gestalt perception is vulnerable to introspection and to attention to details. What must be learned and practiced is the attitude which allows our faculties to perform optimally. If this is achieved, Gestalt perception is a powerful instrument in the analysis of complex phenomena, and an instrument that cannot be replaced by automated quantification. Complex phenomena require a complex technique of assessment and visual Gestalt perception is such a technique.

Again, it was Prechtl in the 1960s who made fundamental contributions to our understanding of the quality of organization of the whole in his elegant research on infant state, operationally defining infant states on the sleep–awake spectrum. This work culminated in his empirical definition of a "coherence index" that from his 8-hour, five-parameter sleep polygraphy, captured the temporal synchrony or asynchrony over time between these five physiological subsystems; that is, their temporal organization. This determination of coherence of function enabled him to predict successfully the subsequent behavioral functioning of the infant in a rearing situation in a long-term follow-up with Kalverboer.

You are undoubtedly aware that it is just here, in the mother's perception of where within the spectrum of states her infant is at any moment of the day, that specificity begins in the framework of caregiving, a specificity that is essential in facilitating her newborn's own self-regulation.

As this becomes a recurrent recognition in the infant–caregiver system, the temporal framework of the day becomes established that begins a shared expectancy for both participants, a common expectancy necessary for that continuity over time that characterizes "enduring coordination." It is in the perception of her infant as it repeatedly, day after day, moves across the spectrum of states, within the familiar temporal framework, where the infant becomes for her a unique and singular entity—a Gestalt perception of the organism as a whole, within a context as a whole.

An important requirement for this specificity, however, lies in the organization of the focus of attention in both infant and mother, in beginning and defining their "moments of meeting." It is in the quiet-alert state of the newborn in which the capacity to focus attention is present and in which the phenomenon of primary intersubjectivity is encountered, depending in turn on the organization of the mother's focus of her attention on her infant. The focus of attention can be thought of as a powerful integrating function in the organizing process. As such a focus meets between two partners, we have the specificity spoken of by Weiss, now on the level of conscious organization.

One of the important observations in Lynne Murray's (1988) study of postpartum depression is the way the mother's state is translated through her behavior to the organizing process in her infant. As Murray said, her postpartum depressed mothers "fail to catch and then to maintain their infant's attention in the experience of an attuned exchange, so these infants have far less experience of there being a relationship between their own action and events in the world." When we couple this with Edelman's ongoing process of synaptic selection, which consolidates neural groupings through the channels needed for recurrent function, the possibility of an enduring impact of the quality of infant experience in these initial relations on brain organization as a whole needs to be considered. This could involve the patterning of such functions as the organization or disorganization of attention, or the differentiating of the reentry loops that mediate singularity patterns of self-awareness and perceptual categorization, as well as in those necessary and idiosyncratic behavioral strategies needed by the infant for his own self-regulation to reach enduring adaptive coordination with the uniquely idiosyncratic characteristics of his particular caregiving context.

One cannot help, at this point, as we consider the primordial shaping of self-regulatory neural groupings that must be defined by recurring context of events which the infant must survive, of thinking of Christopher Bollas's (1987) "unthought known." Before we speak of internal representation, are there primitive adaptive skills becoming assembled (i.e. procedural knowledge)? These would be procedures that become organized, as when one learns to ride a bicycle. These would be easier to spot in the case of noxious or traumatic early experience than in healthy normal development. Might such procedure themes then underlie and later shape recurring themes of self-organization? These would be illustrated in the enduring of themes of early experience that organize the parent who suffered early abuse, who now abuses his child, or the deep-seated terrors of coming apart, being lost or abandoned, that may underlie the discontinuities of the borderline character (as might arise from the persistence of traumatic mismatches in expectancies that have framed the Gestalt of procedural expectancies derived from these earliest experiences).

We have begun by talking about organization—the quality of wholeness of an organism or of a system, and the emergent properties that appear when that quality of unity or coherence obtains. Let us look now at the infant–caregiver system as a whole, within the recurrent framework of the longer dimensions of time that I have referred to. The recurrences and the expectancies such a system establishes give meaning to the word *enduring* in the notion of adaptive coordination, or to *continuity* in the background sense of expectancy over time, as when we speak of Erickson's "basic trust." How is such a framework set up? How early are these qualities of recurrent experience taken up by the infant? How early do "emergent properties" of the system within the regulatory stability of an enduring coordination begin to appear and what are they? (Keep in mind here I am thinking of the "ordinary good-enough" system of the infant and the caregiver in a state of relative health. I am not getting into what constitutes possible individually unique, genetic characteristics, such as resilience or idiosyncracies of organization such as may be found in the premature or disorganized newborn.)

In our work with our noninvasive,[EN3] continuously operating, automatic bassinet monitor of neonatal state, is there any evidence that an infant–caregiver system shows the beginning of being organized as a whole within these first 10 days? Could there be any effect of Weiss's specificity this early, as having the special determining effect necessary to organize infant and caregiver as a coherent system that might then show emergent properties?

From our studies, we got evidence that the natural mother's specificity of recognition includes not only the recognition of her infant's state at the moment, but where the infant is in its organization around-the-clock—over time itself, so to speak. Because of this stability of recurrence, the organization of the sequence of events over an awakening become expectancies. I've had mothers tell me that it is around 3 weeks postnatally when this sense of knowing the patterns of recurrence over the 24 hours, and the sequence of infant state over the span of an awakening, that the mother has the sense of feeling she now "knows" her new baby. In the presence of such a stable background (i.e., in the presence of such a context of enduring, adaptive coordination over time), the mother's attention can become organized about variations in the more immediate day-to-day stabilities and changes in her infant's behavior and organization of attention, and these patterns, in turn, begin to have signal and communicative meaning.

I see this not as a cognitive achievement but as a feature of the organization of the whole, again having the characteristic of an adaptive skill, like riding a bike, or learning to pitch a ringer in horseshoes. Here we are again at the origins of an "unthought known"—the wonderful expression that Christopher Bollas (1987) has given us.

However, the assimilation of the time framework of that enduring coordination of events that is the background stable regulation becomes organizing for the neonate as well as the mother.

This was demonstrated in our "masking experiment" carried out on the seventh day of life. This was back in those days when the usual lying-in stay of mother and infant in the hospital was 1 week in duration. Again, we had been recording infant states and caregiver interaction around the clock from the delivery room onward with our bassinet monitor, using healthy natural mothers rooming-in with their healthy new babies.

On the morning of the seventh day, as the infant first showed signs of transition to the awake state, we asked the mother to put on a ski mask, but otherwise to carry out her caregiving in every way exactly as she customarily had been doing. Thus, at the appropriate moment, she picked up the infant and began her usual sequence of changing the baby's diapers and gown, holding the baby while getting and preparing the bottle for feeding, and finally sitting down and making herself comfortable in the feeding chair. During these procedures the infant looked in the direction of the mother's face repeatedly without the slightest evidence of a change of state. However, now, as the mother found her comfortable position in the chair, with her infant in her left arm, and only at the moment she brought the nipple of the bottle to the infant's lips, did the effect of looking directly at the mother's face transform the infant in a dramatic surprise reaction. Although its lips were now open, there was not the slightest interest in the nipple that the mother was moving gently in and out to try to get the baby to start sucking. The baby continued staring at the mask, looking at it from different angles as it moved its head from side to side. It was almost a minute and-a-half before the infant finally took the nipple and began sucking. But the feeding was not as customary with the infant gradually becoming drowsier and terminating the feeding by falling asleep as in the days previously. Its state now was one of arousal throughout, with feeding interruptions, spitting up, and choking, followed by a long transition from this state of arousal to sleep, requiring from half-hour to an hour after the mother had returned the infant to the bassinet.

I think we can see here by the seventh day the infant had assimilated the background of the time frame of the awakening and its sequence of kinesics. This now had become a familiar context that could set the stage for the profound reaction to the violation of the infant's expectancy of the familiar configuration of the mother's face that we observed, but it was only at a specific point in the sequence—the moment of accepting the nipple for the onset of sucking—that this violation of expectancy could be experienced so profoundly.

What this illustrates for me is that the familiarity and stability of a time framework of recurrent events and sequences also becomes a background organizing the infant's perceptual focus in the foreground that provides the necessary specificity of exchange and expectancy by which the infant maintains the stability of its own state regulation as a whole. Here, again, we have the organization of the whole and the needed specificity of exchange that Weiss pointed to as the biological device necessary to establish and maintain such coherence. The striking thing for me here is that this organization of the system has come together already at 7 days postnatally. (This finding of the masking study was confirmed in a sample of some 30 infants by Dr. Tom Cassell at Wayne State University; see Cassell & Sander, 1975.)

To further illustrate the relation of initial regulation of infant state to the specificity of maternal interaction we turn to the 3 neonatal samples described in chapter 6. The first sample, Sample A, was reared in the hospital neonatal nursery with feeding and caregiving interventions by the nurses made every 4 hours by the clock, without regard to the state of the infant. At 10 days these infants were placed under the care of one or the other of two special duty nurses. Each nurse then served as a 24-hour, around-the-clock surrogate mother caring for only one infant at a time, feeding the infant on demand, not by the clock, until Day 30. She had no other duties during this time and roomed-in with the infant. At Day 30 the infant went to a foster home, where 24-hour bassinet monitoring continued until Day 60.

In the second sample, Sample B, the newborn infant was assigned on delivery, in random order, to one or the other of these same two women for continuous, rooming-in, 24-hour care over the first 10 days of life. At 10 days the infant was then transferred to the other of the two nurses for care until Day 30. The infant then went to the foster home from Day 30 to Day 60. The critical feature of Sample B was that the nurse's caregiving interventions would be contingent to a prior state change in the infant. In Sample B, another interesting feature of the recurrently familiar face during feeding and the infant's generation of its own self-regulatory devices was demonstrated.

You will recall the Sample A infants who were on 4-hour clock time feedings in the first 10 days in the nursery had a different nurse at each feeding over those first 10 days. Thus, whatever self-regulation they were capable of generating could not anchor to the specificity of a particular face. As you will recall, also, the Sample A babies were transferred on day 10 to the care of a single individual nurse around the clock for the next 20 days, and during this time rapidly increased their looking time at the caregiver's face during the feeding. However, at 30 days on transfer to the new foster home, these infants suddenly stopped looking at the caregiver's face during feedings, only gradually regaining this use of the visual modality as a self-regulatory anchor late in the second month.

Thus, the initial adaptive strategy remained underlying, reemerging as the recurrence of a previously familiar encounter with strange feeders was again experienced.

Principles characterizing the organizing process are suggested by the way self-regulatory adaptive organization proceeds in this early prerepresentational period (where, nevertheless, as we have seen in the masking experiment, perceptual categorization of the familiar must already be underway). One such theme is that the organization of a self-regulatory strategy can remain and be available later as part of the repertory acquired by the infant through its own particular experience with the idiosyncrasies of its recurrent context. A second principle concerns the way new skills or "emergent properties" such as the day–night circadian rhythmicity can appear when the necessary background of enduring coordination or regulatory stability has become the established basis of the infant's framework of expectancy over time. A stable background over time allows the differentiation of new and more refined devices in the infant for dealing with changing events in the foreground of time.

This is also illustrated by our observation of the way infants looked at the faces of the caregiver and of a stranger in a visual perceptual test that Dr. Gerry Stechler (1973) carried out twice[EN4] weekly on the subjects of our three samples over the first 2 months of life. The exposure time of the infant to the variety of facial stimuli in the test was that of a full minute duration for each stimulus. It was only as we carried out the study that we realized that for an infant to look at a human face for 1 minute is a test of limits at this age level. This is a test of limits of the infant's capacity to deal with the excitement and agitation the human face arouses as a visual stimulus for the infant. The infants in Group A, those having spent the first 10 days in the hospital neonatal nursery, more often broke down and cried before the minute of looking at the face stimulus was up, thereby disengaging from the stimulus. The infants in Group C, however, whose caregiver was their own mother, regulated their looking and their visual behavior by actively looking at her face momentarily, then looking away, or looking peripherally at hair or ears or neck, and then looking back, and then looking away again.

The total actual looking time at the facial stimulus was actually significantly less for the Group C infant, but their state regulation was more smoothly preserved. At the same time there was significantly more crying in both Group A and Group B infants during exposure to the caregiver's face.

We can think of this principle of the opportunity for differentiation of the infant's more highly specific self-regulatory devices when there is an enduring coordination of specificity in the broader caregiving exchange that provides the stable background for self-regulation of the infant. This in Ross Ashby's (1952) language would be called "disjoin" or "loose coupling" of such more differentiated infant functions.[EN5]

In other vocabulary loose coupling in the infant's agency to actively organize its behavior, within its changing network of engagement, can be thought of as the self-organizing core of primary activity, a generative impetus that Winnicott identified as true-self development, or that Bollas identified as being restored in the analytic situation as genera. This active self-organizing function will engage its context over the lifetime, constructing and maintaining *coherence*—the person as a whole. We are here again at the origins of human identity in terms of the inner experience of the infant: the experience of its own state.

Here we must also ask again what establishes and maintains this coherent whole of the person. I have suggested it is the experience of specificity in being known, a specificity of recognition in moments of meeting, that in development has a progressively inclusive coherence or integration of a whole—a content of inner experience within a framework of context of outer experience.

One has only to be asked by a stranger, "And who are you?" to appreciate the complexity of what it is to be recognized or known. At what level will you answer? We have tried to capture the progression of complexity in this process of specificity in recognition over the first 3 years of life in terms of the specificity of fitness that is being negotiated over the first 3 years of life in the sequence of seven issues[EN6] of adaptive coordination between infant and caregiving environment. Each issue proposes a direction during that particular time span of development, toward which coordination in moments of meeting must move that will confirm the validity of one's singularity of agency for self-organization. Opportunity for such confirmation of the validity of one's agency is recurrently being provided within the spectrum of intersubjectivities that furnish the necessary matrix for the organizing process.

Within the system in a state of stable equilibrium, the goal-organizing agency, the direction of the intention of each partner, can be sensed by the other, and given reinforcement or enter the process of mutual modification necessary to construct an enduring coordination—the adapted state.

The search for such moments of recognition in the analytic process, for example, as described in Evelyn Schwaber's (1983) concept of psychoanalytic listening, needs the context of process over time shared together between analyst and patient in the process of experiencing awareness of own inner states and their changes as they join in the search for specificity of fittedness in the experience of a mutual recognition. Such specificity of fittedness in moments of meeting also can be conveyed in the opposite direction—from infant to mother by the specificity experienced by her in her infant's behavior. This in turn confirms the mother's coherence of her sense of personal identity, within the caregiving context.

NOTE

This paper was presented at the Conference on the Psychic Life of the Infant: Origins of Human Identity, University of Massachusetts, Amherst, Amherst, MA, June 28, 1991.

EDITORS' NOTES

[EN1] Conference held near the University of Massachusetts, Amherst, June 28, 1991.
[EN2] The person that invited Sander to participate in the conference.
[EN3] Presented extensively in chapters 4 & 6.
[EN4] The experiment is reported in greater detail in chapter 8.
[EN5] Such an argument is already tackled by Sander in chapters 7 and 8, to which we refer.
[EN6] See the chapters in the first part of the text.

REFERENCES

Ashby, R. (1952). *Design for a brain.* London: Chapman & Hall.
Bollas, C. (1987). *The shadow of the object: Psychoanalysis of the unthought known.* New York: Columbia University Press.
Cassell, T. Z., & Sander, L. (1975). *Neonatal recognition processes and attachment: The masking experiment.* Paper presented at the biennial meeting of the Society for Reseach in Child Development, Denver, CO.
Condon, W., & Sander L. (1974). Synchronization of neonatal movement with adult speech. *Science, 183,* 99–101.
Edelman, G. (1992). *Bright air brilliant fire: On the matter of the mind.* New York: Basic Books.
Layzer, D. (1990). *Cosmogenesis: The growth of order in the universe.* New York: Oxford University Press.
Murray, L. (1988). Effects of post-natal depression on infant development. In R. Kumar & I. Brockington, Eds., *Motherhood and mental illness* (Vol. 2). London: John Wright.
Prechtl, H. F. R, Weinman, H., & Akiyama, Y. (1969). Organization of physiological parameters in normal and neurologically abnormal infants. *Neuropaediatrics, 1,* 101–129.
Schwaber, E. (1983). Psychoanalytic listening and psychic reality. *International Review of Psychoanalysis, 10,* 379–392.

Stechler, G. (1973). Infant looking and fussing in response to visual stimuli over the first two months of life in different infant caretaking systems. Presented at the Society for Research in Child Development. Philadelphia, PA.

Stern, D. (1985). *The interpersonal world of the infant*. New York: Basic Books.

Trevarthen, C. (1979). Communication and cooperation in early infancy: Primary intersubjectivity. In M. Bullowa (Ed.), *Before speech: The beginning of interpersonal communication* (pp. 321–347). New York: Cambridge University Press.

Von Bertalanffy, L. (1949). *The problem of life*. New York: Harper.

Von Holst, E., & Mittelstadt, H. (1950). Das Reafferenz Prinzip [The Re-afference Principle]. *Naturwiss, 37,* 464–489.

Weiss, P. (1968). The living system: Determinism stratified. In A. Koestler & J. Smythies (Eds.), *The Alpbach Symposium*. Boston: Beacon Press.

Weiss, P. (1970). Whither Life Science, *American Scientist*, 58: 156–163.

Winnicott, D. (1958). Transitional objects and transitional phenomena. In *Collected papers*. New York: Basic Books.

Winnicott, D. (1965). *The maturational processes and the facilitating environment*. New York: International Universities Press.

Part 3

Part 3 opens with an elaboration of Von Bertalanffy's basic principle of organization, essential for life in the living system. The overall perspective organizing Chapter 10 can be found in the way "process" in living systems can move an increasing inclusiveness of complexity toward and increasing coherence and unity of the whole.

Chapter 11 is a brief enlargement on the early development of self-awareness in the infant as the foundation for the experience of self-recognition, as regulation of state in the mother-infant system achieves recurrence, restoration, and continuity. Self-awareness, coupled with the experience of the state of the "other," moves the system toward an increasing level of inclusiveness of coherence.

Chapter 12 presents previously unpublished material. It is an illustration in the life of one individual of the way a common background of principles of process in all living systems provides a context of meaning as we encounter life's uncertainties. Uncertainty in the trajectory of the life span is a powerful element, and inner strength and resilience of the developing person is called upon to encounter, endure, and transcend as life progresses.

This section concludes with an attempt to bring together the sequence of projects and papers accumulated over a life's work and link them to the psychotherapeutic process. The linkage is accomplished through "specificity", an experience in the interaction between patient and therapist that can be seen to be crucial to change in therapy.

10

Reflections on Developmental Process
Wholeness, Specificity, and the Organization of Conscious Experiencing

If you think about the developmental process, you need to open up or dissolve the boundaries between the enclosures formed by our different languages and viewpoints or you might say, our different constructions of how it all goes together.[EN1] The opening of boundaries allows the construction of a new perspective that will have even broader inclusiveness. The act of loosening the constraints that our constructions have set up and experiencing the opening of new vistas can set the stage for a positive experience: the experience of entering a context of greater inclusiveness. As a metaphor for the basic direction of engagement in the living system, we could call it something like "a moment of vitalization."

Obviously, life-span development is a vast complexity. All that my brief comments here can include will be bits and pieces—snapshots taken from a reel of movie film—a moment frozen from the endless flow of an ever ongoing process that is a life story. But, the big question will remain, how do we put snapshots together to make the real movie again?

This brings us to the first thing that intrigues me about long-term developmental processes. It is what you might call the problem of "wholeness"—coherence—in how it all goes together. Wholeness suggests to me the organization of an almost infinite complexity into a single coherent unity. An example is the individual organism in which a certain unity holds together an incredible diversity of components. This is the essential vital requirement for life to exist at all. Organization (in the living organism) depends on a hierarchy, or scaling of lesser component coherences that are nested within larger, more inclusive coherences. The intriguing question is how do we account for the holding together, the coherence of the larger organization, on which life rests? What connects part to part and part to whole? Even more, what holds the organism together over time, while it is engaged in an endless process of exchange with an ever changing, even larger coherence—its ecology?

In his delightful paper, "A Stroll Through the Worlds of Animals and Men," Jakob Von Uexküll (1934), biologist and ethologist early in this century, invented his own language to point out that each creature constructs for itself how it "all goes together." There is not just one space or one time for all the diverse creatures that inhabit the world around us. Each creature is an engineer that operates those tools that it has—its perceptual tools and its effector tools, be they few and simple or many and complex—to construct its *Umwelt,* its subjective or self-world. He wrote, "The organism picks out of the general environment those stimuli *specific* for it, and spins his relations to certain characters of the things around him, weaving them into a firm web that carries his existence."

I am sure many of you have been impressed in the past few years by the flood of new books, authored by some of the world's greatest minds—scientists, Nobel laureates, philosophers, theologians—each trying to "put it all together" from different disciplinary approaches, from uniquely different individual perspectives, using different disciplinary languages so to speak, in their choice of the words and the meanings given them, with which they construct their concepts. Among the Nobel laureates in the past few years, you may have seen Steven Weinberg's (1992) *Dreams of a Final Theory,* or Murray Gell-Mann's (1994) journey from *The Quark to the Jaguar,* or Charles Townes (1997), the Nobel laureate who invented the laser, bringing mind, matter, and spirit together in his book, *Making Waves.* There are others: Henry Stapp (1993), the Lawrence Livermore Laboratory's theoretical physicist and his book, *Mind, Matter, and Quantum Mechanics;* David Layzer (1990), the Harvard astrophysicist, who, in his book *Cosmogenesis: The Growth of Order in the Universe,* goes from the Big Bang to consciousness; E.O. Wilson (1990) *Consilience, the Unity of Knowledge;* M. Mitchell Waldrop (1992) in his story of the work at the Santa Fe institute presents the "Vision of the Whole" in his book entitled merely *Complexity;* with Stuart Kauffman, a Santa Fe Institute scientist, in his book *The Origins of Order,* giving the microbiologist's view of organismic evolution resting on the interaction of the self-organizing system with what he called "spontaneous order"; that is, an ultimate coherence may be the ubiquitous potential of matrices of sufficient complexity. But we can ask, how do we account for so many of us trying to "put it all together"—a "direction" that can be traced from the toddler's dropping his spoon, to experiment with whether or not mother will pick it up, to the theoretical physicists' cosmogenesis? Each seems to be asking: Just how does the system work? Is there some *directionality* inherent in the mystery of wholeness?[1] The coherence of the living organism within its ecology?

Weiss (1970), in effect, proposed a universal principle of matched specificities that determine and maintain the wholeness, the unity implied in the concept of living organization.

Weiss talked about the specificity between two component systems that *meet*, each already configured as to their properties. *Specificity,* for Weiss, is not only the lock-and-key, fitting together, of their specific configurations but the time dimension of their meeting, a sequencing, with a preliminary flow of movements of each that allows them to join at a particular moment to create a more inclusive *coherence* of organization, and a following flow that represents the configuration of consequence.

Most of you have noticed how often the word *coherence* is coming into the language of developmental research. You may have encountered Heinz Prechtl's (1990) *coherence index,* which he derived from his continuous 8-hour, five-parameter, polygraphic newborn sleep state recording. His five parameters were EEG, eye movement, heart rate, respiratory rate, and body movement. In neonatal sleep state recording, each of these physiological subsystems shows a fluctuating rhythmicity as the infants' sleep moves from active, or REM sleep, to quiet sleep and back to REM sleep. The five physiological rhythms are being continuously recorded over an 8-hour run. Prechtl's coherence index is a single number derived from calculation of the exactness of synchrony, or asynchrony, these five rhythms show in the timing of their togetherness as they flow over time within the larger rhythmicity of the infants' sleep states, which an observer is recording and timing.

This measure of synchrony among these physiological subsystems—that is, how coherent the physiology of an observed sleep state is—proves to be an indicator of the well-organized or poorly organized newborn.

Another example of coherence is Mary Main's Adult Attachment Interview (AAI) that she uses in the study of the security or insecurity of attachment, which infants show at the end of the first year of life in the Ainsworth stranger paradigms. From the recorded AAI, she derives a coherence variable, using a complex and inclusive evaluation of this single session. Not only is the mother's developmental history, her early relationships and experience with caregivers evaluated, but the way she tells her story: its clarity or vagueness, or contradictions, her logic of sequencing in her story, as well as how she interacts with the interviewer; in other words, the extent to which she "has it all together" in her life, thinking, and expression.

Main has found that when the AAI is given to a mother during her pregnancy, the coherence variable derived from the interview will predict at a .75 or .80 level of correlation to the assessment of measures of "security" or "insecurity" of attachment that her infant will show at the end of its first year of life in the Ainsworth Stranger Paradigm.

Let us return for a moment to wholeness in the organization of brain function, at the level of the organization of conscious experiencing, that Weiss introduced by referring to the enduring coherence represented by the sense of identity. How do we begin to think about a wholeness con-structed by the brain that would be necessary for the consolidation of a coherent sense of identity? We can begin at that highly complex level of brain function, one that provides a background for perception, the con-struction of the *gestalt*. A familiar example is the Kanizsa figure, in which we "see" a triangle when there are only three correctly angled dots on the page. The profound significance of this elemental capacity of the brain is better illustrated in Heinz Prechtl's newborn research design for assessing the central nervous system intactness of the premature newborn's brain, a brain often damaged in various ways, at or before delivery, by prior genet-ic-developmental events. His method is to observe the newborn's sponta-neous whole-body movement, using the variables of description, such as complexity, fluency, and elegance. With these variables he obtained .90 cor-relation of agreement between observers. Using these variables in assess-ing neurological intactness in samples of premature infants, he obtained a far greater accuracy than can be obtained using elicited movement, or any combination of quantitative measures. In describing his results, Pre-chtl quoted from Konrad Lorenz's paper entitled, "Gestalt Perception as a Source of Scientific Knowledge."[EN2]

We are so attentive to the foreground of perception that we forget entirely about this background of wholeness, which includes the config-uring flow of preliminary sequencing and timing, leading up to an event and its ensuing flow of consequence. Such an organization of gestalts over time translates easily to the language of Sylvan Tomkins: the construction of scenes and their assembly into scripts. If we are to include the language of biology, the enduring existence of living systems depends on adapta-tion, the ongoing fitting together of the configurations of two spheres of organizational coherence (that of the organism and that of its ecology). This is a moving, ongoing fitting together over time, as well as within time. We can think of adaptation at the level of the organization of human consciousness in early development as the fitting together of two spheres of coherence, the gestalts of the flow of sequencing and expectancy in both infant and caregiver. The gestalt within which each acts brings together the complexity of sequencing, and the expectancy that repetition and recurrence previously has generated in each, up to a "now moment of meeting" between them, each such moment enfolding all that has gone before, as each partner organizes to engage the other. If the "meeting" has Weiss's device of specificity[EN3] in their fitting together, we will have a posi-tive moment—a vitalization—or in Tomkin's language an "amplification" or "affluence." On the other hand, in case of a moment of misfit, the reor-ganization that follows in the flow of consequent moments provides the place for the negotiation or the mutual modification necessary to reach the more enduring coordination that the word adaptation has always implied. A third possibility is that the moment of meeting will be a failed moment, with relative disorganization and lessened coherence following.

Walter Freeman's (1994) work with the olfactory bulb of rabbits reveals how the brain functions in just this way. Freeman placed 64 electrodes on the rabbit's olfactory bulb, from which he then obtained recordings of *patterns* of firings that combine the firings of each clustering of neurons that is tapped by each of the electrodes. He then supplied an odor or smell to the rabbit, obtained the patterns resulting, and its updating, as he trained the rabbit in an experimental paradigm initiated by the smell as a stimulus until he obtained a stable pattern. Then he supplied a brand-new odor the rabbit had never been exposed to before. A brand-new pattern was obtained that was "held" by the rabbit brain as such, but, as a consequence of exposure to the new smell, Freeman found that the complex pattern that had been stabilized for the first smell now changed. Freeman proposed from these findings that the brain is in constant function to bring all previous experience, memory, and learning up to a "now" moment, in anticipation of the next step to be taken, the next move to be made.

It seems obvious how crucial such a capability must be for adaptation, as an essential "process for life." If we think in such terms, the *place* of time and moments of meeting between an organism and its ecology become clear. We can have a "now" moment, a moment of fittedness with the association of vitalization, or, we can have a missed moment, including the subsequent flow of a consequent experience, shaping the process of repair and reorganization, or the disorganization of a failed moment. The *vitalization* associated with acts of engaging in opportunities for reaching states of ever more inclusive coherence in now moments of specificity of meeting can be thought of as giving a basic *direction* to evolutionary biology.

Gerald Edelman (1987, 1988, 1989, 1992) has couched his theory of neuronal group selection—his neural Darwinism—in just this framework of adaptation. He demonstrated the way successful fitting together of organism and its ecology on the outside can govern the process of selection or extinction, the shaping of patternings and neuronal groupings going on inside the brain. We can think of such a process of mutual coordination as a further example of a process creating the more inclusive coherence by combining or joining two lesser coherences by the "device of specificity" operating in the configuration of their engagement. Edelman has given us a picture of the way a continuous process in the updating of brain organization can be based on such functions as categorization, mapping, and reentry. Central to the reentry function in the human would be the brain's capacity to be aware of its own function, aware of the moment of its own initiation of the next act, the capacity for self-awareness in the "now" moment of Walter Freeman. The selection process on neuronal grouping that Edelman proposed would emerge from the bias set on the selection process by the limbic system, which he termed "limbic system values," a term to which the word I have used (i.e., vitalization) could be translated.

On the other hand, the vitalization might be provided by the specificity of a "now" moment of meeting of two such states of consciousness, in which the way one would know oneself would be matched by the way one was known by an other.

Recurrent experiencing of recurrent sequences in the flow of engagement between interacting partners, and the expectancies that become shaped by recurrence, would provide additional inclusiveness of specificity or the lack of it that would come to govern experiencing of continuities, discontinuities, and directionality in recurrent engagements. When the directionality of both partners becomes joined, specificity of recognition becomes transforming, giving new continuity of coherence to organization; that is, the organization of individual consciousness and the organization of both partners as a system.

I have given the name recognition process to this "determining" quality of Weiss's matched specificities at the level of human awareness, one that establishes and maintains the coherence of organization implied by the sense of identity.

I know of no better description that is generally available than that of the process Winnicott (1972) described in his book *Therapeutic Consultations in Child Psychiatry*. He described and illustrated with many case examples the interactive process between therapist and child that goes on as each alternates drawings in the game he called "squiggles." Winnicott detailed the drawings by which each embellishes the squiggle of the other, within the context of Winnicott's sensitive clinical observations, to bring them both to a moment of shared awareness, as the child becomes aware that another is aware of what the child is aware of within. This is a moment of specificity in recognition that Winnicott has called the *sacred moment*—a "moment of meeting" that involves a new coherence in the child's experiencing of both its inner and its outer worlds of awareness. The consultations Winnicott described were often single diagnostic sessions, but if the sacred moment of being "known" was reached, there ensued a change in the child's self-regulatory organization that endured over many years, even from just that one experience.

Recognition as a *process* has been chosen to indicate the flow of sequence before and consequence after a potential "now" moment of meeting that child and caregiver negotiate to reach the specificity of recognition. A process of *negotiation* (in the language of biology, this would be the process of adaptation that the biologist refers to as a process of "mutual modification to reach enduring coordination") is a preliminary experience necessary to lead up to a moment of recognition. This is because the participants are in a dynamic system, a system always constrained by opposing forces; we call them now *dialectic tensions*.

A basic polarity of contrasting forces from the very outset to the very end of the life span is that between being together with and being distinct from. From birth onward the whole realm of biologically enabled microsecond synchronies of "primary intersubjectivity" (Trevarthen, 1979) and "attunement" (Stern, 1985) provide the positive affects and behavioral engagements that move infant and caregiver to be together with. On the other hand, the also biologically determined requirement that the infant as a living organism be *self*-regulating and *self*-organizing necessitates recognition in the system of the agency of the infant to initiate action toward these ends. Competence of the infant-as-agent to initiate and self-organize desired states or goals recurrently within the constraints of the infant's own unique context provides the experiencing and the effects of being distinct from. At the same time if such competence becomes an enduring configuration of adaptation in the system, the stage is set for experiencing the continuity of sense of self-as-agent. It is not only the coherence or unity in the sense of sameness we would like to understand, but also its continuity. The experience of continuity must firmly underlie the subsequent development of the sense of identity.

Elsewhere[EN4] I have proposed that, over the first 3 years of life, it is just such a process governing the interpersonal negotiation of central adaptations between child and family context that establishes the organization in the system on which the child's sense of identity can build. I have described seven such adaptations, points of possible bifurcation in the pathway toward constructing the coherence of a valid and enduring sense of identity, but that is another story.

In identifying the pathways of true self and false self development, Winnicott captured both the nonlinear open-endedness and at the same time the enduring consequence of the early engagements that potentially might underlie the identity process for the duration of the individual's entire life. The true self pathway of adaptation establishes self-regulation on the basis of a recognition of inner experiencing, of subjectivity and intersubjectivity. The false self pathway requires a behavioral fitting together based on outer criteria demanded by the child's caregiving context, that is not shaped by the specificity that recognition of subtleties of inner experiencing makes possible.

There is a rapidly emerging interest in psychoanalysis as a dialectically oriented discourse within the spheres both of subjectivity and intersubjectivity. Schwaber's (1983) viewpoint on psychoanalytic process that she refers to as psychoanalytic listening is relevant here. She described the analyst as observant of the flow of the patient's state and especially of shifts in state during the course of the hour, and their context. Concurrently the analyst must be keenly aware of the flow of the analyst's own inner subjective experiencing and the location of its shifts and changes. When a shift in either is encountered, it marks a point of opportunity for further exploration of the patient's associations and meanings, or the opportunity for orchestrating the specificity of a moment of recognition—a "now" moment of meeting—in the ongoing dialogue between analyst and patient.

Perhaps my thinking about "wholeness" in the ever-ongoing process of development over the life span can be summarized, in conclusion, by the argument for wholeness and the implicate order put forth by the theoretical physicist David Bohm (1980) in his book of the same name, in which he *begins* with the statement that his main concern is with "understanding the nature of reality in general, and of consciousness in particular, as a coherent whole which is never static or complete, but which is in an unending process of movement and unfoldment."

Bohm ended with the statement:

> We propose that the basic element be a *moment* which, like the moment of consciousness, cannot be precisely related to measurements of space and time, but rather covers a somewhat vaguely defined region which is extended in space and has duration in time. The extent and duration of a moment may vary from something very small to something very large, according to the context under discussion (even a particular century may be a "moment" in the history of mankind). As with consciousness, each moment has a certain *explicate* order, and in addition it *enfolds* all the others, though in its own way. So the relationship of each moment in the whole to all the others is implied by its total content: the way in which it "holds" all the others enfolded within it.

I think I have tried to communicate to you the way I think about wholeness, and the flow of moments. Specificity in the implicate order of a moment of "meeting" enfolds the whole within it.

NOTE

1. One of the most intriguing things to me about wholeness is, that although it is there at the forefront of it all, we have the greatest difficulty talking about it, or even thinking about it, even though it is what "is," that is, our being. It is there but is not represented. Christopher Bollas (1989) gave us language to use: "the unthought known."

EDITORS' NOTES

[EN1] The contribution was presented by Sander at the American Psychological Association Division 39 Symposium in Santa Monica, CA, April 29, 2005.
[EN2] This topic was covered extensively in chapter 9.
[EN3] See chapter 9.
[EN4] See the chapters in Part One.

REFERENCES

Bohm, D. (1980). *Wholeness and the implicate order.* London: Routledge & Kegan Paul.
Bollas, C. (1989). *Forces of destiny: Psychoanalysis and human idiom.* London: Free Association Books.
Edelman, G. M. (1987). *Neural Darwinism: The theory of neural group selection.* New York: Basic Books.

Edelman, G. M. (1988). *Topobiology: An introduction to molecular embryology.* New York: Basic Books.

Edelman, G. M. (1989). *The remembered present: – A biological theory of consciousness.* New York: Basic Books.

Edelman, G. M. (1992). *Bright air brilliant fire: On the matter of the mind.* New York: Basic Books.

Freeman, W. (1994). *Societies of brains.* Hillsdale, NJ: Lawrence Erlbaum Associates, Inc.

Gell-Mann, M. (1994). *The quark and the jaguar.* New York: Freeman.

Kauffman, S. A. (1993). *The origins of order: Self-organization and selection in evolution.* New York: Oxford University Press.

Layzer, D. (1990). *Cosmogenesis: The growth of order in the universe.* New York: Oxford University Press.

Prechtl, H. F. R. (1990). Qualitative changes of spontaneous movement in foetus and pre-term infants are a marker of neurological dysfunction. *Early Human Development, 23,* 151–159.

Schwaber, E. (1983). Psychoanalytic listening and psychic reality. *International Review of Psychoanalysis, 10,* 379–392.

Stapp, H. (1993). *Mind, matter, and quantum mechanics.* Berlin: Springer-Verlag.

Stern, (1985). *The Interpersonal World of the Infant.* Basic Books: New York.

Townes, C. (1998). *Making waves.* American Institute of Physics.

Trevarthen, C. (1979). Communication and cooperation in early infancy: Primary intersubjectivity. In M. Bullowa (Ed.), *Before speech: The beginning of interpersonal communication* (pp. 321–347). New York: Cambridge University Press.

Von Uexküll, J. (1934). A stroll thru the worlds of animals and men. In C. H. Schiller (Ed.), *Instinctive behavior.* New York: International Universities Press.

Waldrop, M. M. (1992). *Complexity: The emerging science at the edge of chaos.* New York: Simon & Shuster.

Weinberg, S. (1992). *Dreams of a final theory.* New York: Pantheon.

Weiss, P. (1970). Whither life science? *American Scientist, 58,* 156–163.

Wilson, E. O. (1999). *Consilience: The unity of knowledge.* New York: Vintage Books.

Winnicott, D. (1972). *Therapeutic consultations in child psychiatry.*

11

Awareness of Inner Experience
A Systems Perspective on Self-Regulatory Process in Early Development

I would like to offer a few reflections on three quite disparate realms of thought such as the constructionist viewpoint in development, integration, and individual uniqueness, by drawing from three areas of research I carried on over the years.

The first area is that of a detailed observational study of mother–infant interaction over the first 3 years of life. The second major area of research is the study of the development of 24-hour infant state organization and regulation along the sleep–awake dimension over the first 2 months of life. Finally, the third, and perhaps most fascinating research task of the last half-dozen years, is the study of the 25- to 30-year life span of development at outcome on those same individuals we had observed so closely as infants.

From the integration of ideas suggested by this lifetime of research experience, we would like to propose a ground plan for our thinking about the individual's life span trajectory as a unique construction within a unique context. We are presenting these comments as ideas, as reflections, as ways of thinking about life-span development, not as findings, or results of direct empirical analysis.

We are beginning to think differently about early development these days than we did a decade ago. We are moving now from ideas of linear causality to systems thinking and the matter of "organization." Alan Sroufe (1979, 1982) referred to this as the "organizational perspective." We have gone from the search for first causes to the search for process. In living systems it is not organization that develops; we begin with organization. Any enduring existence in nature requires the organism to maintain a regulated, ongoing exchange with the surround. Properly timed and appropriately self-regulatory and self-righting functions arise from an endogenous origin of "primary activity." Von Bertalanffy described two basic properties of living matter: namely, organization and primary activity. This is an endogenous origin of the organism's initiation of action or function that ensures self-activation for the purpose of self-regulation within the specific environment that is that organism's environment of evolutionary adaptation. In short, our search for "process" in the living system leads us to a self-organizing complex (von Bertalanffy, 1952), wherein the initiative for the self-organizing function inherently arises from within the individual organism and cannot be subsumed by any extrinsic condition or other agency. We will expect then that a search to locate the source for the initiation of the organism's action or function will begin our understanding of the organizing process we know as life process.

In taking this organizational perspective, we begin with a great many already established lawful principles that have advanced the understanding of organization in living systems. Major examples of bodies of lawful principles that govern the ongoing exchange between organism and environment are those of regulation, of adaptation (or "fitting together") with a central principle of specificity as the essential ingredient that insures fitting together at every level of adaptation, as emphasized so lucidly by Paul Weiss (1947, 1949).

The integrative design that guarantees coherent function of the diverse and multimodal subsystems of the complex living organisms depends on another domain of lawful biological principles. There are a great number of built-in ways that living systems have evolved as the means to accomplish the necessary integration that ensures organismic unity. These cannot be detailed at this point (e.g., Sherrington, 1923). We will select only one such integrative mechanism in this brief essay, namely, that integration of the multiple physiological, functional, and behavioral subsystems we refer to by the concept of *state*. We can begin with the recurrent and clearly recognizable states of the newborn on the sleep–awake continuum. Here in the healthy newborn there is an integration of a remarkable complexity of physiological subsystems that can be read at once by the observer in a single pattern of behavioral variables. This same phenomenon of the integration of complexity and unity characterizes the emotional states. This is now a subject of great current research interest, at present more often designated by the term *affect*.

We cannot escape the fact that, on another level and for the human organism, inner experience in the domain we call the self also can be a remarkable integration of components and functions. The sense of self is a multidimensional experience including the sense of the body in space, through the sense of agency, finally including what Winnicott termed the infant's sense of "own" or of being oneself. In other words, he is referring here to the infant's sense of self-recognition in the beginning awareness of agency, as effectance in self-regulation of his own state begins to be experienced (Winnicott, 1965). Erikson (1950) long ago suggested, in formulating his final stage of development, that these principles of integrative construction in the organizing process of the living system move us over the life-span trajectory toward a final stage of integration. He labeled this simply *integrity*.[EN1] Conversations in the Boston Change Process Study group have led us now to use the expression *co-creation* rather than *construction*.

CONSTRUCTIONIST VIEWPOINT

We can turn briefly now to the different perspectives offered by our three areas of research. Our study of mother–infant interaction over the first 3 years of life provided the data for our first effort to propose a constructionist view of self-regulation within the organizing process of personality development over the first 3 years of life. We proposed that this organizing process over the first 3 years of life really consisted of the negotiation between infant and caregiver of a sequence of adaptations, or fitting together. By this we mean the achievement by mother and infant of those new and specific coordinations that become necessitated by the advancing levels on which the infant can initiate new behaviors and activities. Each level presents the caregiving system with a new requirement for regulation. Each creates an issue as to how, or in what way, for a unique infant within a unique caregiving system, the unique configuration of specific coordinations necessary to achieve an enduring harmony of regulation will be achieved. Such adaptation of one partner to the other is a matter of mutual modification involving both alloplastic and autoplastic modifications. Our initial formulations proposed seven such issues for the construction of adaptive solutions that will be unique for any given mother–infant pair.[EN2] This epigenetic sequence of adaptive strategies constructed by the participants then provides a framework or logic for describing an organizing process that would lead first to a unique behavioral organization within a particular system and then to character organization in the developing child.

At issue in the negotiation of each of the adaptations in the epigenetic sequence is the extent to which, and the manner in which, the self-activating, self-regulating principles governing the exchange between infant and caregiving environment can generate the conditions necessary for recurrent, coherent inner experiences in the infant (Sander, 1962). The idea is that such recurrent, coherent, and desired inner experiences of the infant, in the negotiation of each level of mutual adaptation between infant and caregiver, establish such inner experience as the inner set-point or goal criterion around which new inputs are matched (in the model of the goal-organized schema; Wolff, 1960). The modifications of behavior necessary for goal realization, when successful, generate the situations associated with the infant's reexperience of familiar or desired states. In other words, in the frequently recurrent regulatory situations in the system, the infant's desired states become his goals. The sequence of seven issues we proposed for the first 3 years of life advanced from adaptations related to initial sleep–awake state regulation, to reciprocal behavioral coordinations, "attunements" as Stern (1985) would describe it, to "recognition" as the sixth issue late in the second year of life (Sander, 1975). This is a time when much interaction is being carried out on the level of perceived or inferred intentions for behavior both by infant and caregiver. At issue here again is the specificity that the infant experiences as the infant becomes aware that another is aware of what the infant is aware of within himself. At issue in the mutual modifications of infant and caregiver, which are necessary to achieve the sequence of adaptive coordinations, is the extent to which the system provides support in enabling the infant to use this inner perception. There will be varying degrees to which an infant can rely on this awareness of his own state as a guide to regulate successfully his own behavior within his particular caregiving system. It is a time in which the infant experiences validation or invalidation by the caregiving system of this awareness of his own inner experience as a reliable guide for the construction of new adaptive schemes in the exchanges with the caregivers.

INTEGRATION

We turn now in this brief commentary to the second area of our research: namely, that concerning the initial regulation of infant states over the first 2 months of life. From this extensive work, which studied infant and caregiver together continuously around the clock as a regulatory system, we were introduced to a whole domain of organizational principles related to biorhythmicity, entrainment, phase synchrony, and especially temporal "coherence" among physiological subsystems. Here again is another domain of lawful principles of integration.

Three central factors in the organization of the infant–caregiver system have stood out from our experience in investigating the basic role of biorhythmicity in the organization of living systems. One condition that the 24-hour (circadian) nature of biorhythmicity sets up for the infant–caregiving system is a daily recurrent situation beginning, of course, with the daily recurrence of four to six awakenings of the infant. This provides an essential condition of repetition over and over of infant state sequences and caregiving events on which habituation and learning can be based. A second essential organizational framework that the phenomenon of biorhythmicity sets up for both infant and caregiver is a time structure of this 24-hour day that they both come to share. It is at the point when a first level of adaptation is achieved, involving stable regulation of infant states on the sleep-awake continuum, that the shared time structure can become the basis for expectancies that are common to both infant and caregiver. This might also be identified as a first level on which the intersubjective world so beautifully described by Stern (1985) might be said to begin, but it would be part of a stably regulated, competent system in a state of adapted coordination and not the property of any single or nonadapted component within that system. Such shared time structure provides for each partner a common basis for the meaning of recurrent behaviors in the day's sequence of events. For example, an important measure for a mother's reading of the meaning of her infant's crying depends on the time at which it occurs in the familiar event structure of the day. A third element that the early temporal structure provides in a stably regulated infant–caregiver system is the experience of the "meeting" of infant and caregiver in states of matched readiness or expectancy. This is not a matter of one eliciting a response from the other, but a temporally synchronized meeting in states of matched expectancy and readiness of one for the other. For example, the breast-feeding mother comes to expect when her infant will soon be waking from his nap because her breasts are becoming filled. The adapted harmony or equilibrium of regulation that sets the temporal synchrony for such moments provides a common experience for both infant and caregiver; the responsibility for regulation does not rest on a necessary prior disharmony or distress within one or the other of interacting partners, but is now a property of an adapted system. This can be viewed as a matter of profound significance in biasing infant expectation for what is "given" in relation to what is to be "gotten," namely, the analog, of the foundation for the emergence of trust.

INDIVIDUAL UNIQUENESS

The third area of our research we mentioned at the outset concerns the study of the life span of the 30 infants we began with in 1954 that led to the formulation of our attempt at a constructionist view of development that we alluded to earlier; that is, the conceptualization of a sequence of issues in the interactional adaptation between infant and caregiver. We will underline only one outstanding lesson here that we have learned from this follow-up research. We have been unable to escape the actuality of uniqueness in every aspect of each subject's data. The closer one looks, the greater individuality is apparent.

The significance of uniqueness is not how one can judge that uniqueness from normative standards but what organizing processes and relationships account for it and depend on it, and what the significance is of recognizing the specific ways an individual is unique. We ask in what degree is recognition of that uniqueness a necessary element in shaping the individual's construction of his life-span trajectory? We can ask, after decades of studying the normative, is it possible that attention to uniqueness will now have a new significance in developmental research instead of our merely continuing to limit ourselves to the repair of tragedies and deficits in this early developmental process? What aspects of that uniqueness will be critical to recognize? It will certainly be central if we are to address the optimizing of early developmental processes for any child. A major effort in the self-psychology approach to the therapeutic process is that of enabling the individual not only to discover his own inner experience but to recognize, validate, and esteem its uniqueness. In what we have touched on in this brief essay, we can see a linkage among biological origins, developmental process, life-span trajectory, and therapeutic process. The integration of processes common to each of these domains we propose centers on the occurrence or experience of specificity in the recognition process. This integration we refer to now as recognition process theory.

The hypothesis that we are looking at in the longitudinal study follow-up is that the configuration of adaptive strategies that the child by 2 years of age has constructed in fitting together with his own particular unique caregiving context provides a configuration that is recognizable in the way that individual at outcome is constructing his ecologic niche and his world of self-regulation. This is a recognizability of configuration, not a correlation.[EN3] What if instead of beginning our conceptualization of psychological development with an undifferentiated newborn, we began with the idea that the organizing process in development begins with specificity in the exchanges between infant and caregiver that are at the highest and most differentiated level of organization of which each is capable? We are referring to the organization of experiences of awareness on which the organization of consciousness would rest. The idea is that "experiencing" is possible from the outset, at least the outset of postnatal life. This experiencing we propose is especially in terms of the infant's own inner state, which, as we have noted in speaking of the biorhythmic structure of organization in the infant–caregiver system, is regularly recurrent. Can we consider that it might be in the way, from the outset, that the highest levels of organization possible can come into a specificity of exchange that may play a critical role in biasing the sequential logic organizing the longer term trajectory of developmental construction? Remember, we are here beginning with prerepresentational experience in the earliest months of life, where the infant's action directly can change his own state, not some representation or symbol of it. If inner awareness is the critical experience in the infant's self-regulation of his own states, construction of adaptive strategies and behavioral organization within the infant's own particular system proceeds as this awareness of his own state becomes the inner criterion or set point of goal-organizing schemata. This would be especially so when such strategies and behavioral organizations come to be based on the infant's experiences of competence as agent in successfully regulating his own desired states. This is achieved in the regularly recurrent interactive situation of the adapted infant–caregiver system as the infant's own desired states become his goals.

SUMMARY

These ideas can be summarized in a framework of five propositions (Sander, 1985). At the moment they can be thought of as a kind of logic of construction by which the individual shapes his longer term developmental trajectory. Very briefly, the five steps run somewhat as follows:

1. The infant's initial inner experience consolidates around the experience of his own recurrent states. The initial ego is not a body ego but a state ego.

2. The infant's own states, where coherent, recurrent, desired, or essential to key regulatory coordinations, become the primary target or goals for behavior. By states we must include emotional states that have their own configurational indicators from birth onward (i.e., the affects).

3. Infant competence in initiating and organizing self-regulatory behaviors to achieve desired states as goals represents a systems competence (i.e., dependent on facilitation of goal realization), as well as providing conditions for the infant's initiation of this goal-organized behavior. Such systems competence ensures a sense of agency in the infant. The emergence of infant-as-agent must be granted by the system because it means a reorganization of the system to admit the newcomer.

4. Each infant–caregiver system constructs its own unique configuration of regulatory constraint on the infant's access to awareness of his own states, his own inner experience, and his access to options to initiate the organization of schemes of self-regulatory behavior on the basis of this criterion of inner experience. These configurations then become a repertoire of enduring coordinations or a repertoire of adaptive strategies between the interacting participants of each infant–caregiving system. These strategies set the conditions in the system by which the infant can construct situations in which he can reexperience a knowing of, or recognition of himself. Construction of experiences, in which one recognizes oneself in terms of reexperiencing familiar states, is the vehicle by which a sense of continuity of self is conveyed. The experience of self-recognition constitutes a parameter that biases the infant's later construction of his ecologic niche in which the same repertoire of adaptive strategies, which now can be called self-regulatory, promise the experience of a familiar continuity of predictable self-recognition.

5. A continuing differentiation of the individual's competence as agent to reconstruct the array of familiar states under widening and changing contextual circumstances is an ongoing life-span process. It remains biased by the organizing logic of the early experience that first confirmed continuity by re-creation of familiar inner experience consequent on individual uniqueness, a repeated process, becoming

ultimately the construction of that individual's life-span trajectory. Differentiation and continuity proceed in a close and paradoxical connection with competence of regulatory coordination in the system. The better regulation is achieved in the system, the better increasing differentiation proceeds and, paradoxically, the experience of continuity.

The reader who is familiar with Brandt Steele's (1983)[EN4] seminal and richly documented paper, "The Effect of Abuse and Neglect on Psychological Development," will have graphically illustrated there examples of the profound effects of derailment of the organizing processes in early development that we have tried to bring together in this brief synopsis. Especially there in his discussion of development of the self is the specific reference to the processes of validation of the infant's inner experience of his own states leading to "a certain coherence of the primordial self." Without this the self is experienced as "irrelevant if not actually erroneous." It is "henceforth in some degree disregarded." Such an infant "remains persistently oriented toward the outside world for cues and guidance, disregarding to a greater or lesser extent his own internal sensations, needs, and wishes." In pathogenesis, as well as in normal development, there is a critical role for what is in the awareness of both infant and caregiver and in the way it enters and shapes their encounter. The organization of consciousness in early experience becomes a central clue to the organization of the developing personality and its construction of the trajectory of the life span over its longer term.

In conclusion, then, an interest in the course or trajectory of the quality of inner experience, or experience of one's own state, is exactly what you might expect of the interest of a psychoanalyst who turns to early developmental research to understand the person of the patient.

NOTE

This chapter originally appeared in *Child Abuse and Neglect: The International Journal* 11.3, 339–346, 1987.

EDITOR'S NOTES

[EN1] Here the integrity of the self is considered a polar opposite to dispersion.

[EN2] See the chapters in the first part of the present volume.

[EN3] Thus, it is not the case that a temporal sequence is identified, but instead a configuration of adaptive strategies (re)proposes itself during the course of life.

[EN4] This writing was composed in honor of Brand Steele's work, who was considered by Sander as a pioneer of psychoanalysis, of evolutionary research, and of infant psychiatry.

REFERENCES

Erikson, E. (1950). Growth and crisis of the healthy personality. *Psychological Issues Monograph, 1,* 50–100.

Sander, L. W. (1962). Issues in early mother–child interaction. *Journal of the American Academy of Child Psychiatry, 1,* 141–166.

Sander, L. W. (1975). Infant and caretaking environment: Investigation and conceptualization of adaptive behavior in a system of increasing complexity. In E. J. Anthony (Ed.), *Explorations in child psychiatry* (pp. 129–166). New York: Plenum.

Sander, L. W. (1985). Toward a logic of organization in psychobiological development. In H. Klar & L. Siever (Eds.), *Biologic response styles: Clinical implications,* pp. 19–37. Washington, DC: APA.

Sherrington, C. S. (1923). *The integrative action of the nervous system.* New Haven, CT: Yale University Press.

Sroufe, A. (1979). The coherence of individual development. *American Psychologist, 34,* 834–841.

Sroufe, A. (1982). The organization of emotional development. *Psychoanalytic Inquiry, 1,* 575–599.

Steele, B. (1983). The effect of abuse and neglect on psychological development. In J. Call, E. Galenson, & R. Tyson (Eds.), *Frontiers of infant psychiatry,* pp. 235–245. New York: Basic Books.

Stern, D. (1985). *The interpersonal world of the infant.* New York: Basic Books.

Von Bertalanffy, L. (1952). *Problems of life.* New York: Harper.

Weiss, P. (1947). The problem of specificity in growth and development. *Yale Journal of Biology and Medicine, 19,* 234–278.

Weiss, P. (1949). The biological basis of adaptation. In *Adaptation.* Ithaca, NY: Cornell University Press.

Winnicott, D. W. (1965). The capacity to be alone. In *The maturational process and the facilitating environment* (pp. 29–36). New York: International Universities Press.

Wolff, P. H. (1960). The developmental psychologies of Jean Piaget and psychoanalysis. *Psychological Issues, 2*(1), Monograph 5.

12

Thinking Differently
Principles of Process in Living Systems
and the Specificity of Being Known

A first glance at the title selected for this symposium suggests that its goal must be to stimulate each of us to try to "put it all together." But as soon as we address the meanings and levels of meaning that can be given to each of the words of the title—Organizing Complexity, Biological Systems, Developmental Process, Therapeutic Process, The Psychoanalytic Framework—we confront the necessity to acknowledge the diversity of meanings we can give to these words, or at least a diversity of ways each of us might think about how one could go about such a task of integration. The limits of a brief essay allow me only to sketch one idea of the way it might be done.

As I see it, even to begin the task, one must begin with the broadest possible perspective, one that could include each of these five domains from the outset. The challenge of integration, then, would be to work out how each relates to the other within that perspective. For me, that broadest of perspectives would be the actuality of life itself, each of us sustained by it even to think about it—something we, for the most part, take totally for granted, but something that remains a mystery to all of us. Furthermore, immediately when we begin to think about life and life process, we are confronted with paradox, and not only one paradox, but many. In what follows, we will be searching for principles in life process that govern the moves toward resolving some of its enigmas. If we find that such principles apply at each of the different levels that our symposium title includes—the biological level, the developmental level, and the level of the organization of consciousness, or the level at which therapeutic process operates—we already will have begun the process of integration we are seeking. It should be evident that, by choosing to begin within the broad perspective of principles governing life as process, we will be beginning at the level of biology, but this is the same level at which our thinking about developmental process must also begin. Then, if we find that the same principles operate at the psychological level, the way will be open to integrate our thinking about the level of therapeutic process. "Emerging knowledge" in each of the several domains included in the title can give the necessary new meaning to the way the word integration can be applied in bringing these diverse domains together.

Each person's life has its own pattern, which is one reason why so many efforts have been made to find a language that allows us to communicate across our diversities. My effort here is to draw on a spectrum of sciences to select powerful terms that can facilitate translation. For example, I have come to rely on the term *coherence* to describe the wholeness in the organization of the complexity of component parts that exists at a hierarchy of levels in the life of the organism and is essential for its continuity. The state of coherence, or wholeness, can be thought of as a goal, or motivating force, for the achievement of what regulation means—at the level both of the individual organism and of the organism within its ecology of life support. This would imply an underlying direction between infant and its surround that makes a widening connectedness possible in their engagement together as the developmental process increases its complexity of functioning.

The experience of specificity in interaction and engagement at the level of consciousness is what I have called *recognition process.* I propose this process as a bridge, at the human level, connecting basic principles of biological process with developmental process—through the negotiation of a sequence of increasingly complex tasks of adaptation, or "fitting together," between the infant and its caregiving environment over the first years of life. This is a sequence of negotiations of connectedness in the interactions between infant and mother that constructs the bridge to organization at the psychological level. By organization at the psychological level, the level of consciousness, I am thinking of the spectrum of ways we experience our own self-awareness within our awareness of our surround. The ever-developing brain, through the infant's experiential engagement with its world, as a self-initiating agent, is now understood as functioning to bring together new levels of integration in the adaptive process (see Freeman, 1995). An example of a new level of integration would be increasing coherence in the experience of sense of "self" within one's context of life support.

The sequence of adaptive tasks we propose as a perspective on early development illustrates the way "the experience of recognition" (i.e., the specificity of a moment of one's knowing that one is "known" by an "other") gradually expands as the infant moves to increasingly complex levels of function. In a healthy environment, expansion of the experience of recognition allows the infant's spontaneity of initiative to emerge through the way the infant's adaptive strategies construct relative harmony in its engagement with both its surround and its significant "other." On the other hand, given the spectrum of healthy-to-unhealthy infant–caregiver systems (in which fitting together becomes increasingly difficult), there would be a spectrum of exchanges that could move from facilitation to inhibition.

In a like manner, the goal of the therapeutic process can be thought of as the facilitation of increasing coherence—one's organization of consciousness through the experience of an expanding specificity of recognition, coconstructed between patient and therapist, that changes awareness of one's sense of self-as-agent within the awareness of what one is doing in the therapeutic interaction and in the world around.

LIFE PROCESS AND PARADOX

Immediately when we begin to think about life and the mystery of life process, we begin to confront paradox, actually a list of paradoxes. For example, we cannot think of any organism, down to the smallest microbe, that lives without having to think of an environment within which it must be in an ever-ongoing interaction. Thus, if we begin with life, we begin not with the living organism itself, but with a "system"—the organism and its environment. However, if we begin with a system—the organism always within an ever-ongoing exchange with its surround—we are thinking of process, a continuing process with many levels of complexity occurring together. A process with many levels of complexity occurring together immediately becomes paradoxical because life process requires both ongoing continuity and ongoing change. What appears to have the stability of the material structure of the body is found to be, itself, within a flow of change. The molecules that make up the body today are not the same molecules that constructed it a month ago. This flow of change, paradoxically, must maintain the organized wholeness of the organism, as its components move through disorganization, removal, and replacement, all the while maintaining the vital coherence of the organism, essential for the continuity of its life. How can all this be done? How can continuity, discontinuity, and wholeness go on together? What we have been accustomed to thinking of as having the permanence of "structure" we now seek to understand as an ongoing process, a process organizing complexity. Later we will come to a way of thinking about this by taking a glimpse at chaos (or complexity) theory, but first let us return to paradox—that, by thinking of life as a process, we must think of the organism actively and continuously engaged with its ecology at a complex hierarchy of levels—that is, we must think of the functioning of a system, not of life as the property of the organism alone.

Let us start with the meaning Webster gives to the word *system:* an assemblage of objects united by some form of regular interaction or interdependence or "a group of diverse units so combined as to form an integral whole." For life to continue over time, the combining of diverse units to form an integral whole also must be continuous over time. If a coherently organized wholeness stops, life begins to fail; if process stops, life stops. We know that in living systems life does stop, but we know also that the new keeps appearing. Thus we must think of process as a flow of input and output in the system through an ever-moving, overarching, organizing process that, through ongoing interaction between organism and surround, is constantly achieving continuity in the face of discontinuity, rather than thinking of the continuity of life as having a kind of given permanence. It is process at all levels of complexity, from the molecular to our ecology within our solar system, that is required to keep the almost unimaginable diversity of parts combining to achieve the "integral whole" that the living system represents.[1]

GENERAL SYSTEMS THEORY: A PERSPECTIVE ON THE PROBLEM OF LIFE

Those familiar with my work will recall that I began my search for principles of process in living systems as part of an effort to bring together the first 3 years of empirical observational data of infants and their families in the Boston University Longitudinal Study of Early Personality Development, begun in 1954. I turned then to the writings of the biologist who launched general systems theory some 70 years ago, Von Bertalanffy (1952). He proposed two principles essential for life: organization and primary activity. By organization he referred to Webster's "integral whole"—the holding together, or coherence, among the enormously complex diversity of parts that make up the living organism. It is because of the diverse ways we can think of the word organization that the title of my paper begins with the words "thinking differently." The meaning I give to the word organization as it applies to living systems includes concepts of an ongoing process—a flow of energy—that, in the healthy systems, brings the astounding complexity of the organism to a coherence, wholeness, or, unity among its interacting components that stems from an essential specificity in the connections between them.

By "primary activity" von Bertalanffy was referring to an organisms's inner, or endogenous, origin of the initiatives for action necessary to achieve and maintain integration of such complexity. Coherence in the organization of the living organism comes from the inside; it is not imposed from the outside. Each living system—each organism—thus is seen as self-organizing, self-regulating, and self-correcting within its surround, its environment. A first step in our way to integrate the biological, the developmental, and the therapeutic would be to see how principles such as organization and primary activity, essential at the biological level, might be applied to each of the higher levels. For example, we now refer to the initiation of self-organizing, self-regulating, self-correcting moves as reflecting the agency of the individual. Achieving a coherent sense of self-as-agent—differentiated, valid, and competent within one's context of life support—brings us to a key goal of both the developmental and the therapeutic processes. I suggest that the process of achieving a coherent sense of self-as-agent is an example of the way "principles of process in living systems" can be applied to the task of integrating biological, developmental, and therapeutic levels we have been assigned.

THE NONLINEAR DYNAMIC SYSTEM

To go a step further, the living system is described now as a nonlinear dynamic system, a system far from equilibrium (to use Prigogine's [1997] term) having the features of sensitivity to initial conditions, the uncertainty of potential bifurcations, and an open-endedness of its trajectory. The nonlinear dynamic system perspective allows us to understand the way both the new and the creative, as well as the disorganizing and the destructive, can be potentials of the same system. Within such a framework, self-organizing, self-regulatory processes must be continuous at a hierarchy of levels of complexity to maintain the essential unity, or coherent wholeness, of the organism that is necessary for life to continue. Even today, as biologist Paul Weiss (1970) pointed out some 30 years ago, biology still has not clarified how the principle of wholeness, unity, or coherence, which the word organization represents, as essential as it is, is accomplished or maintained through "self-organization." How the principle of wholeness, or coherence, operates remains one of the mysteries of the life process, which, for the most part we resist confronting—or of which we remain totally unaware—taking it for granted, without thinking. It is to be hoped that this principle will be clarified as the human genome project progresses in its comprehension of the way the ongoing flow of exchange between genes and environment brings about this essential requirement for life. However, it is a parameter involved at every level of complexity in living systems, and, as we shall see, of special relevance at the psychological level—the level of the organization of consciousness, the level at which the therapeutic process takes place. Let us begin with a look at what can be seen of organization—the "integral whole"—at the cellular level.

Coherence at the Cellular Level

Recently Ingber (1998) introduced the concept of *tensegrity*[EN1] to capture the way the structural wholeness of a cell is maintained when it is exposed to the pressures of a changing dynamic of forces. Although Ingber was referring to the architecture, the mechanical structure, of the living cell, I would suggest that tensegrity might serve as a useful metaphor for conceptualizing the elusive property of coherence at the level of psychological organization. Let us take a moment to see the way Ingber described tensegrity as a principle of process in the living system.

Ingber wrote:

> Life is the ultimate example of complexity at work. That nature applies common assembly rules is implied by the recurrence—at scales from the molecular to the macroscopic—of certain patterns. These patterns appear in structures ranging from highly regular crystals to relatively irregular proteins and in organisms as diverse as viruses, plankton and humans. This phenomenon, in which components join together to form larger, stable structures having new properties that could not have been predicted from the characteristics of their individual parts, is known as self-assembly. It is observed at many scales in nature. In the human body, for example, large molecules self-assemble into cellular components known as organelles, which self-assemble into cells, which self-assemble into tissues, which self-assemble into organs. The result is a body organized hierarchically as tiers of systems within systems. Thus, if we are to understand fully the way living creatures form and function, we need to uncover these basic principles that guide biological organization.
>
> An astoundingly wide variety of natural systems, including carbon atoms, water molecules, proteins, viruses, cells, tissues and even humans and other living creatures, are constructed using a common form of architecture known as "tensegrity." The term refers to a system that stabilizes itself mechanically because of the way in which tensional and compressive forces are distributed and balanced within the structure. Since the molecules and cells that form our tissues are continually removed and replaced, it is the maintenance of pattern and architecture—I reason—that we call life. Tensegrity structures are mechanically stable, not because of the strength of individual members, but because of the way the entire structure contains and manages to distribute and balance—stresses. Tension is continuously transmitted across all structural members. These counteracting forces which equilibrate throughout the structure, are what enable it to stabilize itself. (pp. 48–49)

I suggest that Ingber's conceptualization provides a bridge, a metaphor for our thinking, namely, that a principle of equilibration of counteracting forces within the hierarchical complexity of psychological organization might describe the way a degree of relative order or disorder in the coherence of organization or wholeness of function in the personality of a given individual would be brought about. For example (although not to say how it is done), it is not a great leap to think that an interplay of counteracting forces is required to maintain coherence in one's sense of identity. This would be particularly true as one engages the unpredictability of conflict between opposing forces in one's dynamic system of life support. As Weiss (1970) pointed out at the biological level, we have yet to define at the psychological level the way the strength of coherence in our sense of identity operates and is mediated.

But coherence in one's sense of identity brings us to the next, most difficult, paradox with which thinking of process in the living system confronts us. How can we, as unique self-organizing individuals, remain distinct from an other at the same time that we must be together with that other for our "system"—which is sustaining life for us—to maintain its essential coherence and wholeness (Benjamin, 1995; Seligman & Shanok, 1995)?

TWO ADDITIONAL PRINCIPLES: SPECIFICITY AND RHYTHMICITY

Two additional principles in biological systems—specificity and rhythmicity—provide essential clues to the way life process resolves this difficult paradox: the way the complexity, generated by the uniqueness of self-organizing individuals, still permits the necessary wholeness or coherence of organization of the larger system of which each is a part to be attained and maintained.

Specificity

The first of these principles, specificity, was introduced to me by the work of the biologist Paul Weiss (1947) at the time I was getting acquainted also with the work of von Bertalanffy (1952). Weiss emphasized the critical significance of what he called "the device of specificity" in establishing and maintaining those connections on which the mysterious coherence or unity of living organization rests. He pointed out that the determining quality of specificity is a principle, universally used in the living world. It is essential for communication, recognition, affinity relations, selectivity, and so on. Weiss (1970) described the basic principle as one of matched specificities—"a sort of resonance between two systems attuned to each other by corresponding properties" (p. 162)—and gave several illustrations of the way a principle of specificity operates in the living system, from the level of embryology and the immune system, to the functions of hearing and seeing.

Observing the "Device of Specificity"

Can we see the way specificity functions to connect components as essential coherence is being constructed at the systems level? The mysterious way Weiss's "device of specificity" operates to construct organization, or wholeness, in the living system at its most complex level was brought home to me powerfully decades ago, when Dan Stern offered me the opportunity to review some of the movies of newborn infants that we had taken in our longitudinal study, using his frame-by-frame projector. The scene was drawn from some 3 minutes of movie film taken of our research team out on the lawn during a home visit with one of our new neonatal subjects on the eighth post-delivery day. In that scene one can see a little girl in her father's arms[EN2] standing on the lawn talking with other members of the team run it at normal film speed of 30 frames per second, and this is all one sees.

Over the same few minutes, now run frame-by-frame, one sees the father glance down momentarily at the baby's face. Strangely enough, in the same frames, the infant looks up at the father's face. Then the infant's left arm, which had been hanging down over the father's left arm, begins to move upward. Miraculously, in the same frame, the father's right arm, which had been hanging down at his right side, begins to move upward. Frame by frame by frame, the baby's hand and the father's hand move upward simultaneously. Finally, just as they meet over the baby's tummy, the baby's left hand grasps the little finger of the father's right hand. At that moment, the infant's eyes close and she falls asleep, while the father continues talking, apparently totally unaware of the little miracle of specificity in time, place, and movement that had taken place in his arms.

How do we account for such specificity of connection between father and baby? Was there a "representation" of the father's little finger in the newborn's brain? Did she know "where" it was, to grasp it? As the father's hand came over the infant's body, father extended his little finger, separating it from his other fingers; otherwise the baby could not have grasped it. How did he know the baby wished to grasp it? How could the movements of father and baby fit so precisely in time and in place, 8 days after the baby had been born? Are we looking at some principle of wholeness—that is, building on an underlying principle of specificity in time, place, and movement that joins directionalities between component subsystems—a joining that is necessary to construct coherent wholeness in a "system" that can be said to "live"? Would tensegrity be one illustration of this principle of wholeness? Might this same principle of joining directionality also underlie Stern's (1985a) attunement or Trevarthen's (1979) brain-to-brain communication—or our increasingly employed concept of intersubjectivity?

Self-Assembly at the Psychological Level

When we extend the concept of specificity to the interactions between two people, we begin to have a bridge from the principles of process at the level of molecules to principles of process at the level of persons. How people find and link with one another has become a current interest in the psychoanalytic world. Thus we can turn our search for principles of process in the organization of coherence or wholeness in living systems to the level of the organization of consciousness.

In Tronick et al.'s (1998) "Diadically Expanded States of Consciousness and the Process of Therapeutic Change," drawn from Tronick's research in infancy and using the still-face paradigm, we find exactly the same principles as Ingber described. Tronick et al. wrote:

Each individual is a self-organizing system that creates its own states of consciousness—states of brain organization—which can be expanded into more coherent and complex states in collaboration with another self-organizing system. When the [specificity of] collaboration between two brains is successful, each fulfills the systems principle of increasing its coherence and complexity—the infant becoming capable of performing actions in the dyadic system that the infant would not be capable of performing alone. (p. 296)

Tronick's example thus illustrates the way a principle of process in living systems, such as Ingber's self-assembly, can be applied at the highest level of human complexity—that of human consciousness. As we shall see, the principle of specificity of connection, required for the self-assembly of components into larger wholes at the level of awareness, is basic to what we refer to as recognition process—a process that brings two states of consciousness together in a moment of fittedness.

However, a paradox remains. Specificity of connection must emerge from the resolution of stresses between opposing forces generated by the ongoing flow of change in time, place, and movement both within and among the components that make up the organism's hierarchical levels of complexity. Are there other mechanisms by which specificity of connection can be accomplished? The answer, I suggest at this point, would draw from and extend Weiss's (1947) expression of a device of specificity. We propose that it is through a second additional principle, the device of rhythmicity, that this is accomplished. Let us see how rhythmicity contributes to expanding connections between the infant and his or her world.

Rhythmicity

Relatively stable but resilient "holding together" of the complexity of the biological system is brought about by the entrainment and synchrony of biological rhythms. The living system is a symphony of biorhythmic systems within systems. A simple metaphor in the language of complexity, or chaos theory, gives an overview of the process of construction of rhythm in the nonlinear dynamic system: "When a flow of energy enters a matrix of sufficient complexity that is under constraint by certain parameters, it will emerge as a flow of recurrent pattern, each recurrence of pattern having features, both of self-similarity and of singularity." That is, each recurrence of pattern both resembles previous patterns and is unique in its own way. The creative potential of such a flow of energy might be illustrated in the world of mathematics by the repeated iterations of a simple formula in fractal geometry that constructs the beauty and complexity of the display known as the Mandelbrot set (Mandelbrot, 1982).

Self-similarity in recurrent patterns brings us at once to rhythmicity—and, in the biological system, to biorhythmicity, a fundamental feature of living systems at all levels of complexity from the dino-flagellate to the human. It is a feature in nature that facilitates resolution of one of life's underlying paradoxes—the way a complexity of self-organizing components distinct from each other can reach a coherence or unity in being together with each other.

The Wider Role of Rhythmicity

Let us go a bit further with rhythmicity as part of the basic machinery of self-assembly by which coherence of organization is achieved in the living system. The rhythms of oscillating systems become coupled when they share a common signal. Coupling amplifies the signal, increasing the inclusiveness and strength of coherence in the community of oscillators. The flow of energy is enhanced. This is one reason the construction of a new specificity of connection that expands the inclusiveness of two states of consciousness as they become engaged together can be thought of as motivational. A simple illustration is the nightly onset of flashing rhythms in communities of fireflies (Strogatz & Mirollo, cited in Peterson, 1991). The rhythm becomes increasingly inclusive as the night deepens, until the whole community is flashing synchronously.

A fascinating recent discovery is Young's (1998) finding that there are biological clocks in each of the components of a fruit fly's body—thorax, proboscis, antennae—so that phase-shifting and phase-synchrony of endogenous rhythms may be found to be central to the modifiability needed for its adaptability, as well as for its coherence as a fruit fly. Essential to the coupling between rhythmically oscillating systems is the specificity of the shared signal; that is, the timing and configuration of the entraining cue. In jet lag, for instance, we experience the break in coupling with the disorganization that goes with temporal asynchrony between our internal rhythm and that of our surround. Phase-shifting of rhythm is necessary to reconstruct the specificities of connection that are required to restore our sense of coherent organization within the timing of the new environment. Within a principle of rhythmicity governing both interacting partners, continuity is preserved, because disengagement does not mean disconnection.

A still more provocative perspective on the role of rhythmicity in biological organization is the way each brain puts together unified scenes and meanings from its own widely distributed areas of sensory processing. Gray, Singer, and others (cited in Bower, 1998) proposed that synchronized rhythms of neural firing spark the anatomical connection and chemical processes necessary for perception, memory, language, and even consciousness. Rhythmic electric output among far-flung neuronal groupings lies at the heart of visual perception and perhaps of other aspects of thought, all of which brings us to a key bridge in the integration of the biological, the developmental, and the psychological—the brain.

THE BRAIN AND DEVELOPMENTAL PROCESS

One of the important bridges extending our integration of emerging knowledge of biological processes to newer perspectives on developmental processes is our changing understanding of the way the brain functions. Of special significance is the interplay between an infant's experiencing and the developing morphology of the infant brain. For example, we are learning that the early experiencing of the infant shapes and modifies the morphology of the baby's brain. Thus the door is opened to new understanding, both of long-term effects of certain negative features in an infant's early experiencing, such as trauma and recurrent pathogenic encounters, and, on the positive side, amplifying the development of the brain's potentials.

The Brain and Perception

One of the most basic, but, to me, most incredible of recent findings is that, in its function of perception, the brain first deconstructs its sensory input into the bits and pieces that make up the perception. It places each sensory component of the input into a category—line, color, depth, contour, movement—which the brain then processes, each category in a different brain area. The map of this widely distributed process is then brought back together to construct the whole of the percept, including relevant affective or emotional categories (its limbic system values, as Edelman, 1992, termed them), and from these, the meaning of the percept is constructed for the perceiver. (Perceptual function includes perceiving "direction" in one's interactional exchanges. As part of this process, the infant's repertoire of actual behavioral strategies governing how to "be with" significant others—mother, father, and the like—within the idiosyncrasies of its particular caregiving system is being constructed (see, e.g., Stern, 1985b).

The brain's integrative function in putting together the whole of a percept from the complexity of its input can be seen as a function that provides fundamental motivation for each of us in our flow of engagement with our context to put it all together, each in our own way. The brain's integrative function not only enables each one to carry out idiosyncratic tasks of basic adaptation, but also is an organizing force at the most complex levels of human experiencing—the goal of this symposium (e.g., Freeman, 1999). One has only to look at the flood of new books that are appearing from the disciplines of physics and mathematics to experience the way researchers in these fields also have been trying to put it all together in new integrations stemming from new theories of cosmology, chaos, complexity, and nonlinear dynamic systems.[2]

As mentioned, an example of the way the brain integrates a hierarchy of subsystems to form an integral whole can be seen in its powerful but often unrealized wizardry of "gestalt perception." Those familiar with infant research know about Heinz Prechtl's (1990)[EN3] use of this gestalt function.

The importance of bringing this functioning capacity of the brain to the fore at this point is its relationship to the role of expectancy in this process of fitting together, or adaptation. In fact, long before language and words are available, adaptive, interactive, and interpersonal strategies become organized: "ways of being with the other" (Stern, 1985b) and "implicit relational knowing" (Lyons-Ruth, 1999).

THINKING DIFFERENTLY

If our integration is to begin at the level of the broadest of perspectives, we find that human social culture has, from its historical beginnings, identified a principle of recognition, and the experience of being "known," as essential to the vitalizing human experience of a moment of joining with a larger, more inclusive, whole. To quote from the 139th Psalm, "Oh, Lord, thou has searched me and known me. Thou knowest my downsitting and my uprising, and art acquainted with all my ways. ... For there is not a word on my tongue but thou knowest it altogether."

By beginning with the idea of thinking differently, I am also asking, "Why not begin with uniqueness as a central principle in the organization of a living system?" I suggest, further, that specificity of recognition of that uniqueness—in an interactive system—is key to an organizing process based on constructing the essential specificity of connection between components that is necessary to achieve the coherence or wholeness of the system required for continuity of its life. The same principle of specificity of connection that is essential for Ingber's (1998) self-assembly at the biological level—"hospitalism," as described by Spitz (1945)—illustrates what happens in systems in which such specificity is lacking in early development. At the level to which the complexity of human consciousness brings us, the uniqueness of each of us in the organization of our attention and awareness seems obvious.

Where do we begin, then, in the increasing complexity of recognition of uniqueness? We began our task of integration with Webster's definition of *system* as an "integral whole" and with von Bertalanffy's principle of organization as essential descriptors of systems that can be said to live. The route that gives us operational access (or observational access) to the recognition of the integral whole of the organism within its system is through the concept of state. *State* has a very specific, empirically valid definition as a descriptor of the complexity yet the unity of a living system. It is defined as that configuration of the values of a set of variables that characterize the functioning of the system as a whole at a particular moment in time, a configuration that recurs and that can be recognized whenever that same configuration recurs again. An example at the newborn level would be the range of states on the sleep–awake continuum, observable with a high degree of reliability. At a slightly later point in the developmental process, there is the range of emotional states that express feeling, namely, the affects. *Affects* are observable states, specificity of recognition of which becomes key to regulation, to adaptation, and to communication. It is fascinating to realize that the essential role in the adaptive process made possible by one's ability to perceive the state of an "other" depends on the brain's capacity for gestalt perception that we have just been reviewing. We can presume they have evolved together.

Furthermore, regularities in the recurrence of infant states, within the basic 24-hour periodicity of the larger system, provide a framework—a background—for temporal organization, essential in the process of adaptation. As illustrated in the clinical example presented earlier, recurring states recur within recurring contexts of recurring exchanges between infant and caregiver; thus the stage is set for recurring gestalts within which their interaction is framed—a process configuration—and that becomes characteristic for each system. We propose that—within this familiar framework as unexpected perturbations and their repair in the regaining of new moments of connection construct a flow of recurring sequence from harmony to disharmony to harmony again—the infant begins to experience an awareness of its own state. It is in our capacity for self-awareness that we have a solution for one of the paradoxes with which we began. Within the self-awareness of familiar states in recurring patterns of expectancy for sequence–consequence flow, a sense of continuity can be experienced in the presence of discontinuities. Desired states become motivational goals. The infant's own desired state begins its role in organizing the direction that the initiation of its next move will take in the adaptive process.

With specificity in the recurring recognition needed for the regulation of infant state, a framework is provided also for the recurrence of a most vital event—a "moment of meeting" between infant and caregiver in states of mutual readiness. Stability in the recurrence of meeting in states of mutual readiness is an experience fundamentally different from the infant's elicitation of a response from the caregiver or vice versa. When the adapted state is achieved, it is an essential facilitating condition but also something experienced in the nature of a "given." From the outset the developmental process constructs for the regulation of each system a logic of organization (Sander, 1985) in the unique pattern for that system that defines the balance that will characterize it in terms of what is given and what has to be gotten. The sense of fulfillment that coherence or wholeness in the system brings, and that stable regulation of state provides, can be proposed as a deep source of motivation for both partners in govern-

TABLE 12.1
Adaptive Issues Negotiated in Interaction Between Infant and Caretaker

Issue	Title	Span of Months	Prominent Infant Behavior That Became Coordinate With Maternal Activities
I	Initial regulation	Months 1–3	Basic infant activities concerned with biological processes related to feeding, sleeping, elimination, postural maintenance, and so on, including stimulus needs for quieting and arousal.
II	Reciprocal exchange	Months 4–6	Smiling behavior that extends to full motor and vocal involvement in sequences of affectively spontaneous back-and-forth exchanges. Activities of spoon feeding, dressing, and so on, become reciprocally coordinated.
III	Initiative	Months 7–9	Activities initiated by infant to secure a reciprocal social exchange with mother or to manipulate environment on his own selection.
IV	Focalization	Months 10–13	Activities by which infant determines the availability of mother on his specific initiative. Tends to focalize need-meeting demands on the mother.
V	Self-assertion	Months 14–20	Activities in which infant widens the determination of his own behavior, often in the face of maternal opposition.
VI	Recognition	Months 18–36	Activities (including language) that express perceptions of own state, intentions, and thought content.
VII	Continuity (conservation of self as active organizer)	Months 18–36	Activities rupturing and restoring coordination on an intentional level (intended and directed aggressive behavior in equilibrium with directed initiations aimed at facilitating restoration of interactional concordance).

Note: From Anthony (1975, p. 136). Reprinted with the kind permission of Springer Science and Business Media.

ing their next relational move. In as much as the developmental process is an ongoing flow of change, recognition of state itself must be an evolving process, constructing specificity of meeting in new configurations of increasing complexity as development proceeds.

As summarized in Table 12.1, the first five adaptive tasks engaged in by the infant and its caregiving environment over the first 18 months of life involve increasing complexity in the behaviors and initiatives of action of the infant, which can be observed and experienced directly. It is in the early part of the second year of life that the infant experiences a new level of developmental complexity, an emerging awareness of its own inner sense of intention and direction, well illustrated by Spitz (1957) in his description of the infant's "head-shaking, 'No'" at 15 months of age. We can readily see the stage set for adaptive task 6, which I originally called recognition, with this profound advance in the organization of consciousness—the development of awareness of own state and awareness of own role as initiator of action. We think of the brain's capacity to construct gestalts of expectancy amid the recurrence both of affectively positive moments of meeting and of the affectively negative experience of further constraint to spontaneity of initiative. This emerging developmental step of an inner awareness of the infant's own intention in initiating an act sets the stage for the infant's experience of an "other's" being aware of what the infant is aware of within itself—its states, its expectancies, and the direction of its goals and intentions. The stage is set for expectancy to begin to shape initiative before action occurs.

Thus it is toward the end of the second half of the second year or the early months of the third year that the adaptive process begins to be carried out on the level of inner awareness and sequence–consequence expectancies. The capacity to inhibit spontaneity and conceal intention before action emerges in the older toddler. The mutual modifications and adjustments of the adaptive process begin to be constructed on the basis of the sensitivity to self and other that exists in both partners. Specificity of recognition becomes the clue to success or failure of the adaptive process or, if disruption remains unrepaired, the skewing of organization in the system in the direction of projections and mismatches.

At the same time, the sense of fulfillment (Tronick et al., 1998) or heightened affective moments (Beebe & Lachmann, 1996) of the experience of specificity in moments of meeting between infant and caregiver provide the essential positive motivating pole in the nonlinear dynamic system they are constructing; that is, moving each partner to seek the positive affective accompaniment of being together with the other. It is a small step here to move, in terms of a common basic principle, from Ingber's (1998) many examples of self-assembly at the biological level to self-assembly at the psychological level—two unique brain organizations of mother and infant self-assembling into a larger, more inclusive coherence of conscious organization—as in doing things together. With specificity of connection, the flow of energy expands as states of brain organization in the two partners expand their complexity into new and more inclusive states of coherent organization, enabling the infant to do what it would not be able to do alone. (Again, we are at Tronick et al.'s [1998] "Dyadic Expansion of Consciousness Hypothesis.")

THE LEVEL OF PSYCHOTHERAPEUTIC PROCESS

We began with the challenge of integrating emerging knowledge at the biological, developmental, and psychotherapeutic levels and chose to see if a way to do this might be to find basic principles of process in living systems that would apply at each of these levels. In turning now to the psychotherapeutic level, especially within the psychoanalytic framework, we can think of the therapeutic process essentially as a process bringing change to the organization of consciousness, that is changing the way we are aware of ourselves in the context of what is going on around us, which allows us to put together a new and more inclusive coherence of ourselves within our own particular environment of life support. In the foreground detail of the progression of interactional events that construct the flow of process at the biological and early developmental levels, the question becomes this: What do these principles look like at the therapeutic level? In the integration of the biological with the developmental, we translated from organization to wholeness to state, beginning our list of adaptive tasks in early development with the regulation of the flow of state change in the infant within the 24-hour day–night cycle.

A current example of the use of specificity in recognition of state within the psychoanalytic framework is the work of Schwaber (1983) in her description of "Psychoanalytic Listening." She applies together her sensitivity in perceiving the flow of state and state change, both in her patient and within herself, as the therapeutic hour progresses. Each point of change provides her the opportunity for a moment of inquiry, an opportunity to bring her awareness of change to the patient's awareness of change in the flow of the interaction between them, an opportunity to reach a new moment of meeting as the "direction" and the "intention" of each become clarified.

The adaptive tasks just described, leading from the recognition of state change to the recognition of the process of disembedding of "self" from "other," illustrate the increasing complexity of what specificity of recognition involves as development proceeds. How the experience of specificity of being known or recognized is conveyed obviously is at the heart of what the effective interpretation accomplishes—bringing patient and therapist into new "moments of meeting"—the inclusiveness of new, expanded states of conscious connection.

I would like to conclude with a clinical moment that Lyons-Ruth (2000) described. She related a brief exchange with a self-destructively acting-out adolescent during the early alliance-forming months of treatment. In this session the adolescent was angrily listing her disappointments in all her adjunct treatment providers. Lyons-Ruth wrote, "The patient finally looked at me with a hard querying look and fell silent. I asked what she was thinking that made her lapse into silence. She said, 'You never know what these people are thinking. I mean they're human. They're probably thinking about the errands they need to do, you know, go to the cleaners and things'" (pp. 92–93).

The author notes that the patient's feeling of being unseen by important others had already been a part of the dialogue, so that making a comment about her feeling unseen within the therapy felt sterile and abstract. The therapist reflected briefly on her own experience of feeling attacked and depleted by the patient during these early months of therapy. Then she said, "Would you like to know what I've been thinking about as I was listening to you?" The patient nodded and the therapist continued, "I was thinking what a difficult adversary you are to yourself. You're very thoughtful and disciplined and insightful (all obvious traits in this excellent student) and right now all those strengths are being used against you rather than in the service of furthering your life" (p. 93). At this point, for the first time, the patient began to talk at a very meaningful level about her inner experience of feeling like an abused wife who could not separate from an abusive husband, the "husband" who was embodied in her self-destructive behavior, because she feared he was the only one who could love her.

The author used this exchange to point to the multilayered levels of communication that are inherent in such a clinical exchange:

> My understanding of what had transpired between us had more in common with a theory of complementary fitted action and recognition process than a theory of interpretation. She had brought a central "way of being with" into the treatment room that involved angry opposition to the "unseeing others." But in this instance, it was an opposition in the course of her development that had become directed away from the important others in her life and towards herself. I was improvising as best I could to recognize implicitly a number of levels of her communication to me in a way that opened new avenues for collaboration, without overpowering her defenses or undermining her self-esteem. Over the course of this exchange, a deepening of her willingness to share her inner world with me occurred that was perceptible to us both. However, we did not verbally acknowledge our *shared perception of the moment* until many sessions later. (p. 93)

It was a moment, but one not forgotten.

This example illustrates the specificity of fittedness in therapeutic moments of recognition, in which a complex configuration of interactive elements must become well enough aligned between patient and therapist at a specific point in time to open up new possibilities for what they can do together.

CONCLUSION

The elements of the recognition process model, with its simple core and culmination in the idea of a structure of meetings centered about the experience of specificity in moments of shared awareness is suggested here to underlie and simplify the complexity of the domains of biological organization, developmental process, and therapeutic process. The central idea is a very simple one that describes a key moment of connection that occurs within a framework of recurrent meeting—becoming a "now" moment that changes organization. It is the now moment of knowing and being known in the governing of a hierarchical self-organizing systems process that brings coherence or wholeness to a dyadic system in the process of increasing its inclusiveness of complexity. This is a moment central to regulation, to adaptation, and to integration—to the experience of oneself and the relation of this experience to one's experience of the other.

NOTES

From a paper presented at a Division 39 symposium of the American Psychological Associations (1998) entitled Organizing Complexity Within the Psychoanalytic Framework: Inward Integration of Emerging Knowledge of Developmental Process, Biological Systems, and Therapeutic Process.

1. Beebe and Lachmann (1996) have been on a similar search for principles of process in living systems at the human level, coming up with their three principles of salience: regulation, disruption and repair, and heightened affective moments. The experience of heightened affective moments provides the essential positive affects in our experiencing that accompany being "together with" another. At the psychological level, then, events that generate the experiencing of positive affects become the source of the essential motivating impetus that pushes us to restore connection when it has become disrupted. Without something of this positive dimension as part of our framework of expectancy, we become vulnerable to a lapse into the disorganization of depression or illness.
2. For example, David Layzer (1990) takes the reader from the big bang to the organization of consciousness. See also Stuart Kaufmann (1995), of the Santa Fe Institute; Nobel Laureate Murray Gell-Mann (1994); Ilya Prigogine (1997), who seeks to bring together linear, Newtonian deterministic physics, and the creative, open-ended, probabilistic, nonlinear world of quantum mechanics; and the most recent, Wilson (1999). These references illustrate a strategy of integration in human thought that can take us from a background of the broadest of perspectives to a foreground of detail that exemplifies a particular principle and vice versa.

EDITORS' NOTES

[EN1] Term coined by the architect F. Buckminster Fuller to describe the fusion between tension and integrity.
[EN2] Already extensively presented in chapter 8.
[EN3] Reported extensively in chapter 9.

REFERENCES

Anthony, E. J. (1975). *Exploration in child psychiatry.* New York: Plenum.

Beebe, B., & Lachmann, F. M. (1996). Three principles of salience in the organization of the patient–analyst interaction. *Psychoanalytic Psychology, 13,* 1–22.

Benjamin, J. (1995). *Like subjects, love objects: Essays on recognition and sexual difference.* New Haven, CT: Yale University Press.

Bower, B. (1998). All fired up: Perception may dance to the beat of collective rhythms. *Science News, 153,* 120–123.

Edelman, G. (1992). *Bright air, brilliant fire.* New York: Basic Books.

Freeman, W. (1995). *Societies of brains.* Hillsdale, NJ: Lawrence Erlbaum Associates, Inc.

Freeman, W. (1999). *How brains make up their minds.* London: Weldenfeld & Nicholson.

Gell-Mann, M. (1994). *The quark and the jaguar.* New York: Freeman.

Ingber, D. E. (1998). The architecture of life. *Scientific American, 278,* 48–58.

Kauffman, S. (1995). *At home in the universe.* New York: Oxford University Press.

Layzer, D. (1990). *Cosmogenesis: The growth of order in the universe.* New York: Oxford University Press.

Lyons-Ruth, K. (1999). Two-person unconscious: Intersubjective dialogue, enactive relational representation, and the emergence of new forms of relational organization. *Psychoanalytic Inquiry, 19,* 576–617.

Lyons-Ruth, K. (2000). "I sense that you sense that I sense": Sander's recognition process and the specificity of relational moves in the psychotherapeutic setting. *Journal of Infant Mental Health, 21,* 85–99.

Mandelbrot, B. B. (1982). *The fractal geometry of nature.* New York: Freeman.

Peterson, I. (1991, August 31). Step in time: Exploring the mathematics of synchronously flashing fireflies. *Science News,* pp. 136–137.

Prechtl, H. F. (1990). Qualitative changes of spontaneous movement in foetus and preterm infants are a marker of neurological dysfunction. *Early Human Development.* Prigogine, I. (1997). *The end of certainty.* New York: The Free Press.

Sander, L. W. (1985). Toward a logic of organization in psycho-biological development. In H. Klar & L. Siever (Eds.), *Biological response styles: Clinical implications* (pp. 129–166). Washington, DC: American Psychiatric Press.

Schwaber, E. (1983). Psychoanalytic listening and psychic reality. *International Review of PsychoAnalysis, 10,* 379–392.

Seligman, S., & Shanok, R. (1995). Subjectivity, complexity and the social world: Erikson's identity and contemporary relational theory. *Psychoanalytic Dialogues, 5,* 537–565.

Spitz, R. (1945). Hospitalism. *The Psychoanalytic Study of the Child, 1,* 53–74.

Spitz, R. (1957). *No and yes: On the genesis of human communication.* New York: International Universities Press.

Stern, D. (1985a), Affect attunement. In J. D. Call, E. Galenson, & R. L. Tyson (Eds.), *Frontiers of infant psychiatry* (Vol. 1, pp. 3–14). New York: Basic Books.

Stern, D. (1985b). *The interpersonal world of the infant: A view from psychoanalysis and developmental psychology.* New York: Basic Books.

Trevarthen, C. (1979). Communication and co-operation in early infancy: A description of primary intersubjectivity. In M. Bullowa (Ed.), *Before speech* (321–349). Cambridge, UK: Cambridge University Press.

Tronick, E. Z., Bruschweiler-Stern, N., Harrison, A., Lyons-Ruth, K., Morgan, A. C., Nahum, J. P., et al. (1998). Dyadically expanded states of consciousness and the process of therapeutic change. *Journal of Infant Mental Health, 19,* 290–299.

Von Bertalanffy, L. (1952). *The problem of life.* New York: Harper.

Weiss, P. (1947). The problem of specificity in growth and development. *Yale Journal of Biology & Medicine, 19,* 234–278.

Weiss, P. (1970). Whither life science? *American Scientist, 58,* 156–163.

Wilson, E. O. (1999). *Consilience: The unity of knowledge.* New York: Vintage Books.

Young, M. W. (1998). The molecular control of circadian behavioral rhythms and their entrainment in drosophila. *Annual Review of Biochemistry, 67,* 135–152.

13

Development as Creative Process

What I shall be discussing cannot help but reflect my personal reaction, not only to Ellen Stechler's life and death, but also to my departure from Boston University a little over a year and a half ago and the continuing separation reaction that set in motion. For me, it was a separation from a place where, for over 30 years, I grew up professionally and as a person, side by side during much of this time with Gerry[EN1] and Ellen.

To return now, on this particular occasion, makes it inescapable that discontinuity and its place in the life process must be the topic to which our thoughts naturally gravitate. It is a subject man has contemplated from his beginnings, every individual struggling for his own answers. I can neither give answers nor perhaps say anything new. I can only share the thoughts and feelings these experiences evoke in me—evoke in some chemistry of interaction with my particular life course, preoccupied as it has been with development as creative process, resulting in the differentiated organization of an individual, a unique person.

Curiously enough, over the past 50 years we have generally wanted to divorce ourselves from the two great discontinuities of life: birth and death. A continuing framework of familiar human relationships was eliminated from the labor and delivery room. Encounter with an uncertain process was, as nearly as possible, forestalled. The best care seemed to demand full professional control of what seemed a knowable process.

Now, however, continuity of relationship and experiences is returning to the birthing process. There is a new appreciation of the initial encounter between infant and family as a moment of discovery for each, a moment of special openness of each to unique features of the other. The polarity between certainty and uncertainty goes on, however, as we gain further control of the early developmental process with amniocentesis and ultrasound. What will happen to the moment of discovery when the sex and perhaps the features of the new individual have been known for weeks before the birth, congealing the moment of discovery, of openness?

With the progression of medical knowledge, the discontinuity of death has likewise become a scene of alienation, in which both the living and dying avoid confrontation. Finally, however, we are beginning to look at death as a new and strange encounter that affects both the living and dying—a final encounter that may have as much impact on the creative process of development as the initial encounter.

In man's contemplation of this second major discontinuity, there seems always the suggestion that the way we live reflects the way the recognition of death is organized in our awareness. From the time of a child's first encounter with the actuality of death (of a pet, a parent, or a grandparent), and when one considers our constructions of fantasy and the dynamics of defense, the line is thin that separates our living from our dying. The fact of death guarantees a measure of uncertainty that we must contend with over nearly the full length of our lives.

This lecture, a memorial to the life of Ellen Stechler, deals with the subject of development and the developing person. It is a new structure in the life of Boston University, something to go onward, a new continuity arising from a discontinuity. How universal a response this is to the ultimate discontinuity of death—to create something new that will go onward—whether it be a great foundation, a lectureship, or a simple plaque. We at once find ourselves, in our experience with discontinuity, confronted by its polarity with continuity. In the face of discontinuity, we generate that which is new, which has not existed before.

There is another response we have to a discontinuity: We step back and try to reorganize; we review and try to gain a wider perspective over a longer span of time leading up to the event. The course of a lifetime may be reviewed. We search over time for a reason, a design, a broader frame of reference, or a broader perspective that will resolve the paradoxes that frame our lives.

Traditionally, the Judeo-Christian world has turned to the Book of Job for such a perspective on disaster and loss that reason cannot resolve. If we regard the book as a poem rather than history—one in which the poet conveys insights for others to interpret—we can look on it as an insight into a problem of development, the differentiation of the self. This is the process whereby one's sense of one's own existence, one's integrity, emerges as a creation, standing within the creative process yet independent of every support—and especially differentiated from merit, competence, reason, or any knowledge one might think one possesses.

Very briefly, for those not familiar with it, the story of Job begins when Satan crashes a party God is giving for His sons. God is quite pleased with His work and calls Satan's attention to Job as a really remarkable creation.

Satan does not accept this; he has spotted a flaw in Job's personality. He has seen that every time Job's sons threw a party, Job had gotten up early the next morning to offer burnt sacrifices for each son in case one of them might have done something wrong the night before. Satan sees that Job has some pretty omnipotent ideas about how he is controlling his little corner of the world.

Satan declares he won't spend his time going after Job as long as God is reinforcing Job's fantasies by constantly lavishing good things on him. Satan asserts that Job only looks good but could not stand alone without all this reinforcement. God then makes a bet with Satan and says, "Okay, take away all his possessions and we'll see." So everything Job has is taken away, but Job still keeps his cool and his integrity. He declares that he came into the world naked and would go out naked—and besides, he could get on without all those possessions.

When Satan crashes the next party God is giving for His sons, God boasts a bit more to Satan and says, "Look, Job is still holding fast to his integrity though he has lost everything without cause." Satan again discounts God's pride and says, "Well, that's no real test. You have to get to his body. If you damage his flesh and bones, then you'll see his integrity collapse." "All right," says God, "try it. Anything short of killing him." Then Satan, having taken away Job's possessions and destroying his family, covers him with boils from head to foot. He is at the point of death. Everyone is repulsed by his appearance. Even his wife wishes him dead.

The story continues with a dialogue between Job and his erstwhile friends, who cook up endless reasons for his misfortunes and try to get him to feel guilty and accept blame for what has happened. The poet here is making the point that if Job did accept guilt it would only confirm Satan's assertion that Job had indeed believed himself responsible for his former good fortune because of his pious behavior. However, instead of admitting guilt, Job becomes furious and upbraids God, demanding a direct encounter to put questions and get answers. He wants confrontation.

When his friends fail to dent Job's conviction of his own blamelessness, another character, a young man, reveals his vision of God's action in the creative process, and suddenly Job has his confrontation. But instead of questioning God, it is he who is questioned, and the questions are about the creative process. Here the poet demonstrates Job's ignorance. God asks, "Where were you when I laid the foundation of the Earth?" He taunts Job: "Tell me, if you understand, who determined its measurements. Surely you know." Finally, God demonstrates the fine points of the great crocodile, describing the majestic features that give the creature its terrible power. He asks Job to explain it, intimating that Job himself was created by the same process. Confronted by the awesomeness of the creative process—realizing that he is a product of it but had no part in it—Job is abashed and stands before his Creator with nothing left, not even his argument with God, now fully aware of his own unknowing.

At this point there is no way that Satan can undo Job. God, on the other hand, can maintain that he has a truly remarkable creation—one that can stand in a contrary position to his Creator, in a direct encounter, and know fully that he knows nothing.

Here we can think of the development of the self as it is now being discussed in psychoanalytic circles, and of the vulnerability of the patient, diagnosed as having a narcissistic character disorder, who meets separation or misfortune.

The poet is making at least three points: (a) the self is vulnerable when its continuity depends on performance or knowledge; (b) misfortune without reason should be examined in light of the process of creation; and (c) it is only in direct encounter with the full awareness of one's unknowing that the differentiation of the self, the creation of man, becomes complete.

Curiously enough, it is said that in the beautiful land of New Zealand, where there is secure old age, no unemployment, no poverty, and no pollution, the young people leave to seek their fortunes elsewhere. They create a discontinuity; they confront themselves with an unknown. We say they have to grow up, have to "find themselves," that it is a part of the developmental process. Could it be that uncertainty is a necessary condition for development—that discontinuity in life is a condition necessary for new elaborations by an organizing process within?

We have long been aware that personality development seems to require a graded process of mismatch, of discontinuities, of failures. Consider what Winnicott (1958, p. 238) has written on this:

> If all goes well, the infant can actually come to gain from the experience of frustration, since incomplete adaptation to need makes objects real, that is to say, hated as well as loved. The consequences of that is that if all goes well, the infant can be disturbed by a close adaptation to need that is continued too long, not allowed its natural decrease, since exact adaptation resembles magic, and the object that behaves perfectly becomes no better than an hallucination. Nevertheless, at the start adaptation needs to be almost exact, and unless this is so it is not possible for the infant to begin to develop a capacity to experience a relationship to external reality, or even to form a conception of external reality.

In other words, the ontogeny of perception, awareness, or consciousness, if you will, depends on a degree of inexactness. This poses, then, a considerable paradox—one that Winnicott (1958, p. 240) solved by proposing that it is unsolved—that there is and remains an in-between area where the predictable and unpredictable can be, and are, integrated.

Winnicott continued:

> It is assumed that the task of reality-acceptance is never completed, that no human being is free from the strain of relating inner and outer reality, and that relief from this strain is provided by an intermediate area of experience which is not challenged. This intermediate area is in direct continuity

with the play area of a small child. It is necessary for the initiation of a relationship between the child and the world. Essential to all this is continuity of the external emotional environment and of particular elements in the physical environment.

The discontinuities, in some proper relation to continuity—and this is the key—provide the essential conditions for what we call structure building. Structures include adaptive strategies generated to organize our behavior in the face of the sequence of mismatches, separations, losses, and fumblings that mark the life span. But we don't have a very clear idea of the mechanisms. We have notions of identification or incorporation, notions that we need the integrative posture of a person with whom to identify—one with whom we have a relationship, one who has bridged loss and discontinuity—but we don't make clear where that person got his or her organization.

In our research, we have tried to take apart the machine, but how does it go together as an ongoing working process?

If development is indeed a life-span matter, developmental process and life process must share common mechanisms. Certainly both can be described as processes involving ongoing, endogenously active, self-organizing properties framed within the dynamics of numerous natural polarities. We speak very easily of life as an open system, subject to variations and perturbations of the environment with which it must actively regulate an intimate exchange to survive. But when it comes to development, we find it hard to get away from our orientation to the idea of linear causality. We look at early events to find causes for later ones; we frame our histories and data in terms of cause and effect. We tease apart variables and analyze interactions to determine the contribution of each isolated variable to the outcome. As clinicians, we look to the developmental histories of our patients to explain the origin of their conflicts. We then "analyze" these conflicts in an attempt to resolve them, leaving it only implicit that what we are really trying to do is strengthen the patients' integrative functions and capacities.

However, there is now a turning point in developmental research. It is a turning point that has come with the challenge to prevent deviations in development—even more, the challenge to discover how we can optimize development, beginning with the sick and malfunctioning newborn. We struggle now with how best to intervene in a given rearing environment without derailing the integrative factors that are already operative, as impaired as they may be. It is to that process that developmental research is now turning for integrative mechanisms.

We have conceptualized integration as an ego function without needing to define what the mechanisms of integration might be. We say the ego has an organizing function without saying just what that organization is or how it operates. In the privacy and sameness of the consultation room, it is easy to think of organization as the property of the individual rather than the individual as the property of an active process in an individual–environment system—a system with endless variation for which the person generates ever changing solutions—solutions, which if they are to be solutions, involve some next order of organization.

The problem of understanding organization, or the mechanisms by which the unity of the organism (or person) can be achieved or maintained, is not an easy one. The awesome dimensions of the problem can be strikingly illustrated at the psychological as well as the biological level.[EN2]

Paul Weiss is pointing out that the problem of understanding the relation between complexity and unity at the psychological level—the problem of accounting for the enduring uniqueness of "person"—has an awesome precedent in the understanding of the living system, and that both may well depend on the elaboration of common basic principles.

Efforts to understand the maintenance of the unity of "person" go back almost as far as human records. The word for person in ancient Sanskrit—*perusha*—appeared nearly 4,000 years ago and is defined as "consciousness constructing for itself a form." Even at that time, apparently, there existed the idea of an active, creative, self-organizing process. However, it seems we are only now getting into a position to begin to examine to what extent our understanding of this process may have relevance for today.

At this point, I would like to discuss the viewpoint of the developmental process that has evolved from the research carried out at Boston University Medical Center over the past 25 years. The viewpoint emerged from the psychoanalytically oriented clinical psychiatry in which most of us at the Medical Center have been trained and have spent our professional lives.

This will be only a sketch to highlight a few points that related to the questions we have raised so far. There is not space to show data, trace ideas to their origins, place them in chronological order, relate them to each other, trace precursors, distinguish the influence of endowment from that of environment, or cite all those who have made similar points or hold similar ideas. Suffice it to say that at the beginning was the contribution and tradition of Freud, Hartmann, Erikson, Spitz, and others who turned to biology and embryology to gain insight into life processes—to gain ways to think about the developmental process, the relation between structure and function, or the organization of behavior and thought.

Our initial task was to assemble the data from the longitudinal study to compare the observations we had made on 30 infants and their mothers over the first 36 months of life. Just as biology can understand the organisms only in exchange with a surround—an environment of life support—so the infant and its caregiver were viewed as a system of semi-independent, self-regulating components related to each other by the nature of their exchanges.

It was because we had such systematically detailed and multifaceted data of these exchanges that we sought for clues as to mechanisms by which mother and infant began to get together, to adapt to each other after birth. Mechanisms of behavioral adaptation are obviously based on mechanisms of behavioral regulation. The aim was to understand—from a systems point of view—the mechanisms of, and relationship among, regulation, adaptation integration, and organization—and changes in organization over the first months of life. This approach drew on and combined a variety of conceptual frameworks—such as cybernetics and information processing, as well as evolutionary and ethological principles—as necessary tools to describe the initial behavioral regulation of the newborn and mother.

The instrumentation we had developed to monitor states of sleep and wakefulness around the clock focused our attention by biorhythmicity as a mechanism of state regulation over the 24-hour day, and as a clue to the understanding of the initial adaptive fitting together of two partners, the infant and mother, disparately organized in time—a fitting together based on rhythm, entrainment, and phase synchrony.

The approach to regulation and adaptation in terms of the temporal organization of semi-independent components, each with its own periodicity, provided an avenue to the conceptualization of complex organization in terms of attunement and coherence, equilibrium, and tight or loose coupling. The behavior of the well-organized and poorly organized infant or system could be described in these terms, as could the significance of redundancy in the recurrent situations that constitute the caregiving process.

The framework of cues and temporo-spatial configuration so established provides a highly specific temporally organized context for the infant's active organization of his behavior, each awakening and caregiving interaction constituting a new adaptive trial. Perhaps the most remarkable finding to me was the importance of the first 10 days in this process of establishing temporal organization in the infant–caregiver system.

Even within the first month of life, days of predictably organized behavior could be seen set off by days of disorganization. New and relatively more stable organization then appeared after the discontinuity. By 3 weeks after birth, during which time the infant's mother had been the sole caregiver, adaptive coordination between them was becoming a multimodal, sensorimotor, spatiotemporal configuration of great specificity.

To give some picture of how this adaptive coordination looks—between the rhythm of sleep and awake states and the aim and sequence of caregiving activity—I refer to Figure 13.1. This represents the situation toward the end of the first month of life, when, in the average normal instance, a mother will say she now "knows" her baby. The entire 24 hours of the day have reached some recurrent familiar pattern of length and timing of awake periods, and of the onset of naps—a familiarity that, incidentally, both infant and mother now share in common as their background of temporal organization.

The heavy line in Figure 13.1 represents the course of change in the infant from cycles of active and quiet sleep subphases, through the major

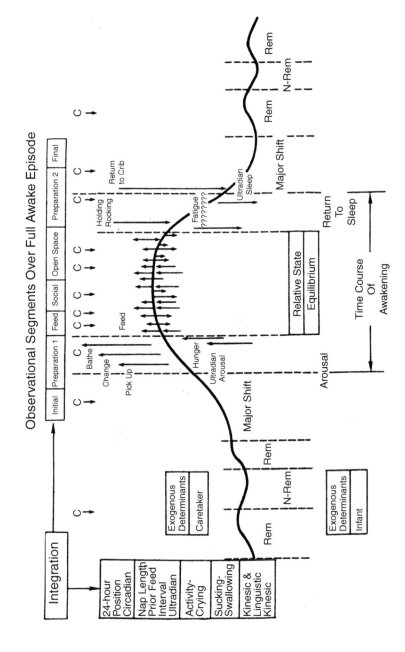

FIGURE 13.1 Sequence of caregiving behavior over an infant's sleep-wake cycle.

shift from sleep to wakefulness, through the state changes during the wakeful span, and, finally, through the major shift from wakefulness to sleep again. The maternal influences affecting the course of this sequence, and their respective durations, are represented by arrows above the line. Infant influences are represented by arrows below the line. The effects of these influences on the course of the state sequence are indicated by the direction of the arrows, whether up toward arousal or down toward drowsiness. A similar direction indicates coordination; an opposite direction may indicate a discordance, or an effect of one to produce an effect on the other.

The "adapted state" in the system can be thought of as a meeting of readiness and direction not experienced by mother and infant as caused by either. The experience of meeting validates one's perception of expectancy of the other, the basis for trust. In the absence of this meeting, one or the other must behave so as to attempt to produce the conditions regulating state course. In respect to state regulation, control then exists in a polarity with trust. An infant with a precarious ego development must manipulate an environment to affect his own state regulation—an environment that has not modified itself to arrive at such a mutually coordinated (adapted) temporal organization.

The seven segments at the top of Figure 13.1 represent the natural sequence in caregiving behaviors during an awakening. The open space[EN3] indicates a time of disengagement—when infant is fed, changed, dry, comfortable, but not ready to return to sleep—during which a mother may put the baby in its reclining seat where he can watch her go about her own activities.

Integrations that the mother is making to arrive at her caregiving decisions are indicated by where she is in the horizontal sequence of caregiving segments and by the vertical list of rhythms of various period lengths that are phase synchronized as she reaches coordination with the infant.

The open space, then, is a span of time provided by a background of adapted coordination in the system. Over this span there exists a dynamic, richly coupled equilibrium in which action is not preempted by a necessity for restoration or regulation (i.e., the infant's initiation of behavior can become partially and temporarily disjoined from the usual regulatory linkages, and free to organize in relation to inner criteria and motivational states). Here infant initiation can begin to establish a differentiated "agency" within the system as the infant actively explores stimuli of low intensity and organizes expectancy schema.

The open space, then (to follow the language of relativity), is a space in time, a discontinuity in the system necessary to admit a new semi-independent agency in the regulation of exchange in the family system. In this day of mother–infant "bonding," there is a tendency to forget that there must be both engagement and disengagement if bonding is not to become bondage. The open space is an initial site for the infant's active integration of inside and outside. I think of it as a precursor of Winnicott's intermediate area, an integrative site from which new goal-oriented behaviors are initiated as the infant generates the richness and complexity of his adaptive coordination. This in-between area is a necessary, private space in time where the self begins to take shape. It depends on a balance in the system, like that of riding a bicycle or flying an airplane.

For each new behavior the infant can introduce into the exchanges within the system, an adjustment or adaptation with his partner must take place if an enduring harmony of coordination is to be achieved between them.

To represent such a sequence of new initiations over the first 3 years of life, we proposed an epigenetic sequence of issues of adaptation. The observations of infant–caregiver interaction were arranged longitudinally in terms of this sequence. These then served as the basis of between-subject comparisons of the longitudinal courses that were observed in the different infant–caregiver systems.

Such an epigenetic sequence can be thought of as a sequence in the development of interpersonal schema—an epistemology of the interpersonal world, so to speak, based on the specific characteristics of specific people in the infant's environment. This parallels Piaget's sensorimotor sequence in cognitive development, by which the characteristics of the infant's relation to the world of inanimate objects becomes known to him. It is epigenetic in as much as all these interactional elements have been present in some degree from the onset. However, the extent to which they will characterize regulation of interpersonal exchange in the system is negotiated in sequence, in "decisive encounters," to use the expression first suggested by Erikson. For me, they provide a start in thinking about mechanisms connecting regulation, adaptation, integration, and organization over the first 3 years of life.

We can mention seven negotiations.[EN4] The first, as we have seen, refers to the mutual modifications necessary to achieve this initial meeting in time—the harmonious coordinations that establish basic regulation of states of sleep and wakefulness, feeding, elimination, and so on.

The second concerns the mutual, active adjustments needed to achieve fitted reciprocations, especially apparent in face-to-face smiling play (which Robson, Stern, Tronick, and Brazelton described so beautifully as a rhythmic engagement and disengagement of gaze and gaze aversion).

Reciprocally adjusted organization of behavior is also seen in spoon feeding or diapering. A voluntary timing and control is required of each in a process of assimilation and accommodation, leading to temporally organized schema of interpersonal interaction. Gerry Stechler has shown quite wonderfully the disturbance of the infant confronted by a nonreciprocating still face—especially before the point, at 5 to 6 weeks, when smiles begin to appear—and especially in those infants who have not learned to look away to regulate the excitement that accompanies confrontation with the face.

The exuberance of affect generated by tuned up, social reciprocation—the affect of delight—must be mentioned. It can be seen as an important mechanism of integration in which the infant brings into action his entire motor system with squeals and vocalizations. Strangely enough, the occurrence and extent of joy and delight in interpersonal exchange within different dyadic systems has not been studied longitudinally to discover its longitudinal course or its essential role in integration.

As this reciprocal tuning up is accomplished, the motor development of the infant allows him to introduce an increasingly wider range of options, to initiate action both toward and away from the caregiver. Here the third issue arises—the negotiation of the extent to which the system can adjust to this independence and allow the infant to retain a sense of "agency" in actively producing effects in his world.

To the extent that space for the infant as active agent can be established in the system, the infant then carries forward a production of effects on the mother. Here ensues the fourth issue—the infant's discovery of the mother's limits, the extent of her availability to his specific and intentional demands.

If a stable and broad enough base is provided, the infant explores the world at increasing distances, with investments of attention, and with delight in mastery.

In the average case, each of these issues is negotiated for each system in the presence of its own idiosyncrasies—in its mismatches of expectancy and discontinuities in previously adapted coordinations—that provide the context for inner reorganizations of new behavioral programs. This is an elaboration of Winnicott's initial description—the necessary interpersonal condition for development as a creative process; the infant arriving at individual solutions to unending adaptive necessity.

A new kind of discontinuity characterizes the fifth issue in the first half of the second year. The toddler can organize his activity on the basis of his own inner goals and intentions, which now often may be in opposition to the context of the familiar interactional coordinations he has established with his caregiver. The issue now is self-assertion—a time Spitz proposed in relation to the head shaking "No"—when the toddler can stand in opposition to his nurturant world—a time when bonding to the outside is uncoupled and self-awareness consolidates, based on the consequences of his own inner intentions to initiate action.

This is a time when the regulation of behavior in the system and new adaptive coordinations often rest on inference as to intentions. Here the reading becomes difficult. Accuracy depends on the foundations constructed from previous mutual coordinations between infant and caregiver—the mutually shared contexts for behavior, gradually built in the negotiations of previous issues. It is a time when the inner perceptions of the child regarding his own affective state and motivations can be validated or invalidated; when parental projection can see goodness or badness, disaster or mastery, in what is inferred of the inner-held intentions of the toddler. For him it is a time of ingenuous openness. Concealment has not yet been achieved. Direct encounter is the rule. (We can wonder what preserves this capacity for encounter.)

We have proposed at this age a sixth issue, that of recognition—a meeting of infant and caregiver on a new level in the adaptive process of fitting together. In this open ingenuous encounter, the toddler can be aware that another is aware of what he is aware of within himself. He comes to know himself as he is known. Here there can be a fit or a miss. It is this issue in the epigenesis of regulation and adaptation that we have proposed as critical to the consolidation or repudiation of the sense of self—of one's own sense of agency—vis-à-vis one's environment. A confirmed self-system will continue as a site for new integration and self-regulation in the guidance and organization of the toddler's new behavioral adaptations.

At this point, recognition rests not only on an epigenesis of integrative mechanisms that require the reading of affective and motivational states of each by the other, but also on the structure of meanings they now share—a common context for action. Words begin to orient both to the focus of attention that exists in the exchange and to the direction of the other's intention. Language makes possible a quantum jump in the integration of more and more complex configurations.

There is now a bifurcation in what is rewarding and reinforcing for the toddler. Will it be the achievement of his own goals and inner intentions and wants, or will it be the fitting together again with the caregiver in a familiar coordination? This leaves him in an in-between—a state of ambiguity and uncertainty. Validation or invalidation largely depends on the toleration of ambivalence by the caregiver. Recognition or validation of the infant, while he is in a state of uncertainty, bears directly on the extent to which control or trust will characterize his future orientation toward new encounters and situations of uncertainty.

It is here, in this in-between state, that the intermediate area or transitional relatedness plays its critical role in preserving the infant's sense of agency in the integration of inner and outer worlds. Even at this level, it is dependent on system characteristics of relative balance or equilibrium of regulation. Coming at a time when the self is jelling, the intermediate area, under favorable circumstances, comes to reside within as a functional configuration characterizing the self—a site of continuing privacy, or continuing integration of inside and outside for the never-ending adaptive process.

One final issue we have termed simply reversal to indicate an analogy to Piaget's sixth issue of sensorimotor development—a time when the idea of the act begins to be abstracted from its performance. Spitz suggested such a process of reversal in the second year in relation to the emergence of the self. Proposed is a mechanism by which continuity of the sense of self as an inner configuration of regulation and adaptation can be disembedded or "conserved" (again to use a term of Piaget's not intended for this use).

Behaviors here concern the place of aggression—provocative and destructive behavior—and how it impacts on the system during these second 18 months of life. The toddler elects to do exactly what he knows he should not do. He takes a contrary position to his world and experiences his own disorganization as the limits are set to the programs he can intend and initiate. He elects a discontinuity of both competence and organization.

Under favorable circumstances, this posture is one from which he can retreat intentionally to reestablish the familiar coordinations that reconstruct the continuity of his sense of agency in the system. Mother forgives and accepts his reversal of direction. Next time the rules of the system will be further incorporated. We call this the process of socialization. If the issue is negotiated, the experience of inner continuity or discontinuity can remain within his sense of agency—a matter of option, not surrender. On the other hand, without a favorable epigenesis of coordinations, it can mean disastrous discontinuity and the impossibility of again taking a contrary position.

In such an eventuality, continuity of self becomes dependent on performance that pleases the caregiver and on other outer criteria that must be met. The openness to direct encounter that so characterizes the 2- or 3-year-old can be closed in a defensive world of control because of the new capacity to anticipate. Before their expression in action, inner intentions can be inhibited or modified due to anticipation of the effects of their outcome.

Again one needs to propose a systems model to account for this balance between the polarities that construct the framework of exchange between the partners; to account for the richness of their coordination, the finality of discontinuities, the epigenesis of regulation and adaptation to this point. In line with what I have merely touched on before, much depends on the extent to which exchanges of joy and exuberant confirmation with the caregiving world balance the discontinuities that function to disembed the self from its interpersonal matrix (the latter, nevertheless, being a necessary step in its differentiation).

From the point of view of development as an actively organizing process within the exchanges of a particular system, we can propose regulatory and adaptive mechanisms in the consolidation of the self. These can leave it with a capacity for direct encounter—a relative openness to the world with its uncertainties and hazards of discontinuity—or in a protective, vigilant posture of anticipation and control.

In the development of "person" over the life span, one can see the construction of the self at some point in this continuum between the polarities of trust and control. On the position of this point depends the organization of perception, awareness, and consciousness that will be ready, as Pribam suggested, to permit participation and openness to the new, or preparation that narrows attention to aspects of the surround or to one's own inner states that are to be controlled. In meeting the ever-present discontinuities as they are encountered within a matrix of the necessary continuities, we can envision the developmental process as disembedding the self-regulating core from the matrix, creating a differentiated yet enduring "self."

How near we are to *perusha*—consciousness constructing for itself a form. From the systems point of view, there is always a natural polarity of focus and rhythms framing the adaptive encounter, ensuring uncertainty, variation, and discrepancy; requiring reorganization, often after painful discontinuity and disorganization. Instead of avoidance, protection, and retreat, it is the capacity for encountering uncertainty and discontinuity that the continuing creative process requires. We pursue certainty with every ounce of strength, yet it is only our capacity to endure uncertainty and discontinuity that enables us to continue the search.[EN5]

We must better define what kind of developmental experience enables us to remain open and permeable, and, in direct encounter, to know our own unknowing—to face the creative process as one of uncertainty and yet preserve our integrity.

The persistence of family interpersonal regulatory dynamics and strategies, originally set up in negotiating the sequence of adaptations necessary to include the new individual in the family system, is evident in the pilot work on the 20-year follow-up of the subjects studied as infants. The most difficult influences on development to assess in family systems are long-term factors (e.g., values, goals, adaptive potentials, and strengths of family members). Higher level organizations of shared meanings and significance must come into play as the integrative task requires more and more of life experience, with its vicissitudes and paradoxes, to be included at later points of critical action and decision.

We are at a strange moment in time as we pass from science as a reference of certainty to science as a doorway to uncertainty. As we celebrate Einstein's centennial year, there is much to read of his life and character. Einstein is described as having been unwilling to accept a universe of uncertainty, but he could not forestall the uncertainty that his relativity theory revealed. Today, the nature of subatomic particles becomes more and more uncertain, and determinism fades toward a matter of probabilities. After more than a decade of sophisticated measurement, it is uncertain what direction the universe is taking.

A Cambridge University cosmologist is quoted as saying, "One of the most amazing things is that the universe should be so close to the dividing line between collapsing and expanding." Again, John Archibald Wheeler, director of the Center for Theoretical Physics at Austin, Texas—a longtime colleague of Einstein's—declared, "What is so hard is to give up thinking of nature as a machine that goes on independent of the observer. No phenomenon is a phenomenon until it is observed. For our picture of the world, this is the most revolutionary thing discovered; we have still not come to terms with it."

We remain faced with the apparent paradoxes of relativity: that from randomness must come order; from uncertainty, knowledge; and from chaos, creation. In the face of these dilemmas, strangely enough, the present consuming effort of physics is to arrive at unity—a single explanation of the four forces of nature, a unified field theory. Man seems determined to integrate complexity and unity, harmonize polarity, and, at the same time, confront ever greater uncertainty.

The insights of ancient prophets into the life process are at times astounding. Isaiah announces the necessity of facing uncertainty and discontinuity as being in the design of things. He rails against those who, for self-preservation, rely on the competence of their own hands or the reason of their own minds. In Isaiah's words, God says, "Behold, I am doing new things: now it springs forth, do you not perceive it? From this time forth I make you hear new things, hidden things, which you have not known. They are created now, not long ago; before today you have never heard of them, lest you should say 'Behold, I knew that.'"

How can openness of encounter be preserved in the paradox of a developmental process that sets up the necessity to know—to organize and reorganize toward an increasing richness of specific coordinations—yet lead us further and further into uncertainty and awareness of our unknowing? Only one way: by our internalization of and identification with those persons of courage with whom we have relationships; those who have themselves becomes courageous enough to elect to encounter uncertainty and discontinuity.

Yet how do we account for them?

I wrote to Gerry as I was thinking about this lecture and asked him if any personal mention of Ellen would be appropriate. He wrote a beautiful letter in response, one I shall always treasure. In it, he said Ellen wanted to be remembered as healthy and vibrant. I think, in addition, she will always represent to me one who elected to walk, with her eyes open, toward an active encounter with uncertainty, with the unknown, and with a final experience of discontinuity.

I have known only one other person like her. It was a relationship that changed me, changed my perspective on death and its role in the organization of my living.

One who is close to development is also close to the stress, turmoil, anxiety, loss, and loneliness of childhood's painful encounters with the repeated discontinuities that frame the creative process of life. The tone of this life journey is nowhere better expressed for me than in T.S. Eliot's "Four Quartets." These lines evoke the experience of one who dares to encounter the journey directly, all the way to its end:

> Home is where one starts from. As we grow older
> The world becomes stranger, the pattern more complicated
> Of dead and living. Not the intense moment
> Isolated, with no before and after,
> But a lifetime burning in every moment
> And not the lifetime of one man only
> But of old stones that cannot be deciphered.
> There is a time for the evening under starlight,
> A time for the evening under lamplight

(The evening with the photograph album).
Love is more nearly itself
Where here and now cease to matter.
Old men ought to be explorers
Here and there does not matter.
We must be still and still moving
Into another intensity
For a further union, a deeper communion
Through the dark cold and the empty desolation,
The wave cry, and wind cry, the vast waters
Of the petrel and the porpoise. In my end is my beginning.[EN6]

Gerry concludes his letter with these lines: "The final tribute to her life and death is that all of us—Amy, Nancy, and I—were so free to go on with our lives after her death."

They go on, I would think, not unchanged, but each having experienced the creative process in a further differentiation of self—in a wider perspective of inner resources of continuity, and a greater freedom to encounter whatever those realities and actualities will be as the context within which they will continue. They have participated in the creative process by virtue of having accompanied a loved one who had the courage to stand in her integrity before a complete unknown and encounter ultimate uncertainty—the final discontinuity in her life's journey.

NOTE

Originally presented as the first Ellen B. Stechler Memorial Lecture, Boston University Medical Center, March 28, 1979.

EDITORS' NOTES

[EN1] That is Gerald Stechler, Ellen's husband, who, at the time of the conference, worked at the Department of Infant Psychology and Developmental Psychology at the Boston University Medical Center.

[EN2] For more on this, see chapters 9 and 10.

[EN3] Sander already discussed this in chapters 7 and 8.

[EN4] See the summarizing table in chapter 4.

[EN5] Here it refers to a research that, while certainly including scientific research, is not confined to it and extends more widely to the existential search for meaning.

[EN6] Excertp from "East Coker" in Fourth Quartets, copyright 1940 by T.S. Eliot and renewed 1968 by Esme Valerie Eliot, reprinted by permission of Harcourt, Inc.

REFERENCES

Winnicott, D. W. (1958). Collected Papers—Through Pediatrics to Psychoanalysis. Chapter 18, pp. 229–243. New York: Basic Books Inc.

Epilogue

It is my hope that readers have experienced this limited selection of papers as an illustration of a way of thinking in terms of living systems. At the present time we tend to see ourselves as existing within a fixed context, rather than as within an ongoing creative process. A new perspective would be to view living systems as being within an ongoing, creative, evolutionary process from which, over billions of years, the human being as "person" has emerged and is now at the center of the evolving direction. It is a way of thinking in terms of the impetus toward growth in living systems as being one that moves the system toward a gradually increasing inclusiveness of complexity, yet with an increasing coherence, or unity of organization.

For example, what is becoming increasingly known about stem cells and the morphology and development of the brain is that in new experiences the potential for new brain capacities and functions can expand. The connection between infant experience and its role in shaping the morphology of the developing brain is an ongoing demonstration of the potential for this creative process. Our growing understanding of the way the unique person emerges over the human life span can be described as part now of an ongoing evolution of consciousness, integrating in the person an increasing self-awareness, within increasing awareness of the complexity and life-amplifying, or growing, process within which the life and living of each individual is embedded.

The significance of such increasing complexity and coherence of organization, in our growing awareness of self and other, is that it opens avenues of potential—and the possibility of our joining in a new and ever larger awareness of the evolutionary process that we are within—a process heading toward further evolution of the human brain and consciousness that in time will open the potential of as yet unknown possibilities.

Author Index

Subject Index

T - #0005 - 101121 - C0 - 229/152/16 [18] - CB - 9780881634648 - Gloss Lamination